STANDING WITNESSES

sanguis martyrum semen ecclesiae

Thorbjörn Campbell was educated at Ayr Academy and Glasgow University and was a teacher of English and Classics for many years. Latterly he was active in the field of urban conservation and he is now a free-lance writer. For this book he has visited all the principal memorial sites in the country over a period of years, and uncovered often dramatic and tragic stories, such as the shooting of John Brown of Priesthill.

STANDING WITNESSES

*A guide to the Scottish Covenanters
and their Memorials with a
Historical Introduction*

by

Thorbjörn Campbell

SCOTLAND
ALBA

SALTIRE
SOCIETY

EDINBURGH
1996

First published 1996
by The Saltire Society,
9 Fountain Close,
High Street,
Edinburgh EH1 1TF

The publisher acknowledges
subsidy from the Scottish Arts Council towards
the publication of this volume

A catalogue record
for this book is available from the
British Library

ISBN 0 85411 061 5

The cover shows a detail from
The Martyrdom of John Brown of Priesthill
by Thomas Duncan (1844), reproduced by permission of
Glasgow Museums: Art Gallery and Museum, Kelvingrove.

Cover & Text Design and Layout by
Smith & Paul Design Associates Ltd, Paisley

Printed and bound in Scotland by Bell & Bain Limited

Contents

Foreword

Over the last few years repeated calls have been made for the cataloguing of war memorials throughout the United Kingdom because of their rapid deterioration. Serious damage to stone-built monuments erected as recently as after the Second World War has already been caused not only by wind and weather, but also by characteristically modern pollutants— acid rain and exhaust fumes — and by vandalism.

If modern monuments are already in crisis, concern should be very much greater in respect of the Scottish Covenanting memorials, most of which are at least 100 years old, and some of which are very much older. These are among the earliest which can be classed as war memorials, referring to a period which is, so to speak, on the edge of public memory —in many respects a very obscure period, and yet one that has major historical implications for Scotland and for the rest of the kingdom. Several of these monuments have disappeared, many have been mutilated by pollution and vandalism, and those that have survived have often done so because of negative factors such as inaccessibility or public neglect.

This gazetteer aims at recording the inscriptions of Covenanting memorials (including those that are no longer *in situ*) and making them available to the public, together with a description of each monument and its surroundings and selected historical and traditional material. Each entry has an OS reference and, where necessary, a map pin-pointing the site. A historical introduction tries to set the period in context and draw some general conclusions.

The actual monuments dealt with in the gazetteer can be grouped under various sub-headings: grave-monuments within regular burying grounds and in other places marking either known burial sites or the conjectured site or even locality; monuments to martyrs and occasionally to non-martyrs; monuments commemorating deaths sometimes widely separated from the burial site, for instance, local monuments to martyrs executed in Edinburgh or drowned in Orkney; memorials commemorating battles and other significant events; and so on. Occasionally an entry deals with a site interesting in itself but with no erected monument—for instance, the Enterkin Pass.

In no case, except possibly, and rather doubtfully, in Dunsyre, is the inscription on the existing stone contemporary with the deaths commemorated.The Society People did not take a decision to erect monuments throughout the country until 1701, thirteen years after the Glorious Revolution had brought an end to the persecutions, although by then some monuments had been put up, notably in Glasgow. The original version of the Martyrs' Memorial in Greyfriars Churchyard in Edinburgh (now at Huntly House Museum) was erected in 1706. A few stones have survived since the early part of the eighteenth century, and some genuine "Old Mortality"* recarvings from the end of the century are still in existence; the majority of the stones now in position, however, are nineteenth-century replacements for older stones — some of which still stand or lie beside them.

During repeated renewals, then, the inscriptions have often been tampered with, sometimes innocently, for instance in up-dating spelling— and sometimes not so innocently. The evolution of the inscriptions thus becomes part of the problem: which is to be regarded as authentic — the inscription in its current state on the present stone, or the words as recorded in *A Cloud of Witnesses* or even in J H Thomson's *Martyr Graves of Scotland*? Quite often, in the case of double or multiple renewals, I have had to rely upon Thomson, even though his own accuracy is questionable. (See e.g. the entry for Magus Muir.)

Above all, however, the weathering of the inscriptions is now the greatest problem. John Law's stone, on the precinct wall of the Ducat Tower in Newmilns, has been renewed at least four times, the last time perhaps in 1930, and yet the inscription is barely decipherable even with the aid of Thomson. Other inscriptions, for instance that for Algie and Park at Paisley, have simply been worn smooth, so that one sees the shadow of lettering only, without any chance of deciding what it has been.

Perhaps it would be suitable here to make the point that it is positively dangerous, as well as misleading, to employ artificial methods of enhancement of lettering. Chemicals and paint can damage stone irretrievably, and techniques of rubbing are equally suspect. Many inscriptions, such as the one at Priesthill, have been "picked out" in paint—but this method, besides being potentially deleterious, relies upon interpretation too: a half-sensed squiggle on the rough surface of the stone can be over-excitedly interpreted as a letter (often an "e") or alternatively passed (and painted) over when it should not be. Thus, at Priesthill and elsewhere, there are several worrying departures from the text as given in printed sources. It is no easy task to arrive at a definitive version of every inscription, and I must not pretend that I have achieved this, although I have visited nearly every site in the country and photographed the inscriptions in their present state.

* For an explanation of "Old Mortality" see entries for Balmaclellan and Dunnottar Churchyard.

Of course, this is not the first attempt to produce a comprehensive survey of Covenanting memorials in Scotland. A century ago J H Thomson produced *The Martyr Graves of Scotland*. Thomson's work deserves to be better known not only for its painstaking fullness, but also for its vivid picture of travelling conditions in Victorian Scotland, now as remote from our imagination as the Scotland of the Covenanters themselves. J H Thomson was a minister originally of the Reformed Presbyterian Church in Eaglesham and then of the Free Church in Hightae near Dumfries. He spent his summer holidays over nearly quarter of a century—from 1870 to 1894—visiting and writing up as many Covenanting memorials as he could get to. Often he was on foot, sometimes he used horse-drawn vehicles, and sometimes he travelled by train where nowadays no civilized conveyance exists at all. The monument at Auchencloy, for instance, was easily accessible a century ago from a railway siding now long gone at Loch Skerrow. Of this access, admittedly, Thomson himself says,

"How a railway was ever taken through the bleak and desolate and repulsive wilderness between New Galloway and Dromore stations, when it might have taken a shorter route through an inhabited country full of attraction from the beauty of its scenery, is a question for the shareholders and not for us to answer.."

More typical, however, is his visit (written up in the same chapter) to Alexander Linn's tomb at Craigmoddie in 1881, when he was able to rely upon the kindness of a brother minister to organize a carriage party to drive the ten miles or so from Kircowan Station. This tomb was recently shown in a fleeting helicopter shot during a television programme on the Southern Upland Way, and for all I know the air may well be the favoured mode of access in the coming century.

Thomson's work is long out of print, and a new, less anecdotal approach would be desirable in any case for a modern readership. Yet, of course, detailed research is wanting even now for much of the Covenanting period, and the surviving material is often so episodic and fragmentary that the best way to present it may be to embed it, like the scraps of ancient architecture or sculpture, in the smooth plaster-of-paris of a gazetteer. In the present work the historical introduction may go some way towards making the overall picture more coherent.

Coherence is certainly lacking in the case of the first real historian to investigate the Covenanting period, Robert Wodrow. His attitude to his data may be compared with that of a squirrel hoarding nuts, and his attempts to organise his enormous dossier were rarely more than half-hearted. His published work, principally in four huge volumes, and his vast collection of unpublished material together form an invaluable mine for later researchers, but even in his published *History* pieces of

A

CLOUD OF WITNESSES,

FOR THE

ROYAL PREROGATIVES

·OF·

JESUS CHRIST:

OR, THE

LAST SPEECHES AND TESTIMONIES

OF THOSE WHO HAVE SUFFERED FOR THE

TRUTH IN SCOTLAND,

SINCE THE YEAR 1680,

WITH A

COPIOUS APPENDIX.

Rev. vii. 14. These are they which came out of great tribulation, and have washed their robes, and made them white in the blood of the Lamb.

A NEW EDITION.

GLASGOW:

PRINTED FOR J. & A. DUNCAN, J. & M. ROBERTSON,
AND J. & W. SHAW.
1796.

(Illustration: Reproduction of title page of 1796 Edition of A Cloud of Witnesses)

information relating to the same subject are often widely separated, dates are often wildly at variance with each other, and relative weighting of subjects by importance is non-existent. Wodrow's motto seems to have been, When in doubt, quote the Act of Parliament in full. All in all, he is not an easy author to read.

Clarity and incisiveness about Covenanters had to wait for nineteenth-century historians-—from opposite sides, as it were: the Reverend James King Hewison, who leans to the Presbyterian side, and Professor C S Terry, whose biography of Claverhouse goes a long way towards rehabilitating its subject.

Hewison's *History of the Church in Scotland* is still incomparably the best-organized detailed account of the whole sweep of development from the Scottish Reformation onward, and quibbles about interpretations of particular matters should not make us withhold our admiration. His attitude, however, while not as hagiographical as that of Howie of Lochgoin or *A Cloud of Witnesses*, may cause discomfort to less strenuously engaged readers of our own time. On the other hand C S Terry, a professional academic, produced studies of Claverhouse and of the Pentland Rising that are models of research technique.

Turning to the present work, I hesitate to make any scholarly claims for it, since my use of primary and especially manuscript sources has unfortunately had to be minimal. However, I must acknowledge especially the help and guidance that I have derived from reading the works of two great modern scholars, David Stevenson and the late Ian B Cowan, as well as those of the late Gordon Donaldson, HM Historiographer in Scotland. These, with the works of many other writers both past and present, are detailed in the bibliography on pp 211-214. I owe a more direct debt of gratitude to the staff of the following institutions: Cunninghame District Library Headquarters in Ardrossan, Glasgow University Library, Glasgow District Council Parks and Recreation Department, Huntly House Museum, Edinburgh, Kyle and Carrick District Council Library Headquarters (Ayr Carnegie Library), Kyle and Carrick District Parks and Recreation Department, the Ewart Library, Dumfries, and Dumfries and Galloway Libraries generally, Kilmarnock and Loudoun District Museums (the Dick Institute and Dean Castle Museum), the Lochgoin Covenanting Museum Trust, the National Library of Scotland, Edinburgh, the Royal Museums of Scotland, Edinburgh, Saltire Society Headquarters, Edinburgh and the Scottish Covenanting Memorials Association. The portrait on p149 of John Graham of Claverhouse, Viscount Dundee, by David Paton, is reproduced by courtesy of the National Galleries of Scotland; the portrait on p158 of Jean, Viscountess Dundee, by an imitator of Sir Peter Lely, is reproduced by courtesy of the City of Dundee District Council Art Galleries and museums (McManus Galleries).

I have also to thank Mr Gilbert Gordon the artist, for his beautiful renditions of my photographs.

I must particularly thank the Carnegie Trust for the Universities of Scotland for coming promptly to my assistance late in the production process.

Among individuals to whom I owe many thanks are Mrs R Airlie (Euart Library Dumfries),Mrs Greta Aitken (Jerviswood House, Lanark), Mr J Andrew (Upper Welwood), Mr Ken Andrew (Prestwick), Mrs Sheena Andrew, the Rev. Charles Armour, (Parish Church of the Holy Trinity, St Andrews), Mr J Blackwood (Nether Welwood), Mr Bob Brooks, the Rev James Crichton (Crosshill and Dalrymple), Mr H Eagle (St Andews), Mr Tom Findlay (Muirkirk), Mrs W Gibb (Threepwood Farm), Mr John Sibbald Gibson, Mr James Hunter (Kilmarnock), Mr Tom Johnston (Sanquhar), Miss Annie Joss (Dalmellington), Mr Robert Kirk (Dundonald), Mr J Kirkwood (Symington), Miss H McArthur (Dumfries), the Rev Fraser McNaughten (Fenwick), Mrs McLaren of Glenearn (Ecclesmagirdle), Mr Marr (North Berwick), Professor Rosaland Mitchison, Mrs Kathleen Munro (Saltire Society), Colonel William Munro (Lochgoin Trust), Mr and Mrs Robin Porter, Mr Bob Robertson (Forgandenny), the late John Samuel, Mr George Scott (Cumnock), Mr and Mrs Donald Smith of Skerrington, Cumnock, and Mr Allan Young of Barshare. In addition, since I do not possess the skill of driving, the success—indeed, the possibility—of this endeavour has rested with a band of devoted motorists who have been prepared almost at a moment's notice to drop what they were doing and career through thick and thin to the most unlikely locations in "bleak and desolate and repulsive wildernesses": these include Mrs Catriona Gregson, my sister Mrs Aase Irvine, the late Kenneth Lumsden, Mr Murray McAllister, Mr Calum McLean, Dr Keith Martin, Mr Bill Ovens, Mr Marsden Ovens, Mrs Mary Cuthbertson and Mrs Faridhe Wiseman. To all of these, my most profound thanks. Finally, I should like to thank all the farmers, landowners, ministers, planners, architects, tourist officers, hill-walkers, inn-keepers and other local contacts without whose helpful advice and directions this task would have been considerably more difficult. If I have omitted any person whose help I should have acknowledged, I apologize.

Historical Introduction

The Covenanters were a force in Scottish religion and politics between 1638 and 1688, deriving their name and their strength from two documents, the National Covenant of 1638, and the Solemn League and Covenant of 1643. In the main their memorial stones refer to the period between the Restoration of King Charles II in 1660 and the flight into exile of his brother and successor James VII and II in 1688. Before 1650 the star of the Covenanters had been on the rise, and they had even formed the Government of Scotland. Under Oliver Cromwell, however, the Covenanters came under pressure, and after the Restoration they were subjected to sustained Government persecution. It has been said that the character of the movement changed radically during the later years; certainly the *geographical focus* of the movement seemed to change, but the radicalism of the West of Scotland was a constant factor even in the early days: it only appeared to grow starker as the West became isolated in virtual schism and the Government's use of military repression became extensive.

The National Covenant

King Charles I's introduction of alien practices ("innovations") into the Scottish liturgy provoked riots in 1637 and then, in February 1638, the signing of the National Covenant in Greyfriars Church in Edinburgh. This great manifesto was drawn up by Alexander Henderson, the Minister of Leuchars in Fife, and by a young and fanatical Edinburgh lawyer, Archibald Johnston of Wariston. It has been seen by some as the first modern declaration of Scottish nationhood, but it is primarily a religious document, reaffirming the reforming impulse in Scotland against the Anglicizing and Romanizing innovations. The original copy was signed on 28th February and 1st March 1638 in Greyfriars Church by principal noblemen, lairds, ministers and burgesses. Other copies were carried round the country and signed by most leading men, sometimes under compulsion and even, in less fervent Covenanting areas such as Aberdeenshire, under armed threat.

The National Covenant does not openly object to bishops.[1] Yet the existence of bishops was one of the main points of contention between the King and the Covenanters. Both sides saw rule by bishops as a method of royal control. King James VI and I had said, "No Bishop, no King," and his successors held by this. Many Scots, however, preferred to organize their worship on *Presbyterian* lines, that is to say, with equality of all ministers under the divine headship or kingship of Jesus Christ, eliminating the need for the merely human leadership of King, bishops or Pope. Ministers themselves should be organized in a hierarchy of *courts*, starting with kirk sessions and presbyteries and ending with the General Assembly of the Church.

By November 1638, when a General Assembly was held in Glasgow Cathedral, positions had hardened. The Scottish Bishops did not dare to attend the Assembly. The King's Commissioner, the Marquis of Hamilton, protested against the Assembly's discussing the legitimacy of bishops and other constitutional matters; when he was overruled, he tried to dissolve the Assembly, and when this had no effect, he withdrew in dudgeon. The Assembly went on without him to vote the bishops out of existence ("the abjuration and removal of episcopacy from the Church"[2]) on 8th December, 1638.

War was now inevitable. Both sides had been arming themselves since before the November assembly. Many Scottish soldiers who had been taking part in the great religious conflict, the Thirty Years' War, at that time raging in Germany, now came home to take sides in the Bishops' Wars.

The King lost both Bishops' Wars, in 1639 and 1640. He had not counted on much support from inside Scotland, but relied upon invasion from England, and since the English Parliament denied him money, he was effectively hamstrung from the start. On the other hand, the Covenanters were well organized in a governmental system of "Tables" or Committees through which leading Covenanters controlled every aspect of national life including defence and propaganda. Right from the beginning the Covenanters were headed by some of the greatest men in the kingdom, principally the Earls of Argyll, Rothes, Montrose and Loudoun. Against these, the King's supporters, the Marquis of Hamilton, the Marquis of Huntly and the Earls of Traquair and Roxburgh, have a distinctly "second-eleven" look. The formal instrument of royal control in Scotland, the Privy Council, had long merely rubber-stamped the King's decisions taken in distant London, and it was moribund and divided. One fairly serious threat to the Covenanters came from the West, from the MacDonalds of the Isles and their Irish relatives, the Macdonnels of Antrim. They, however, were more anxious to recover the lands lost to Clan Campbell and the Earls of Argyll than to support the King.

The first Bishop's War was a matter of shadow-boxing rather than of actual fighting: the Marquis of Huntly's nerve broke — or he had little nerve to begin with—and so Aberdeen, the one major centre of anti-Covenant feeling, was occupied by Covenanters, as were most of the royalist establishments in the Lowlands. The King brought an army up to the Borders but prudently decided not to attack the strong Covenanting forces on the other side of the Tweed. So, after the arrest of the Marquis of Huntly and a few minor skirmishes, the King settled for a truce signed at Berwick on 18th June, 1639.

In the second War, the Scots invaded England on 20th August, 1640, and occupied Newcastle ten days later. The Newcastle garrison fled without firing a shot. Major royal fortresses in Scotland, including Edinburgh Castle, surrendered, and Charles I was forced to sign another humiliating treaty at Ripon on 26th October, 1640. One of the terms of this treaty was that the King should pay for the upkeep of the Scots army that had defeated him.

In all this, the Covenanting movement had supplanted and in fact become the Government of Scotland, brushing aside the legitimate forms of government such as the Privy Council and the primitive Scots Parliament. It was still very much a nobleman's movement, with the lesser people following the lead of individual feudal superiors. A sizeable radical grouping within the covenanting ranks was, however, developing around such issues as the holding of conventicles (private prayer meetings); this grouping derived its support from the south-west of Scotland, its leadership including men like David Dickson of Irvine and Samuel Rutherford, one-time minister of Anwoth in Kirkcudbright.

The Solemn League and Covenant (1643)

This treaty between Scotland and England represents the next phase in the evolution of the Covenanters. When the great English Civil War broke out in 1642, the Scots found themselves in demand as a fighting force which could tilt the balance either way. After their recent experience the Scots feared that the English, as the larger nation, would always make their influence predominate in religious matters as in others north of the Border, unless an initiative were taken. Characteristically, under the circumstances, the Scots decided that the best thing to do was to export their revolution[3], and when the English parliament invited them to lend their assistance against the royal power, they seized the opportunity to make terms about religion: they would give military aid on condition that England and Ireland became Presbyterian. In return for armed intervention by the Scots on the Parliamentary side, the Solemn League and Covenant agreed "the preservation of the reformed religion in

Scotland" and "the reformation of religion in England and Ireland"[4] — a phrase that the Scottish plenipotentiaries thought implied Presbyterianization, but their English counterparts interpreted differently. The treaty led to the setting up of the Westminster Assembly and the drawing up of the Westminster Confession, whose thirty-nine articles serve as the constitutional basis of the Church of Scotland to this day.

This, then, was the second of the two great Covenants by which those who were known as Covenanters were motivated. Perhaps it was more influential than the original National Covenant as a factor in the crusading zeal and anti-government intransigence of the later Covenanters.

However glad the English were to receive military aid from the Scots, the Solemn League and Covenant never represented a seamless joint between the two nations. Although there was a considerable Presbyterian party in the English parliament, by far the most important element in the English forces ranged against the King was the Independent party, well represented in Parliament[5]. Independency was the ruling spirit in Oliver Cromwell's New Model Army. To the Scottish Covenanters, however, the Independents represented a quite intolerable religious point of view, and they grew to detest each other cordially in the months following the signing of the Solemn League and Covenant. Add to this the mutual suspicion and scepticism prevailing at military, political, diplomatic and constitutional levels, and we have a recipe for the unbearable tension that in fact ruptured the alliance. By and large the Scots were unable to deliver the military goods—and if they had been effective, the English would have hated and feared them even more. On the other hand, the English were obviously thinking in terms of the deposition of the King—a King of Scotland and of Scottish family; such an idea had never even crossed the minds of most of the Scottish covenanters, however radically they opposed his encroachments on their liturgy[6].

At first, indeed, the alliance prospered, and the King's position went from bad to worse, from the Battle of Marston Moor in 1644, where the Scots did play a decisive part, to the Battle of Naseby in 1645, where Cromwell trounced him without Scottish assistance.

The King's misfortunes contrasted at first with the career of the Marquis of Montrose in Scotland, who had changed sides and won a string of victories against the Covenanters in 1645, ending with a complete rout at Kilsyth not far from Glasgow on 15th August. The only thing which prevented a royalist regime from being established in Edinburgh was a terrible outbreak of plague, which effectively barred the capital to Montrose's army. The Covenanters, however, summoned their armies back from England and regrouped. Montrose was taken off guard at Philiphaugh near Selkirk and soundly defeated on 13th September.

The disintegration of the Covenanting movement

In 1645, therefore, anti-royalist forces held the field both north and south of the Border, and in 1646 the King had to acknowledge defeat. Desiring to play off one set of enemies against the other, however, he surrendered to the Scots rather than to the English. This manoeuvre brought into the open the split between the allies, the Covenanters and the English Parliamentarians, that had been threatening for months. In the end the Scots' desperate lack of money prevailed: they retired from England to Scotland in return for a large down payment from the English parliament, and they left Charles I to the mercy of the English. Yet now a powerful party of Scottish Royalists came to the fore, and these were the people who brought about something previously quite unthinkable: a treaty of armed assistance between the Scots and the defeated and captive King— in return for token religious concessions to Presbyterianism falling well short of the terms of the Solemn League and Covenant[7].

Radical Covenanters, especially those in the West of Scotland, vehemently opposed the Engagement (as the treaty was called), but for the time being the Engagers prevailed.

During all this time, influence had been gradually slipping away from the first, aristocratic leaders of the Covenanting movement, and this led to what has been seen as a change in its character. Scotland had been exhausted by almost ten years of warfare, culminating in the devastating campaigns of Montrose; one of the worst outbreaks of plague ever to hit the country had taken its toll, and there had been savage economic difficulties. Principal landowners could no longer command the automatic loyalty of their feudal inferiors. Many magnates rallied to the Engager cause, while increasingly on the other side stood smaller landowners and tenants, artisans, landless men, professional classes, the urban and rural poor, the womenfolk of all these, and above all, a new generation of ministers: these ministers strongly opposed alliance with the King, and held out for full implementation of the Solemn League and Covenant, including the provisions about presbyterianizing England and Ireland. These radicals were strongest in the south and west of Scotland[8].

The break with the English Parliament became irreparable and a new war loomed on the horizon. The Engagers were faced with the task of raising a new army to march south and help Charles I back to his throne. Large areas of the country simply refused to comply with the new levy, and many Scotsmen avoided conscription by fleeing to Ireland and elsewhere[9]. Others banded together to resist the levy. In the main incident large numbers of horsemen gathered at Mauchline in Ayrshire to oppose the Engagement. No obvious leadership emerged, so that when a party of Government soldiers came down from Glasgow and confronted them, they were easily defeated and scattered (Battle of Mauchline Muir, 12th June, 1648)[10]. This was to set the tone of relations between the West of Scotland and the authorities for the next forty years.

At length, however, the Engagers gathered an army and marched away south in support of Charles I. They were under the leadership of the same Marquis (now Duke) of Hamilton who had withdrawn as King's Commissioner from the Glasgow Assembly ten years earlier. In a series of battles around Preston between 17th and 19th August, 1648, Oliver Cromwell defeated them very thoroughly.

As soon as news of the Engagers' defeat at Preston came through to the west of Scotland, the radical extremists who had been dispersed at Mauchline on 12th June came together again and, by 28th August, were marching east. This time there was a decisive leadership, the Ayrshire Earls of Loudoun, Eglinton and Cassillis. They had the active support of the Earl of Argyll. The "Whiggamore Raid", as it came to be known, drove the Engagers out of Edinburgh and established a clerical dictatorship from September 1648. The term "Whiggamore", soon to be shortened to "Whig", now began to come into use to mean a diehard Covenanting Presbyterian opposed to royal government.

The two-year rule of the Kirk Party (September 1648 to September 1650) represents the high point of the Western wing of the Covenanting movement. Its greatest achievement was the Act of Classes, a statute reinforcing already existing legislation to exclude from public service all who were unacceptable in the sight of the Lord by reason of their loose living, erroneous religious beliefs, or support of the Engagement or of the Montrose campaigns. In this purge they were accorded the support of Oliver Cromwell, who had come north after the Battle of Preston to ensure that Scottish government was in the hands of people he could rely on[11]. They were also supported by the *Western Association*, a military grouping based in the Western shires of Scotland, monitored by the Earl of Argyll and generally representing the radical covenanters who had taken part in the Whiggamore Raid[12].

Charles II and the collapse of the Scottish government

Hardly had the Government been established in Edinburgh when a new external event upset the delicate balance of Scottish politics once more. The Scottish Parliament passed the Act of Classes on 23rd January, 1649. On 30th January Charles I was beheaded outside his own banqueting hall in Whitehall. In spite of the extreme opinions of the radical Covenanters in power in Edinburgh, the execution of a Scottish king by the English proved too much for the Scots. Two days after the news came from London, the Scottish Parliament proclaimed the Crown Prince as King Charles II of England, Scotland and Ireland, and ruptured diplomatic and military relationships with the English Parliament. The Scots Commissioners in England were arrested after they had issued a denunciation of the execution and the simultaneous abolition of the monarchy and of the House of Lords. Yet, in Scotland, the purging instituted by the Act of Classes continued, and the Scots made it clear that their new King should subscribe the Solemn League and Covenant before taking up the reins of power. They were determined that the King should guarantee the Presbyterian way of worship for Scotland and impose Presbyterian uniformity throughout the three kingdoms[13].

After much haggling, King Charles II came to Scotland under terms on 23rd June, 1650, and immediately became the virtual prisoner of the Covenanters. His principal lieutenant, the Marquis of Montrose, had just been captured and executed after trying to repeat his successes of five years before. Indeed there was no way for Charles to establish any kingship in Britain except by bowing the knee to the Scottish Covenanters.

Events now moved fast. Having secured the King, the Scots prepared to invade England but were forestalled by Cromwell who invaded Scotland on 22nd July, 1650. Things did not go all Cromwell's way to begin with, but on 3rd September, 1650, the English army defeated the numerically stronger Scots at Dunbar. The Scots were demoralized by too much purging — the Act of Classes had been applied to the Army too — and their generals had a habit of making wrong decisions at crucial moments.

Cromwell took over Edinburgh, but found that he was not in a position to consolidate his grip immediately upon the rest of Scotland. The two component parts of the Covenanting regime, the Committee of Estates and the Commission of the Kirk, retired first to Stirling and then to Perth, where they prepared for further resistance but soon were being pulled apart by internal quarrels.

Before the Battle of Dunbar the King had been undergoing preparation for coronation on the Covenanters' terms. That coronation had had to be postponed, but the relentless pressures on the King, a young man of only twenty, had continued. The ministers tried to brainwash him, and repeatedly purged his friends and his servants in an endeavour to isolate him as far as possible. Many people tried to manipulate him, some for their own ends, like Argyll, who engineered his own promotion from Earl to Marquis. At the same time ministers and politicians did not bother to conceal their dislike and contempt for him. The Kirk feared as well as disliked him, and went so far as to order him away from the Army encampment at Leith in case his evident popularity with the soldiers should increase their "carnal confidence" (Johnson of Wariston's phrase)[14] at the expense of their confidence in God.

In early October 1650 the King decided that he could no longer stand all this, and literally ran away in what became known as "the Start". He meant either to raise a royalist revolt or, failing that, simply to get out of the country, but his decisiveness and organizing ability were unsurprisingly paralysed after the prolonged mental bombardment to which he had been subjected. After only two days he was caught and taken back to Perth in a dismal state of demoralisation. Oddly enough, the Start operated to his advantage, for it had shown the Covenanting government what its real danger was: losing the one ace up its sleeve, the King himself—the only factor which might give the appearance of cohesion and national unity to the Covenanters' increasingly desperate endeavours.

In the meantime the extreme Covenanters, backed by and perhaps largely consisting of the Army of the Western Association, came together in Dumfries and produced a document of protest or "Remonstrance", with which they confronted the Perth regime on 22nd October, 1650. These radicals, who continued to press for complete fulfilment of the original Solemn League and Covenant, and who were intensely suspicious of the King, held that the reason for the defeat at Dunbar was not too much purging but too little: the Scottish army had not found favour with the Lord because there were still too many former Engagers and other anti-Covenant elements in it. They spelt out these and other criticisms in the Remonstrance.

The Perth government rejected the Remonstrance, whereupon a large minority of ministers on the Kirk Commission, almost half of those present on 28th November, 1650, walked out of the Commission. From this walk-out may be dated the virtual schism of the Church of Scotland into radicals ("Remonstrants" and later "Protesters") and moderates. The latter party passed resolutions in the Kirk Commission repealing the Act of Classes, and so they became known as "Resolutioners".

The Remonstrants, having presented their case, promptly collapsed as a military force. The Army of the Western Association under Colonel Gilbert Ker was unwisely tempted into battle at Hamilton against a superior force of English under General Lambert on 1st December, 1650, and was utterly routed. Not that military defeat eclipsed the party: throughout their subsequent history until 1688, the tough grassroots opposition of the western radical covenanters to royal authority, prelacy and moderate Presbyterianism was unmodified either by their patent military ineptitude or by any prudential leavening of pacifism.

Meanwhile the Resolutioners, having opened the floodgates to former Engagers, Malignants, supporters of the King and even former supporters of the executed Montrose, were organising a patriot army to march south under the nominal command of the King to reclaim his major kingdom. At last they succeeded in bringing him to be crowned at the traditional coronation site, Scone, the last monarch to be crowned there, on 1st January, 1651.

Charles had to submit to sign the Solemn League and Covenant, with its stipulation about "the preservation of the reformed religion in the Church of Scotland", and its ambiguous phrase about the "reformation of religion in the kingdoms of England and Ireland", which the Scots took to mean presbyterianizing these two countries. Earlier, on 16th August, 1650, Charles had been obliged to sign another pre-coronation document, declaring that

> "he [doth] desire to be deeply humbled and afflicted in spirit before
> God, because of his father's hearkening to, and following evil
> counsels, and his opposition to the work of reformation, and to the
> Solemn League and Covenant, by which so much of the blood of
> the Lord's people hath been shed in these kingdoms; and for the
> idolatry of his mother..."[15]

Charles II believed that these signatures had been extorted from him under duress and that therefore he was not bound by them. He never forgot or forgave the people who had compelled him to insult the memory of his executed father and his living, Roman Catholic mother, in this manner. Argyll's head fell after the Restoration; Guthrie and Wariston were hanged. Charles resolved not only to have no truck with Presbyterians ever again, but to establish episcopacy firmly and uniformly throughout his three realms.

On the other hand the Presbyterians believed that his signatures were simply a part of the Coronation Oath, and that Charles committed perjury in disregarding them. They held that Presbyterianism was the only form of church government acceptable in the sight of the Lord. As such it was open neither to negotiation nor to compromise. The scene for thirty years of struggle after the Restoration was thus set.

In 1651, however, these things lay in a very dark future. King Charles at the head of his army by-passed Cromwell and marched south to utter defeat at Worcester and thereafter to perilous escape and nine bitter years of exile. Cromwell mopped up the last pockets of resistance in Scotland

and built a formidable string of fortresses throughout the land to keep the rebellious natives in their place. In his rough and ready military fashion he hammered out the first effective union between England and Scotland, imposing a measure of peace upon the warring factions. There was even a whiff of toleration in the air, but the Resolutioners and the Protesters continued their bickerings; on one occasion, 20th July 1653, they held rival General Assemblies in St Giles's Church in Edinburgh separated only by a thin partition, and were suppressed by the Commonwealth authorities with a party of soldiers. The spirit of the age may be gauged by the following words taken from a prayer offered up by a leading Protester in Glasgow on 3rd August, 1657:

> "Lord forgive the countenance that was given to the late proclamacion which invites men of erroneous oppinions to have liberty provided they live peaceably. Is this the practice of Christian magistrates? The Lord lett not my soul enter into their Councells that set upp such things by a law. God forgive the countenance that was given to this thing, in other places as well as here."[16]

The Restoration of Charles II

At the Restoration in 1660 the two Covenanting parties found themselves in an equally disadvantageous position. They got off to a bad start with the defection to the Episcopalian side of James Sharp, Minister of Craill in Fife, who had been deputed to look after Presbyterian interests in the Netherlands and London in the run-up to the Restoration. Sharp, a devious and crooked character, allowed himself to be bought by the promise of the Archbishopric of St Andrews, and was not above soothing the increasing suspicions of his co-religionists in Scotland until it was too late, by a series of deliberately misleading dispatches. By the time that both wings of the Covenanting movement, Resolutioners and Protesters, had woken up to the fact that the restored monarch would threaten the very existence of Presbyterianism, Charles's clamp-down was too far advanced to be averted. The Act Rescissory annulling all Acts passed since 1633 was pushed through, and the Covenants were declared illegal. A General Assembly of the Kirk was pointedly not called. Presbyteries and synods were forbidden to meet, and actual meetings were broken up by force and the threat of force. Leaders such as Guthrie, Wariston and Argyll were picked off and executed. The King announced his intention of restoring and actually restored the system of bishops' rule in Scotland.

Finally, the Act of Presentation and Collation of June 1662 made it impossible for any presbyterians to continue to worship legally without episcopal sanction. Under this Act every minister had as it were to reapply through the bishop before being allowed to continue his ministry in his parish.

The Act, according to the airy prediction of its sponsor (Archbishop Fairfoul of Glasgow), should have picked off no more than ten or twelve extremists at the most[17]. The new government seems to have been genuinely taken aback to discover that in certain areas of the country a majority of ministers were prepared to forsake their livings rather than conform to Episcopalian government. Charles's first Parliamentary Commissioner, the Earl of Middleton, "cursing and swearing", is reported to have asked, "What will these mad fellows do?"[18] It is clear that besides the inextinguishable hatred of the various parties for each other, sheer stupidity, lack of imagination, incompetence and mutual incomprehension played a very large part in bringing about a near civil war situation.

A good three hundred ministers, nearly a third of the total Scottish establishment of 952, were eventually "outed" as a result of the reckless application of the Act of Presentation and Collation. The West of Scotland was particularly badly hit. The Synod of Glasgow and Ayr lost two thirds of its ministerial establishment, and the Synod of Dumfries lost more than half[19]. Both wings of the Presbyterian church, Resolutioner and Protester, were affected. The determining factor was the degree to which a minister's conscience would allow him to tolerate state interference with the Church or (as it was labelled) Erastianism; many Resolutioners as well as Protesters found that they could not stomach a state of affairs in which the secular kingdom was formally accorded pre-eminence over the spiritual.

To depose ministers or ensure their resignation was one thing; to silence them effectively and to destroy their natural popularity was quite another. The men who were hastily drafted in to replace the "outed" incumbents had the reputation of being unspiritual and dissolute. Popular feeling against these "curates" and the bishops was intense. In spite of this, however, the Government persisted in its efforts, becoming more and more heavy-handed, with fines and imprisonment for "recusants", people who would not go to their regular parish church. The deposed ministers took to holding conventicles which were now often very large-scale meetings held out of doors. Conventiclers were singled out for harsh treatment, including imprisonment and deportation. Many of the famous names of Covenanting legend, Peden, Welch and Blackadder, first come to prominence at this time, itinerant field preachers who built large followings wherever they went.

The Pentland Rising

In 1665 Great Britain went to war with the Netherlands, where many exiled ministers had found a haven, and the government began to suspect that an insurrectionary plot might be hatching with Dutch support. This, and the hot-headedness of Archbishop Burnet of Glasgow, led to the introduction of military repression throughout the Lowlands. In spite of the seriousness of this step, the authorities did not send out sufficient men for the vast areas they were supposed to cover: barely 140 men under Sir James Turner to patrol the whole of Dumfries and Galloway. Later, after February 1666, the numbers began to increase under Tam Dalyell of the Binns and Sir William Drummond, but they were still far too few for efficient policing. When soldiers are over-stretched, nervous and un-popular, their behaviour can become harsher and more oppressive, and this is what happened in south-west Scotland. Their commanders, besides, were both brutal and cynical, and under their terms of service they could hardly avoid being corrupt. Conditions were ripe for a revolt.

In November 1666, while a party of radical Conventiclers was passing through St John's Clachan of Dalry in Galloway, a small group of Sir James Turner's soldiers was maltreating a poor peasant for non-payment of a fine for recusancy. The commotion was loud enough to be overheard by the Covenanters, who immediately set upon and overpowered the soldiers, shooting and wounding one of them. The principle of "in for a penny, in for a pound" was applied, and a surprise attack upon Turner's headquarters at Dumfries ensued, Sir James himself being captured in his nightgown. A small army was hastily organised, gathering a little strength as it passed through Ayrshire and Lanarkshire. The leaders of the revolt may have hoped to emulate the Whiggamore Raid, when Western Covenanters marched on and took over the seat of government, but in 1666 arms, supplies, adequate planning and leadership itself were all wanting. Morale fell, desertions became a haemorrhage and, by the time the insurgents reached the outskirts of Edinburgh, their fate was sealed. On 28th November, 1666, at Rullion Green near Penicuik, the Pentland Rising collapsed under the onslaught of the famous Major-General Tam Dalyell.

After the surrender, the Scottish Privy Council under the presidency of Archbishop Sharp decided to treat the prisoners as traitors and to try them for their lives, in spite of the indignant protests of Dalyell, on whose terms they had laid their arms down. Several of the rebels were sent to their home towns to be executed *in terrorem*, as an example to their fellow citizens[20]. This happened in Glasgow, Ayr, Irvine and Dumfries, giving us our first batch of funerary monuments. (See entries for the named towns and also for Kilmarnock, Hamilton, Newmilns, and Fenwick.)

The next thirteen years after the Pentland Rising are a story of alternating repression and indulgence — specifically, *Indulgences*, or licences to certain previously "outed" preachers, permitting them to exercise ministerial functions under certain conditions and in certain areas. The Indulgences of 1669 and 1672 were the brainchildren of a new moderately-inclined Scottish government under the control of the Duke of Lauderdale, a member of Charles II's CABAL administration. He was by no means an enemy to Presbyterianism but had to steer a middle course between the extremes of episcopalianism and the Covenanters. It seemed to him that the heat would be taken out of the Scottish situation if terms were offered to the opposition. The heat remained and even intensified, but the policy may be said to have had some success in that it sowed dissension among the Covenanters. Quite a number of ministers accepted the terms of the Indulgences, but were bitterly denounced by their colleagues as weak-kneed Erastians and traitors to the Covenants.

At the same time as offering the Indulgences, the policy of the government was to intensify the persecution of the Conventiclers and especially of those who organised or attended the great field conventicles. Field preachers became liable to the death penalty, and fines or imprisonment for those who attended became commonplace. One of the most resented measures made land-owners responsible for the good conduct of their tenants, and liable to prosecution if they did not report conventicles held on their land. Another hated statute made men liable for fines incurred by their womenfolk attending conventicles. Measures of this kind had the effect of strengthening the solidarity already existing since before the Cromwellian period between the lesser gentry, their tenants and the landless folk such as artisans and labourers. Especially in the West of Scotland the grassroots dimension comes to the fore in the 1670s, giving the Covenanting resistance an identity unusual in those times as a mass movement.

Constantly harried by informers and dragoons, many worshippers rode armed to the conventicles, which often became permanent outdoor assemblies with their own systems of look-outs and defence. The authorities, trying to quell whole disaffected districts, evolved a kind of collective punishment by military occupation whereby soldiers were billeted on towns, villages and individual families, to plunder and destroy at will. One of the best-known examples of this treatment was the so-called "Highland Host" of 1678, under which Ayrshire in particular suffered grievously.

The Archbishop's murder and its aftermath

The mixture of oppression and resistance became gradually more explosive as pressure increased. At length a spark to ignite the atmosphere was generated. On 3rd May, 1679, Archbishop James Sharp of St Andrews, by many seen as the chief architect of the anti-Presbyterian measures and as a turncoat who had sold out his fellow Presbyterians for an Archbishopric, was dragged from his coach and assassinated on Magus Muir near St Andrews. The murder itself was a particuarly gruesome and long-drawn-out affair, and the shock-waves spread far and wide. The perpetrators of the deed fled to the West, where they joined a party of radical Conventiclers led by Robert Hamilton, a prominent layman. On 29th May, 1679, the King's birthday and anniversary of his restoration, Hamilton and eighty armed followers rode into Rutherglen, extinguished the celebratory bonfires, and nailed a manifesto "against the iniquity of the times" to the Market Cross there.

At this point the great and sometimes hated figure of John Graham of Claverhouse appears on the Government side. He was a brilliant young officer recently returned from the service of William of Orange and apparently high in the favour (because recommended by William) of James Duke of York, the Catholic brother and heir of King Charles II. Claverhouse had been employed since 1678 "dissipating and interrupting" field-conventicles, those "rendevouzes of rebellion" in Dumfriesshire and Annandale[21]. On 29th May, 1679, he was already on his way north, and by 31st May he was in full pursuit of Hamilton and his men. Hamilton got away, but Claverhouse, after taking some prisoners at the town of Hamilton, set out on the track of a large conventicle reported to be gathering near Loudoun Hill in Ayrshire.

On the morning of Sunday 1st June, 1679, Claverhouse and his dragoons came upon the armed conventicle at Drumclog. When the minister, the Reverend James (or Thomas) Douglas, was warned by the look-outs, he finished his sermon, supervised the withdrawal of the women, children and old men, and said to the young fighting men, "Ye have got the theory; now for the practice!"[22].

When drawn up in line of battle, the Conventiclers outnumbered Claverhouse's little force by about four to one; they had the advantage of the ground, which was unfamiliar to Claverhouse[23]. The dragoons fired wildly, but the Conventiclers threaded their way across a stretch of seemingly boggy ground, and attacked the Government force at close quarters. The dragoons broke and fled, leaving as many as 36 dead on the ground. It is related that one of the freed prisoners taken at Hamilton, the

Rev. King, called after the retreating Claverhouse, "Are ye no bidin' for the efternuin preachin'?"[24]. The Government troops had to fight their way through the narrow streets of Strathaven, whose inhabitants turned out in force to deny them passage. They were a weary and dispirited band by the time they met a relief column under Lord Ross outside Glasgow.

Drumclog was to be the only set-piece battle won by Covenanters against Government forces during the Restoration period. Only a handful of Covenanters fell. (See entries for Loudoun, Newmilns, Strathaven and Lesmahagow.)

"This," Claverhouse wrote, "may be counted the beginning of the rebellion." Large numbers of Whigs (as the Covenanters were now generally called) came together after Drumclog and marched on Glasgow, but Robert Hamilton's generalship proved seriously defective and after some skirmishing they withdrew without securing the city. At Hamilton town, where they encamped, they divided into two sections, the "honest" party (under Hamilton) and the Indulged, and promptly started to quarrel.

Robert Hamilton's irate suspicion of those who had in any way moved towards acceptance of the Government's Indulgences recalls the effect of the Act of Classes a generation earlier. In that case the Covenanter government in Edinburgh had purged the army of all elements held to be unworthy in the sight of the Lord, and this was probably a major contributing factor in their defeat at the hands of Oliver Cromwell at Dunbar in 1650.[25] At Hamilton in 1679 the interminable squabblings simply blinded the participants to the need for adequate military preparations. Meanwhile, the Government forces had rallied under the leadership of the Duke of Monmouth, King Charles's illegitimate son, and, at Bothwell Brig on 22nd June, 1679, they fell upon the Whig forces and routed them after a brief battle. Claverhouse pursued some Covenanters as far as Ayr. (See entries for Galston and Cambusnethan.)

After Bothwell Brig the Government, under the short-lived influence of Monmouth, was initially disposed to be merciful. Then Monmouth was relieved of his command and James Duke of York, the Catholic heir to the throne, arrived in Scotland in November 1679. Under his guidance repression gradually hardened again. The end of the moderate policies of the Duke of Lauderdale was formally confirmed by his removal from office in October 1680. The Drumclog/Bothwell rebellion signalled the collapse of conciliation even as a long-term objective of the Scottish Government.

The Cameronians and James Renwick

Among the extremist Covenanters of the West of Scotland morale fell to a very low ebb after Bothwell Brig, and conventicling, especially out of doors, was largely discontinued. However, in October 1679, a young preacher named Richard Cameron returned to Scotland from the Netherlands where he had been since 1677. He was implacably anti-Erastian—opposed to State interference with Church affairs—and violently hostile to those who had accepted the Government's Indulgences. He was outraged by the presence of the Duke of York in Scotland, and preached fiery sermons at some of the very few field conventicles still being held (e.g. at Darmead and Auchengilloch).

Early in 1680 two extreme associates of Cameron, Donald Cargill and Henry Hall of Haughead, were involved in a fracas at Queensferry. Cargill escaped but Hall was killed, and on his body was discovered the notorious Queensferry Paper. This draft manifesto declared, among other things, that church government should be exercised "not after a carnal manner by a plurality of votes, or authority of a single person, but according to the word of God"[26]. This kind of language seemed to presage a clerical dictatorship on the part of the Cameronians, and it alarmed not only the Government but also moderate Presbyterians, now clearly in the majority, who were beginning to feel their way towards an accommodation with the Episcopalians. Then, on 22nd June, 1680, the anniversary of the Battle of Bothwell Brig, Richard Cameron himself made an actual declaration of war at the Market Cross of Sanquhar, surrounded by his armed followers. He disowned King Charles II and his brother the Duke of York, and vowed to fight them "as enemies of our Lord Jesus Christ, and his cause and covenants"[27].

If Cameron hoped to provoke a general rising in this fashion, he was to be disappointed. The Curate of Ochiltree informed the authorities of the movements of the Cameronians and, on 20th (or 22nd) July, 1680, about 120 dragoons under Bruce of Earlshall caught up with Cameron and 60 of his followers at Airdsmoss just west of Muirkirk in Ayrshire. After a fierce battle, the Cameronian resistance collapsed. More dragoons than Cameronians littered the field, but among the nine Cameronians killed were Richard Cameron and his brother Michael. One of the prisoners was David Hackston of Rathillet, who had been among Archbishop Sharp's murderers. and he was taken to Edinburgh and executed. (See entries for Airdsmoss, Sanquhar and Cupar.)

The sense of tension that Cameron had created now ebbed, and peace might have begun to return to the battered Presbyterian communities of the West, but from the other side the Government began to tighten the screw of repression anew. The Test Act of 1681 required every office-holder to swear loyalty in terms that were uncompromisingly Erastian: the King's supremacy had to be acknowledged in all matters temporal and spiritual. Moreover, the Act of Succession, passed at the same time, made inescapable the succession of the Catholic Duke of York. Government agents throughout the country, including Claverhouse, compelled people to take the Test, often irrespective of whether they were office-holders or likely to be. Systematic military repression continued to grip the land, and there was a mounting total of fines, imprisonments, deportations and executions.

Under these circumstances it is not surprising that the embers of the Cameronians were fanned into flame one more. Donald Cargill, who had excommunicated the King and other Government leaders at Torwood in October 1680, was taken and hanged in 1681, and for some time there was no visible leadership for the uncompromising extremists, now reduced to a few hundred individuals. Yet the "remnant" of these radical Presbyterians formed themselves into several praying societies who held a convention at Logan House (near Lesmahagow) on 15th December, 1681, and thereafter published a fire-eating declaration at Lanark on 12th January, 1682. (See entries for the places named.) They decided to strengthen their mutual bonds by forming a "correspondence union", and in fact laying the foundations of an underground resistance network[28]. When the new young leader James Renwick came across from the Netherlands in his turn in September 1683, he found the means ready to hand to relight the torch of Richard Cameron.

Renwick's mission soon became known to the Government, and their counter-measures became harsher and more vindictive than ever[29]. Sir Hew Campbell of Cessnock near Galston was accused in 1684 of encouraging the rebels at Bothwell Brig in 1679; even though the prosecution case broke down, and their star witnesses withdrew their testimony against Sir Hew in open court, he was sent to the Bass Rock, then used as a prison island[30]. Captain John Paton of Meadowhead near Fenwick, a hero of every Covenanting battle from Mauchline Muir onward, was taken in his old age: General Tam Dalyell, himself aged and near death but still Commander-in-Chief of the Government forces, took the distinguished veteran in his arms and promised to do all he could to spare him the death penalty. Paton said, "You will not be heard!" and sure enough, despite Dalyell's pleas, John Paton was hanged in the Grassmarket, Edinburgh, on 9th May, 1684.

The Killing Time

In fact it is from about this point, the summer of 1684, that we begin to see a progressive deterioration leading to the explosion of violence known as *The Killing Time*. What caused this spiral intensification of trouble is not really clear—whether it originated in some act or decision on the part of the Government or the Covenanters, the return of Renwick or Government apprehensions about the Argyll conspiracy—or whether the whole series of events simply snowballed out of control from disregarded beginnings.

Whatever its cause, the process began to accelerate on or around 10th June, 1684, when John Graham of Claverhouse interrupted his own wedding celebrations in Paisley to go in pursuit of a large party of conventiclers who had fled from the Blackloch conventicle in Slamannan "under the spiritual leadership of Renwick"[31]. (See entry for Paisley for further details.) Claverhouse chased them the length of Ayrshire and into Nithsdale, but by 14th or 15th June it was obvious that the conventiclers had got clean away, and Claverhouse and his men seem to have retired northward in bafflement. However, Claverhouse was a zealous, indefatigable and intelligent tracker, and it is suspected that the Enterkin Pass incident of July 1684 involved the liberation of some of the Blackloch conventiclers who had been captured after 15th June. They were among a party of prisoners who were being taken from Dumfries to Edinburgh for trial under armed escort provided by part of Claverhouse's troop. A well-planned ambush at Glenvalentine on the Pass resulted in several deaths and the liberation of most or all of the prisoners. Claverhouse later personally ran to earth and arrested a number of the participants in the ambush, including the organizer of the affair, James "Long Gun" Harkness.

Harkness subsequently escaped, but the other captured men were hanged in Edinburgh on 15th August, 1684. The ugly vindictiveness of trying and hanging these men on the same day has been noted, and it is clear that the Government was losing patience. (For further details, see Appendix IA and entries for Dalgarnock, Durisdeer, Dalveen and Enterkin.)

In other respects a rigid application of legal apparatus brought the criminalization of whole swathes of the population appreciably closer. In October 1684 landowners were rounded up *en masse* and held in places like Ayr Tolbooth under unspeakable conditions until they should "offer to take the Test" and to pay a substantial sum of money[32]. In the background the soldiery were poised menacingly.

Under these circumstances James Renwick, now the clear successor to Richard Cameron and lurking in Friarminnion above Kirkconnell, was impelled to issue his Apologetical Declaration (28th October, 1684) threatening death to spies and collaborators[33]. This was published in the usual way by being affixed to church doors and market crosses. Then, on 28th November 1684, two soldiers notorious for harassing Presbyterians were assassinated as they left a tavern at Swyne Abbey in West Lothian (near Bathgate).

This act alarmed and infuriated the Privy Council, who now took what has often been described as a step of odious tyranny: they framed and promulgated the *Abjuration Oath* — a loyalty oath directed against the supporters of James Renwick: any person refusing to swear on demand could legally be put to death in front of two witnesses.

The terms of the Abjuration Oath are as follows:

"I A.B. doe hereby abhorr, renunce and disoune, in presence of the Almighty God, the pretendit Declaratione of Warr lately affixed at severall paroch churches in so far as it declares a warr against his sacred Majestie and asserts that it is laufull to kill such as serve his Majestie in church, state, army or countrey, or such as act against the authors of the said pretended declaratione now shewne to me. And I doe hereby utterly renunce and disoune the villanous authors thereof who did (as they call it) statut and ordaine the same, and what is therein mentioned, and I swear I shall never assist the authors of the said pretended declaratione or ther emissaries or adherents in any poynts of punishing, killing and makeing of warr any manner of way as I shall answear to God."[34].

It will be seen that some care has been exercised in the framing of this oath. It is directed against Renwick's Apologetical Declaration only in so far as that manifesto declares war and states that it is lawful to kill. Nobody, of course, would deny that it is monstrously if not recklessly tyrannical to undertake to kill any person who refuses to swear in a given form of words on demand. Whatever else it is, however, the Abjuration Oath is not intrinsically an instrument of religious persecution. An objection might be and no doubt was raised against the Erastian form of referring to "such as serve his Majestie in church", but the consequences of refusing this oath fell only upon people who, for whatever reason, were unable to make a formal renunciation of killing and war as means of obtaining their particular ends. As we go on in this story, we may be able to discern a reason for this.

The framing of the Abjuration Oath was followed by the murder of the Curate of Carsphairn (11th December, 1684), a raid upon Kirkcudbright Jail by over 100 men in which one guard was killed and the prisoners released (16th December), and the Bridge of Dee skirmish in which

Claverhouse himself was nearly killed, but which ended with the death or capture of eight Covenanters (18th December). (See entries for Kirkcudbright, Auchencloy and Dalry for further details.)

The man who nearly got the better of Claverhouse, Black James McMichael, had taken a leading part not merely in the Carsphairn murder and (probably) the Kirkcudbright prison raid, but also in the Enterkin Pass ambush, along with James "Long Gun" Harkness. Accordingly the Bridge of Dee/Auchencloy action may be seen as a follow-up and response by the Government to these previous deeds; it may also be seen as another twist in the spiral of violence that was now gathering intensity: the Killing Time is often dated from the Bridge of Dee action. After this time, the whole of the south-west of Scotland was virtually on a war footing.

The scope of Government action, at first mainly directed against the Renwickian "remnant" of extreme Covenanters, now widened to include the whole spectrum of Presbyterianism. Many previously indulged ministers suddenly became victims of persecution, and legal and administrative means of attacking Presbyterians of all shades were upgraded. One "spite" execution which represents this hardening of Government attitudes was the hanging in Edinburgh of the great, dying scholar Robert Baillie of Jerviswood.

Above all, however, the period from January 1685 is marked out by a series of field executions of (mainly) unarmed peasantry suspected of being Renwickites. It is from this time that the storm of violence in the south west, The Killing Time, is at its height. In it, the Abjuration Oath played a significant part: once this instrument was in place, it could be argued, executions were bound to become more frequent. It could also be argued that the period covers the death of King Charles II on 12th February, 1685, and the accession of his brother the Duke of York as James VII and II: tension was bound to increase at such a time. But in our search for an underlying motivation for the Killing Time, a most important point to consider, covering both the previous points, is that the duration of the Killing Time coincides more or less exactly with that of the ill-fated Argyll Insurrection.

The duration of the Killing Time may, in fact, be dated with some cautious precision. Statistics from this period of history should always be treated with reserve, and some of the data are incomplete. For instance, out of 43 single or multiple killings or other deaths including field executions in the south-west of Scotland between December 1684 and December 1685 involving 89 victims[35], we have no clear day or month for 12, involving 15 victims. Yet from the remaining 31 executions it can be seen that there is a rising curve from December 1684 to May 1685.

The Killing Time
Dec 1684 - Nov 1685

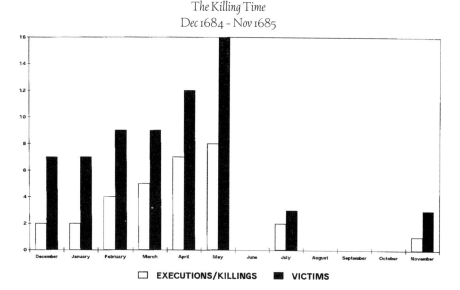

Using this chart with caution, then, we may say that the most intense phase of the Killing Time seems to have come to an end with the shooting of James Kirk (or Kirko or Kirka) at Dumfries on 13th May. The preceding fortnight, from 28th April, saw the executions of 20 people, including John Brown the Christian Carrier, John Browning and his four associates, the Ingliston five, the Polmadie three (buried at Cathcart) and the two female Wigtown martyrs. After 13th May there occur only two or perhaps three isolated executions in July, involving four victims; after July no field killings at all are reported, at least with certain dates, until November, when a shoot-out — not an execution — took place near Fenwick. (This led to the execution in Edinburgh in December 1685 of the hard-core activist John Nisbet of Hardhill.)

Although it is obviously not impossible that some of the executions for which no day or month can be assigned took place after 13th May, the balance of probability is that field and other summary executions did stop abruptly around this time. Why this abruptness?

The immediate reasons for the executions are in many respects as enig-matic as the reason for their cessation. The standard tomb inscriptions, with their references to death inflicted as a punishment for "the covenanted work of reformation", "for owning Covenanted presbytery" and so forth, are not very helpful. In some cases literary sources indicate random killings, notwithstanding the epitaph, which invariably indicates deliber-ate martyrdom. (See, for instance, the entry for Colmonell.) In many cases the standard formulae obviously cover death inflicted after the Abjuration Oath had been tendered and refused. John Brown's tomb at Priesthill is a case in point. In this famous instance, Claverhouse's own testimony (letter written from Galston, given in Appendix III) shows fairly conclusively that the Abjuration Oath and the execution itself were used to put pressure on a third party, John Browning, to reveal his own part and that of others in the Newmilns prison raid of April 1685 and other sensitive information. (For further details, see entries for Newmilns, Priesthill and Mauchline.)

In the light of this case, and of the clustering of executions in late April and early May, it is tempting to see all the executions of the late Killing Time as interconnected, as evidence of some extensive conspiracy whose members were tracked down and summarily disposed of in this fashion. Direct evidence, however, is still lacking.

It is possible, however, to set the Killing Time in a wider context, and this yields certain clues. For a long time plans had been hatching for an insurrection in Scotland to be led by the fugitive Earl of Argyll, who had been living in the Netherlands since being sentenced to death in Scotland in 1682. Sir Hew Campbell of Cessnock, mentioned above as the target of Government persecution in 1684, was involved in the Scottish (and London) ends of this conspiracy, together with Sir John Cochrane of Ochiltree and others. After the unexpected death of King Charles II in February 1685 and the accession of his brother as King James VII and II, who was openly committed to re-Catholicizing Britain, panic measures were taken by the Argyll conspirators to bring forward their invasion of Scotland and to synchronise it with the corresponding Monmouth rebellion in the south. They met in Amsterdam to finalise plans on 17th April, 1685. On 2nd May, 1685, the day after the execution of John Brown, Argyll and the core of his rebel force set sail, putting in first at Kirkwall, Orkney, where the alarm was raised. The Killing Time was reaching its crescendo while the Earl was on the high seas. On 20th May, a week after the apparent sudden stop of killings, Argyll landed at Campbeltown, complete with printing press, and began his hopeless preparations.

On 28th May, 1685, a convention of radical Covenanters, including James Renwick, met at Blackgannoch[36], a remote farmhouse in the Friarminnion area of east Nithsdale. They adopted certain resolutions which Renwick, at the head of 200 armed and mounted followers, proclaimed later that day from the Market Cross in Sanquhar. However, this "Protestation and Apologetical Admonitory Declaration", unlike its Cameronian predecessor, was not followed by a warlike challenge and a suicidal battle. Of course, it uses standard phrases against James VII and II, "a professed papist and excommunicate person ... a murderer ... who hath shed the blood of the saints of God"; yet, through all the fire-eating rhetoric we may discern something more than caution, even an undertaking: "disclaiming (likewise) all Sectarians, Malignancy, and any Confederacy therewith ..."[37]

Decoded, this and similar hints meant that they would not join with the Earl of Argyll, whose attachment to the Covenants had been less than whole-hearted. Argyll's rebellion collapsed before 18th June, when he was captured by a civilian. On 30th June, 1685, the Earl, like his father before him, lost his head on the guillotine ("the Maiden") in Edinburgh.

Whether any fifth-column or maquisard assistance from the Society People in south-west Scotland could have saved the dreadfully rickety Argyll venture may be doubted. Nevertheless it looks as if the Government in Edinburgh were taking no chances on that; at least it is clear that they increased pressure on the south-western extremists in the spring of 1685: then, having made their point, it is not hard to think that the Government would introduce a little "adversarial diplomacy" into the situation, coupled with a dramatically sudden easing of the pressure. A bargain may have been struck, as a result of which the Sanquhar Declaration appeared: the price of the ending of the Killing Time was that the Renwickites and the Society People would not involve themselves in the Argyll Rising.

To make a suggestion like this is not to acquit the Government of a premeditated policy of atrocity—something which the sudden cut-off of the flow of killings after May, as it were with a tap, only serves to accentuate. This suggestion would merely confirm what has already been evident from the terms of the Abjuration Oath, that the motive behind the persecution was not exclusively or even mainly religious. Fear of insurrection whipped up from abroad, even fear of invasion from the Netherlands, had long haunted Scottish administrations and, as we have seen in the case of the Pentland Rising, had once before led to a military crack-down in south-west Scotland, in the 1660s.

The suggestion made above would have to be confirmed with harder evidence than I have so far been able to uncover. Yet alternative explanation would have to account for the increase and, after the middle of May, the sudden falling-off in the numbers of killings. If a bargain was made, the Government seem to have kept their side of it: after May 1685 persecution of Covenanters diminished markedly and permanently. Activists like John Nisbet of Hardhill continued to be picked off, but the general situation eased so much that there was only one execution in 1686 and in 1687 King James brought in two new Indulgences. Not that this did him much good with the Covenanting diehards, who did not fail to notice that the real effect of the Indulgences was to ease restrictions on the Catholics. The Covenanters denounced the 1687 Indulgences as "sinful toleration".

Whatever the extremists' opinion, so many previously "outed" preachers were now readmitted by Indulgence that mass desertion of the officially-sponsored "curates" by their congregations became commonplace. The Indulgences also had the effect of demonstrating how isolated and unrepresentative the Cameronian/Renwickite hard-liners really were. The conventicling spirit flagged, and it was during one of James Renwick's more desperate attempts to maintain the tradition in the Edinburgh area that he himself was captured in February 1688. He was put to death with abominable cruelty, but this was the last major execution of the period. Soon James VII and II seemed to over-reach himself altogether, and at the end of 1688 he had to flee abroad, while his daughter Mary and her husband William of Orange became joint sovereigns in his place. After thirty years of strife the tables were turned, Episcopalianism was made illegal in Scotland and Presbyterianism was established (in so far as any non-Erastian form of church government may be said to be established) on the basis of the thirty-nine articles of the forty-five year-old Westminster Confession.

The Cameronians held themselves aloof for many years after the Glorious Revolution of 1688. Persecution of extremist Covenanters dwindled away almost to nothing, if it did not disappear altogether. The only really significant personage on the other side, John Graham of Claverhouse (ennobled by King James as Viscount Dundee), found it difficult to turn his coat, and raised the standard of what was to become known as Jacobitism against the Dutch usurper in 1689. William's forces were soundly defeated at the Battle of Killiecrankie that year, but Claverhouse was felled by a lucky sniper's bullet at the beginning of the battle. Without his characteristic energy, confidence and overall strategic vision, the pro-Stuart forces fell to pieces in a few days. Otherwise history might have been written very differently.

[1] Stevenson D 1973 p85
[2] Peterkin p46
[3] For the idea of "exporting revolution" compare Stevenson D 1973 p299ff and 1988 p53.
[4] APS vi pt i 41 para 1
[5] Stevenson D 1977 pp54-55
[6] Stevenson D 1977 pp86-87

7   Stevenson D 1977 *loc cit*
8   Stevenson D 1988 p56
9   Turner p53 and Stevenson D 1977 p108
10 Stevenson D 1973 (MM) pp8-13
11 Stevenson D 1977 pp123-124
12 Stevenson D 1977 p125
13 Stevenson D 1977 p132
14 Stevenson D 1977 p174
15 As quoted in Wodrow i 66n
16 Quoted in Dunlop pp33-34
17 Cowan p50
18 Wodrow i p284
19 Cowan pp52-53
20 Wodrow ii p51
21 Terry *Claverhouse* p39
22 Torfoot p3
23 Aiton p54
24 Creichton p32
25 Stevenson D 1977 p179
26 Donaldson p240; Wodrow iii pp207-211
27 Donaldson pp241-242; Wodrow iii pp 212-213
28 Compare Cowan pp110-111
29 Wodrow iii p446; iv plff and passim
30 Fountainhall ii pp510-512; Wodrow iv p71ff, pp224-225
    It is not denied, of course, that Sir Hew Campbell of Cessnock was implicated with Sir John Cochrane of Ochiltree and others in the London end of the Argyll conspiracy.
31 Hewison ii p426 (quoting Erskine *Journal* p65)
32 Wodrow iv p126
33 For complete text see *Vindication* pp96-100; cf Wodrow iv pp 148-149 and *Hind* pp160-161; Donaldson p242 gives a short extract.
34 Privy Council pp564-565
35 This total omits the case of Blackadder (who died on the Bass Rock in late 1685) and the cases of the Dunnottar victims, the unknowns at Old Dailly and at Windshields,the tailor Mowat, Morris and Brown at Craignorth (see Corsgellioch), and the Allan's Cairn enigma.
36 Hewison ii p484
37 *Vindication* p105; cf p106 and p22; also *Hind* p165 and Wodrow iv p446.

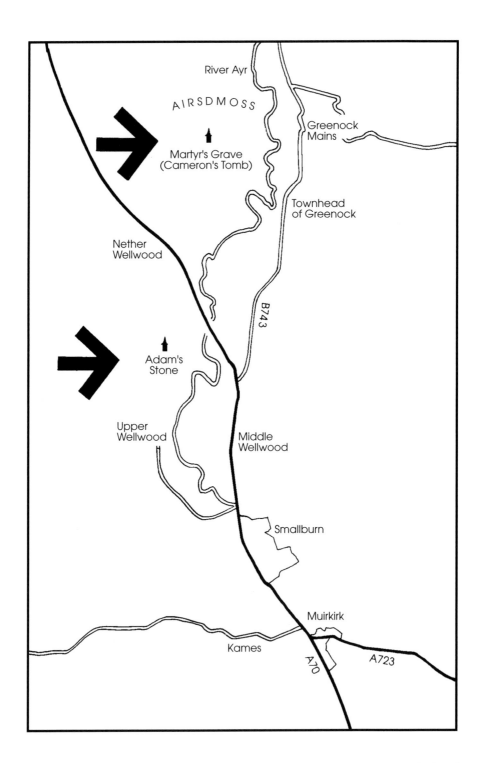

Airdsmoss and Wellwood

Gazetteer

Each site has a map reference based upon the Ordnance Survey Landranger Series (1:50,000).

Airdsmoss (also Airsmoss, Ayrsmoss) (NS 643 259)

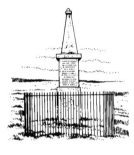

This is the scene of the Cameronians' first and last stand, on 22nd (or 20th) July, 1680. A month previously, on the anniversary of the Battle of Bothwell Brig (22nd June, 1679), Richard Cameron and his followers had declared war at Sanquhar against King Charles II and the future King James VII and II. The Cameronians then formed themselves into a small fighting force, and it was here that about 60 of them fought a pitched battle with 120 Government dragoons led by Bruce of Earlshall. The Government forces won, and Richard Cameron was killed, together with his brother Michael and eight of their followers. Five were captured, and of these, two died of their wounds and three were taken to Edinburgh and executed; they included David Hackston of Rathillet, a participant in the murder of the Archbishop of St Andrews the previous year (3rd May, 1679). See also Introduction and entries for *Magus Muir* and *Cupar*.

Inscription (as recorded in late 1990)

SACRED
To The Memory   1837
The Revd RICHARD CAMRON
MICHAEL CAMRON
JOHN GEMMEL
JOHN HAMILTON
JAMES GRAY
ROBERT DICK
CAP^T. JOHN FOWLER
THOMAS WATSON

ROBERT PATERSON

(*Hand with sword*)
(*Open book with* HOLY BIBLE *and* REV 11-12 *on opposite pages*)

M   C

Here lies the Corpse of that famous
[? and] faithful preacher of the gospel
MR RICHARD CAMERON With
[? the] corpse of seven others who were
conquered by the bloody enemies of
Truth and [? Godlin]es

Halt curious passenger Come and read
Our souls triumph with Christ our
glorious Head in self defence we
murdered head do ly For [? witness]
against this nations Perjury
1680

Other stones at the site are even less legible than the foregoing. Presumably one of these stones bears the older version recorded by Thomson, the first four (five) lines framing the remainder of the inscription:

Here Lyes the Corps of that famous and faithful
preacher of the Gospel Mr Richard Cameron who with
several others fell
here in an encounter with the bloody enemies
of Truth and Godliness July 20 Anno 1680

Halt, curious passenger, come here and read
Our souls triumph with Christ our glorious head
In self defence we murder'd here do Ly
To witness against this Nations perjury.

M
R.   C.

Michael Cameron	Robert Dick
John Hamilton	Cap. John Fuller
John Gemmel	Robert Paterson
James Gray	Thomas Watson

Airdsmoss is a large tongue of land extending east towards Muirkirk between the River Ayr, which runs parallel to the B743 to the north, and the Boshead Lane and the A70 to the south-east. Intending visitors to the martyrs' grave should contact Mr Blackwood (farmer at Nether Wellwood: Tel 01290 661101).

Allan's Cairn (NS 698 009)

*Aftor a photograph
by K.M. Andrew*

The event which this stone commemorates is very mysterious. Even the date of its occurrence is not given in the inscription, which is not contemporary with the majority of Killing Time epitaphs. It may be that 1857, the year when this stone was erected, was also the first time that the fate of the two victims was recorded otherwise than in oral tradition[1]. The martyrdom is unusual in that it involves the shooting of a woman[2].

Allan's Cairn is in a particularly remote and mountainous part of the Southern Uplands, high above Tynron, but it is nowadays relatively accessible because the Southern Upland Way runs right past it, at the eastern shoulder of Forty-penny Hill (Low Countam). A convenient access would be from the B729 (Carsphairn to Moniaive) at Stroanpatrick, from where Allan's Cairn is about 10 kilometres northeast. A number of streams have their head-waters near the site, the Water of Ken running south and west, the Shinnel Water running south and east to Tynron, and, from the Afton Reservoir (lying north-west), the Afton Water running towards New Cumnock.

On older OS maps a feature called The Whigs' Hole is marked on the side of Altry Hill, and this may correspond to the inscription's "Fawns of Altry". ("Fawn" = a rough, wet place on a hill [Chambers's Scots Dictionary].) TheWhig's Hole is apparently a kind of banked platform where people might well be able to lie in concealment but where they might be taken by surprise or fall victim to long-distance sniping.

Inscriptions

(1) *Four sides of base of apex*
IN MEMORY OF
GEORGE ALLAN AND
MARGARET GRACIE WHO
FOLLOWED CHRIST TO MARTYRDOM.

(2) *Four sides of apex pyramid:*
OF WHOM THE WORLD WAS NOT WORTHY Heb. XI. 38
Erected by the proceeds of a Sermon preached here
by the Rev. Peter Carmichael Scarbridge, Penpont
on 2nd Sabbath of July 1857.

(3) *Four sides of column:*
Ye ministering spirits who are hovering over

Guarding the dust neath its mossy cover
We raise not this stone to relieve your cares
Or discharge you from keeping your vigils here.

When all that are in the graves
shall hear his voice and shall come forth
It is expected that this spot
Shall yield up their dust.

They were shot by the Dragoons of
Coupland, and Lagg. near the fawns of
Altry, in the days of the Covenant.

Watch, till the trumpet peal aloud
Watch, till the Judge appear with the cloud:
Then guide your charge to the gathering throng
When the judgement is set to avenge their wrong.

A. D. 1857

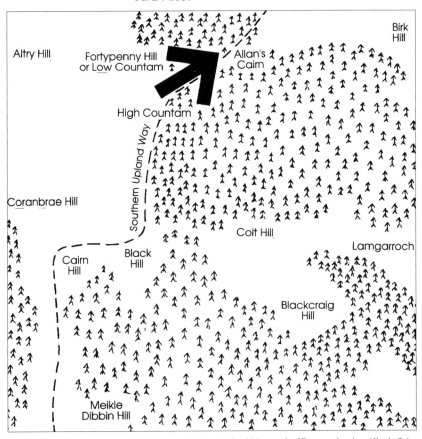

The Southern Upland Way north of Tynron, showing Allan's Cairn

[1] A Covenanting Memorial: Allan's Cairn by James King Hewison (Dumfries1936)

[2] Relevant traditions dealing with the shooting of women elsewhere are mentioned in the entry for *Corsgellioch Hill*. It is noteworthy that one of the women has the Christian name Margaret, and that the place of her martyrdom, said to be Closs, also occurs as Glass; Glenglass is a remote farm about 6 kilometres north of Allan's Cairn. The story is that she was shot on her way to Cumnock to find out what had become of her brother David Dun who had been shot at Cumnock in 1685. He may have been arrested at Corsgellioch. Cumnock and Corsgellioch are only about 20 kilometres north of Allan's Cairn.

Anwoth (NX 583 563)

Anwoth is a charming south-coast village off the A75 near Cardoness Castle and Gatehouse of Fleet. On the Boreland Hills above the village stands a tall obelisk commemorating the Rev. Samuel Rutherford (1600-1661), sometime Minister of Anwoth. In Rutherford's old churchyard John Bell of Whyteside lies buried.

Rutherford, originally a Tweedside borderer, was a vigorous pamphleteer and publicist of the radical Kirk Party who suffered internal exile (to Aberdeen) as early as 1636. He was appointed Professor of Divinity at St Andrews in 1639, and was one of the Scottish delegation who went south in 1643 to participate in the Westminster Assembly. He was one of the radicals who supported the Act of Classes which purged the Army and other public bodies of elements unworthy in the sight of the Lord. Rutherford permitted himself to rejoice when a Scottish army in which the purging had not been sufficient was beaten by Oliver Cromwell at Dunbar in 1650[1].

His book *Lex Rex (The Law and the King)* had the distinction of being burnt by the common hangman in 1661, and he himself only escaped being tried for treason by dying; when he was summoned to the bar of Parliament in Edinburgh, he was already on his deathbed, and said, "I have got summons already before a Superior Judge and Judicatory, and I behove to answer to my first summons."[2] (See also *St Andrews*).

John Bell of Whyteside was shot by the notorious Sir Robert Grierson of Lagg in February 1685 along with four others on Kirkconnel Moor north of Kirkcudbright. (See also *Balmaghie, Girthon, Kirkconnel Moor* and *Twynholm*.) Bell, a local laird, had been dispossessed in the aftermath of the Battle of Bothwell Brig in 1679, and was one of those charged with being implicated in the murder of Archbishop Sharp. He had been a fugitive ever since then. When Lagg prepared to have him shot, he begged for a little time to pray. Lagg is reported to have said, "What the devil have you been doing? Have you not prayed enough these many years in the hills?" —and had him shot immediately[3]. Viscount Kenmure was Bell's step-father, and when he met Lagg socially, he took Sir Robert up on this brutality. Lagg replied with typical coarseness, "Take him, if you will, and salt him in your beef-barrel!" Kenmure drew his sword and tried to run Lagg through, but Claverhouse, who happened to be with them, parted them[4].

Bell's tomb is on the south side of the church, which now is in ruins.

Inscription

(1) *Framing main inscription along four edges of flat (table) stone:*

> HERE LYES JOHN BELL
> OF WHITESYDE WHO WAS BARBAROUSLY SHOT
> TO DEATH IN THE PAROCH
> OF TONGLAND AT THE COMMAND OF LAG 1685

(2) *Main inscription:*

THIS MONUMENT SHALL TELL POSTERITY
THAT BLESSED BELL OF WHITESYDE HERE DOTH LY
WHO AT COMMAND OF BLOODY LAG WAS SHOT
A MURDER STRANGE WHICH SHOULD NOT BE FORGOT
DOUGLAS OF MORTON DID HIM QUARTERS GIVE
YET CRUEL LAG WOULD NOT LET HIM SURVIVE
THIS MARTYR SOUGHT SOME TIME TO RECOMMEND
HIS SOUL TO GOD BEFORE HIS DAYS DID END
THE TYRRANT SAID, WHAT, DEVIL! YE'VE PRAY'D ENOUGH
THIS LONG SEVEN YEAR ON MOUNTAIN AND IN CLEUCH
SO INSTANTLY CAUS'D HIM WITH OTHER FOUR
BE SHOT TO DEATH UPON KIRKCONNEL MOOR
SO THUS DID END THE LIVES OF THESE DEARE SANTS
FOR THERE ADHERENCE TO THE COVENANTS.

[1] Hewison ii p 15
[2] Hewison ii p94
[3] *Cloud* Appendix p386; Wodrow iv pp241-242
[4] Shields p37; Thomson p412; cf Wodrow iv p242

Auchencloy (NX 603 708)

On 18th December, 1684, Claverhouse and his dragoons came upon an armed party of Covenanters near the Black Water of Dee. Forty-eight hours previously a large body of men had stormed Kirkcudbright Tolbooth and sprung all the prisoners, killing a guard in the process. Claverhouse had followed their tracks north and now he had found what he was looking for.

The Covenanters fled incontinent, but Claverhouse overtook them before they got beyond Auchencloy Moor. Both parties dismounted, and a general melée ensued. The leader of the Covenanters, a tall, grim, black-avised man with an impressive reach, took on Claverhouse sword to sword. Since Claverhouse was small if doughty, he soon found himself overmatched and fighting for his life.

"Somebody help me quick!" called Claverhouse, parrying away.

"Claverhoose cannae fecht!" crowed the big man. "Whaur's yer nursemaid, ye shilpit wee cratur? If ye werenae wearin' yon morion .... Aaaagh!" He pitched forward on his face, his skull split from behind by a dragoon's sword.

Later, as the victorious dragoons were relaxing at their temporary headquarters at St John's Clachan of Dalry, someone (let us say, the sergeant) approached Claverhouse. "Excuse me, Colonel Graham," he said, "but do you know who you and Macmillan killed this afternoon at Auchencloy?"

"No," said Claverhouse, taking a bite of his pasty. "Who was it, then?"

"Black McMichael," replied the sergeant.

Claverhouse choked on his ale. "Carsphairn!" he gasped. "Enterkin!"

"Airdsmoss too," said the sergeant. "Hand in glove with Cameron."

"How do you know this?" Claverhouse inquired. "Who told you?"

The sergeant gestured towards the village. "The relatives are burying the body now."

"Howk him out!" snapped Claverhouse. "Give him the treatment. I'll have no traitors in hallowed ground. *Laesa majestatis* - Mackenzie's book ..."

And Black James McMichael's body was exhumed forthwith and hanged on a gibbet.

The above dialogue, needless to say, is apocryphal, although McMichael seems to have jeered at Claverhouse in some such terms before he was cut down[1], and Claverhouse knew and applied the legal treatise *The Laws and Customs of Scotland* written in 1679 by Sir George Mackenzie of Rosehaugh, the Bluidy Advocate "who, for his worldly wit and wisdom, had been to the rest as a god." (Scott)

Black McMichael's was the hand that fired the shot that had killed the Curate of Carsphairn, Peter Pearson, only a week previously, on 11th December, 1684 — an act promptly disowned by the Society People as resembling murder too closely. He had also taken a leading part in the organisation of the Enterkin Pass rescue in July 1684 with John Grierson (also killed at Auchencloy), James "Long Gun" Harkness and others, and seems to have been responsible for at least one death then. (See *Dalveen, Dalgarnock, Durisdeer* and *Enterkin* for further details).

Some confusion exists about the precise numbers of men killed and captured at Auchencloy — caused, no doubt, by the exhumation, which might result in no trace being left of a burial. One man is buried at Auchencloy and two at least at Dalry; James McMichael's burial is unrecorded, as is that of a fifth man, Archibald Stewart, mentioned by Defoe (Robert Stewart, according to Wodrow)[2]. Defoe also says that three men were taken down to Kirkcudbright for trial and execution, but only two men — Smith and Hunter — seem to be buried at Kirkcudbright (besides Hallume, who is not connected with Auchencloy).

Inscriptions at Auchencloy

(Gravestone)

> HERE LYES
> ROBERT FERGUIS
> SON WHO WAS
> SURPRIZED AND
> INSTANTLY SHOT
> TO DEATH ON THIS
> PLACE BY GRAHAM
> OF CLAVERHOUSE
> FOR ADHEARANCE
> TO SCOTLANDS

(Reverse)

MEMENTO (*Skull and Crossbones*) MORI

REFORMATIONE
COVENANTS
NATIONALL
AND SOLEMN
LEAGUE 1684

(Obelisk [1834])

ERECTED
IN MEMORY OF THE MARTYRS
R. FERGUSON, J. M'MICHAN
R. STUART AND J. GRIERSON
WHO FELL ON THIS SPOT 18 DEC 1684

[A fifth name, possibly Archibald Stewart, is omitted here. "M'Michan" is McMichael. For further details, see *Dalry* and *Kirkcudbright.*]

The obelisk at Auchencloy stands on a mound in a small clearing now in the midst of a sea of conifers. The gravestone is nearby, at the foot of the mound. They are inaccessible except to hill and forest walkers. The site is about 5km west of Loch Ken and the A762, which the traveller should leave at Bennan Cottage, branching along the so-called Raiders' Road Forest Drive; this should be left in turn at Craigdoon, where a track inaccessible to wheeled vehicles leads away south-west to a bridge across the Black Water of Dee at Barney Water. The fifth forest ride to the right is marked by a large free-standing conifer at the entrance: the visitor must proceed slowly and with caution down this ride, through waist-high grass which conceals many roots and boulders, for about a mile until a transverse ride is encountered; the clearing lies immediately to the left on the transverse ride. If the expedition is undertaken in the summer, the walker is beset by an intolerable cloud of insects, including clegs and hornets — and some of the most beautiful dragon-flies I have ever seen; if it is winter, or in the slightest rainy, the ride is simply impassable. The obelisk loses nothing in impressiveness through its isolation, silence and inaccessibility.

[1] Defoe p286; Thomson p381; Hewison ii p449; cf Wodrow iv p177
[2] Defoe p250 and Wodrow iv p177; cf Terry *Claverhouse* pp177-178.

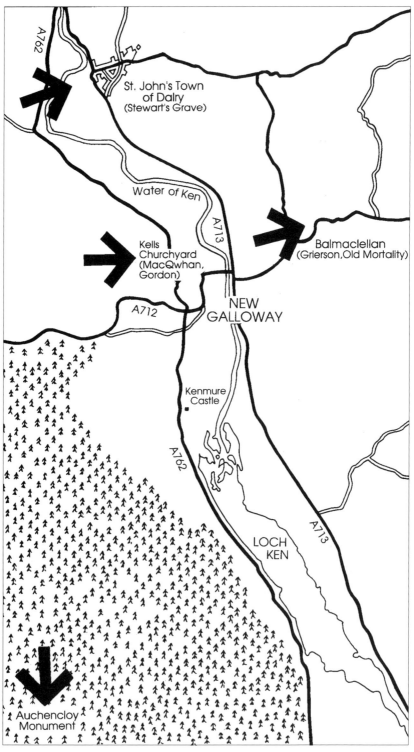

Auchencloy with Balmaclellan, Dalry and Kells.

Ayr (NS 338 219)

In Covenanting times, this provincial capital was the scene of much tension between the Government and the local population and their representatives, whose sympathies were often with the Covenanters. In Ayr, it was said, the health of the Devil was drunk at the market cross at midnight on Christmas night 1662 by the dissolute members of the Earl of Middleton's entourage on their tour of the south-west in support of the hated bishops[1].

In 1666, after the battle of Rullion Green, eight men were sent to Ayr to be executed *in terrorem*. The Ayr hangman ran away when he learnt what his task was to be, and the Irvine hangman, brought to Ayr as a substitute, also refused point blank. This man, named William Sutherland, had got into the executioner's trade via the burning of witches. Someone had learnt him his Bible and, when ordered to hang Covenanters, he argued against the task with skill and fluency, to the fury of the authorities. They set him in the stocks and even fired a volley over him in mock execution, to no avail. In the end they were reduced to bribing one of the prisoners, Cornelius Anderson, "to become burrier to the rest", and after he had been made drunk he duly hanged them[2]. (See also *Irvine*.)

Alexander Peden, the Prophet of the Covenants, was imprisoned in Ayr Tolbooth for a while in 1673[3], and John Graham of Claverhouse is listed among the Freemen of the Burgh[4]. It was, however, more than a little precarious to be a leading citizen of Ayr in those days. We read of an Ayr provost who got into hot water for helping an outlawed preacher to minister to a woman about to be hanged in Ayr Tolbooth[5]. Another was proceeded against for admitting into the town a large body of rebels under the leadership of another outlawed minister, and arranging for them to be billeted and fed[6]. Complex court cases witness to the Ayr magistrates' defiance of the Government in the matter of the Test Act after 1681, and in 1684 local landowners were rounded up and imprisoned under unspeakable conditions in the Tolbooth and in Ayr Kirk until they took the Test and paid a substantial fine. One Ayr minister, William Adair, a veteran of Mauchline Muir (1648) and the Battle of Dunbar (1650), managed to continue in his parish when hundreds of other ministers in the country were "outed", but even he was eventually ejected in 1682, two years before his death. His effigy, dressed in a typical late-seventeenth-century preaching gown and cap, still kneels in prayer at the north external wall of the Auld Kirk of Ayr.

There are two monuments of Covenanting interest in Ayr Auld Kirkyard — the renewed tombstone of the seven rebels mentioned above, and the renewed but decaying effigy of William Adair.

Inscriptions

(1) *Rullion Green rebels*

Here lies the Corpse
of
JAMES SMITH, ALEX^R McMILLAN
JAMES McMILLAN, JOHN SHORT,
GEORGE McKERTNY, JN; GRAHAM
and JOHN MUIRHEAD who
Suffered Martyrdom at AIR 27th.
Dec^{br} 1666 For their adherance
to the Word of GOD and Scotland's
Covenanted Work of Reformation.

This Small Tribute to the Above
was done by the Incorporate
Trades of AIR Anno Domoni 1814
For the Righteous shall be Keept
in everlasting rememberance.

(reverse)

Here lie seven Martyrs for our Covenants
A sacred number of triumphaint Saints.
Pontius McAdam th' unjust Sentence past
What is his own the world will know at last
And Herod Drummond caus'd their Heads affix
Heav'n keeps a record of the sixty six.
Boots, thumbkins, gibbets were in fashion then
LORD let us never see such Days again.

(2) *Adair monument*

MW   AD

M^R GUL. ADAIR Antiquissimae Familiae de KINGHILT frater legitimus Ecclesiae Aerensis per annos 44 Pastor fidelissimus quod caducum habuit hic depositum reliquit Feb. 12 1684 aet.70
(Mr WILLIAM ADAIR, of the very ancient family of KINGHILT, a lawful brother of the Kirk of Ayr, a most faithful minister for 44 years, left his mortal remains buried here on 12th February, 1684, aged 70.)

(3) A tombstone to Andrew McGill, a Ballantrae man "apprehended by the Information of Andrew Tom" and executed in Ayr in November 1684, seems to have disappeared. This stone was erected "at the gallows foot" but no trace of it has survived at any of the several known gallows sites in Ayr. According to *A Cloud of Witnesses* (1741), the inscription on the stone read as follows:

> Near this abhorred Tree a Sufferer lies
> Who chus'd to fall, that falling Truth might rise.
> His Station could advance no costly Deed,
> Save giving of a Life, the Lord had need.
> When Christ shall vindicate his Way, he'll cast
> The Doom that was pronounc'd in such haste,
> And Incorruption shall forget Disgrace
> Design'd by the Interment in this place.[7]

A covenanting flag is held in Ayr Carnegie Library (Library Headquarters, Kyle and Carrick District Council). Little is known of it. Although not on public display, it may be seen on application to the Reference Department staff.

[1] Wodrow i p282
[2] Wodrow ii p53ff. See also Sutherland *Genuine Declaration* etc. (See Bibliography).
[3] Mackenzie 1953 in Dunlop *RBA* p112
[4] Robertson i p286
[5] Wodrow iv p44
[6] Fountainhall *Historical Notices* pt. 2 pp533-534
[7] Cloud 1741 Appendix p401

Balmaclellan (NX 652 792)

Balmaclellan was the scene of the second significant incident leading to the outbreak of the Pentland Rising. On 14th November, 1666, the day after the Dalry episode, the insurgents took prisoner 16 soldiers and, according to Kirkton, killed one of them. The insurgents then moved on to Irongray[1]. (See *Rullion Green* and *Dalry*.)

Balmaclellan Churchyard is the resting place of Robert Grierson, one of the five men who, as recorded in *A Cloud of Witnesses*, were discovered in a cave at Ingliston on 28th April, 1685, by Colonel James Douglas and his men and shot out of hand. See also *Glencairn* and *Ingliston*.

Near the church is a memorial stone to the aged Cameronian Robert Paterson who travelled around Scotland renewing Covenanting grave inscriptions in the eighteenth century and who, under the sobriquet "Old Mortality", figures in the introduction to Sir Walter Scott's novel of that name[2]. Paterson is buried in Caerlaverock, but his family lived in Balmaclellan. A now mutilated sculpture of Old Mortality and his horse stands in the grounds of Holm House, Balmaclellan. The original (1840) of this sculpture will be found in an octagonal lantern in the grounds of Dumfries Museum. A complete copy will be found outside the museum at Newton Stewart.

Inscriptions

(1) *Grierson*
(a) *(Along the four edges of the flat stone, framing the main inscription)*
HERE LYETH ROBERT
GRIERSON WHO WAS SHOT TO DEATH BY COMMAND OF
COLANEL JAMES DOUGLASE
AT INGLES TOUN IN THE PAROCH OF GLENCARN ANNO 1685

(b) *(main inscription)*
THIS MONUMENT TO PASSENGERS SHALL CRY
THAT GOODLY GRIERSON UNDER IT DOTH LY
BETRAY'D BY KNAVISH WATSON TO HIS FOES
WHICH MADE THIS MARTYRS DAYS BY MURTHER CLOSE
IF YE WOULD KNOU THE NATURE OF HIS CRIME
THEN READ THE STORY OF THAT KILLING TIME
WHEN BABELS BRATS WITH HELLISH PLOTS CONCEAL'D
DESIGND TO MAKE OUR SOUTH THEIR HUNTING FIELD
HERE'S ONE OF FIVE AT ONCE WERE LAID IN DUST
TO GRATIFY ROME'S EXECRABLE LUST
IF CARABINES WITH MOLTEN BULLETS COUD
HAVE REACHED THEIR SOULS THESE MIGHTY NIMRODS WOUD
THEM HAVE CUT OF; FOR THERE COULD NO REQUEST
THREE MINUTES GET TO PRAY FOR FUTER REST.

(2) *Paterson*
(a) (outer wall of churchyard):

OLD MORTALITY
LIVED
17 HERE 68

(b) TO THE MEMORY
OF ROBERT PATERSON, STONE ENGRAVER,
WELL KNOWN AS OLD MORTALITY WHO DIED AT BANKHEAD
OF CAERLAVEROCK, 14 FEBRUARY 1801 AGED 88.
ERECTED BY THOMAS PATERSON HIS GRANDSON
1855

Balmaclellan is about two kilometres from New Galloway on the A712.
(See map on p   )

[1] Terry *Pentland* pp7-8; Kirkton p231
[2] Scott, *Old Mortality*, Introduction.

Balmaghie Church

Balmaghie (NX 723 664)

Balmaghie Churchyard is remarkable for containing the graves of two Covenanting martyrs with the same name, David Halliday, shot within five months of each other in 1685, as well as that of George Short. The first David Halliday was shot by the Laird of Lagg with four others on Kirkconnel Moor. (See also *Anwoth, Girthon, Kirkconnel Moor* and *Twynholm*.) The other David Halliday was also shot by Lagg when the latter was operating with the Earl of Annandale in Twynholm not far from Kirkconnel.

Inscriptions

(1) *Two David Hallidays*

HERE LYES DAVID HALLIDAY, PORTIONER OF MEIFIELD WHO
WAS SHOT UPON THE 21 OF FEBR 1685, AND OF
DAVID HALLIDAY ONCE IN GLENGAPE WHO WAS LIKEWISE
SHOT UPON YE 11 OF JULY, 1685, FOR THEIR ADHERENCE TO
THE PRINCIPLES OF SCOTLANDS COVENANTED
REFORMATIONE

BENEATH THIS STONE TWO DAVID HALLIDAYS
DOE LY WHOSE SOULS NOU SING THEIR MASTERS PRAISE
TO KNOU IF CURIOUS PASSENGERS DESYRE
FOR WHAT, BY WHOME AND HOU THEY DID EXPYRE
THEY DID OPPOSE THIS NATIONS PERJUREY

NOR COULD THEY JOYN WITH LORDLY PRELACY
INDULGING FAVOURS FROM CHRISTS ENEMIES
QUENCH'D NOT THEIR ZEAL THIS MONUMENT THEN CRYES
THESE WERE THE CAUSES NOT TO BE FORGOT
WHY THEY BY LAG SO WICKEDLY WERE SHOT.
ONE NAME, ONE CAUSE ONE GRAVE ONE HAVEN DO TY
THEIR SOULS TO THAT ONE GOD ETERNALLY.

(2) *George Short*

HERE LYES
GEORGE SHORT
WHO WAS PURSUED
AND TAKEN AND
INSTANTLY SHOT
TO DEATH UNDER
CLOUD OF NIGHT
IN THE PAROCH
OF TONGUELAND
BY GRIER OF LAG

(reverse)

(Skull and Crossbones)
MEMENTO MORI

AND THE EARLE
OF ANANDALE
BECAUSE OF HIS
ADHERENCE TO
SCOTLANDS RE
FORMTION COVE
NANTS NATIONAL
AND SOLEMN
LEAGUE 1685

Balmaghie Church lies almost opposite Crossmichael on the western shore of Loch Ken. It can be approached either from the A713 north of Castle Douglas, turning west along B795 at Townhead of Greenlaw just short of the Loch and turning north at Glenlochar; or turning off the A762 at Laurieston and driving east along B795 to Bellymack.

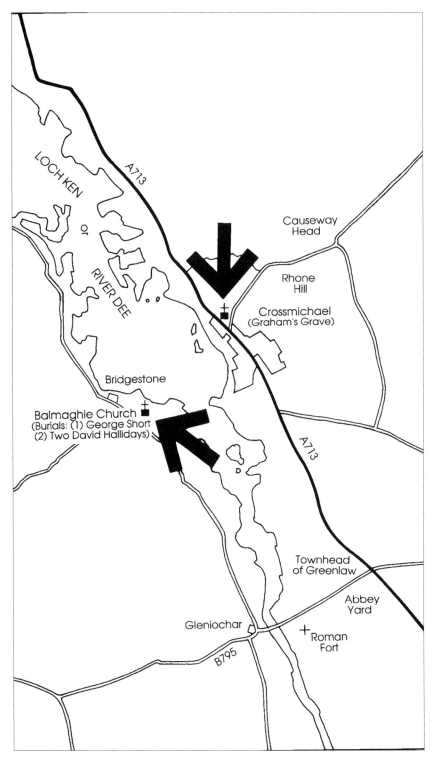

Loch Ken (the River Dee) south of Balmaclellan showing Crossmichael and Balmaghie.

Barr (NX 276 943)

An early source states that on 28th February, 1685, Edward McKeen was taken at Barr with "a flint stone upon him" and this being at least part of a firearm was sufficient for Cornet James Douglas to shoot him forthwith[1]. However, other sources state that McKeen tried to escape from Dalwine Farm on the River Stinchar and that Cornet Douglas had surrounded the farm under cover of night with a party of soldiers[2]. The same sources state that a series of questions preceded the execution, and, taking into account the phraseology of the epitaph coupled with the date of the event, we can be reasonably certain that this is a case of refusal of the Abjuration Oath. (For the significance of the timing etc. see Introduction pp 20-23.) Thomson's editor Hutchison, quoting a Girvan source, states that "being seized by the soldiers [McKeen] was compelled to confess or deny his sympathy with the persecuted. Hitherto he had not openly identified himself with that party, but now, being thus charged, he dared not deny his sympathy with them, and was shot without any further trial."[3]

The graveyard in Barr is separate from the existing church. McKeen's, together with another white-coloured stone commemorating John Campbell, a returned deportee (d 1721), is easily to be found near the entrance.

Inscription

1685
HEAR . LYES . EDW
ARD . M'Keen . W
HO . WAS . ShoAT . IN
THIS . PAReSh . BY . C
ORN: . DOUGLLAS . F
Or . ADherANCE . TO
THe . WOrD . OF . GOD
AND . SCOTLLANDS
COVeNATED .WOrK
OF . ReFOrMATION.

(reverse)

Sandglass and hand-held banner with words:
Be FAITH
FUL UNT
O DeA
THe &c.

Barr is little more than 5 kilometres south of Old Dailly on the B734. Dalwine Farm is about the same distance east of Barr on an unlisted road that runs beside the River Stinchar.

[1] Shields p36
[2] Wodrow iv p241
[3] Thomson pp316-317 (Hutchison: D Mackie of Knockgarran)

Barrhill (NX 233 818)

A Cloud of Witnesses states that "Lieutenant-general Drummond commanded without any process of trial, John Murchie and Daniel Micklewrock *(sic)* to be instantly shot after they were taken [near the Cross Water of Duisk], in the parish of Colmonell in Carrick, anno 1685. At the same time," the *Cloud* continues, "his soldiers did shoot dead Alexander Lin."[1]

Traditionally, Murchie and Meiklewrick were shot merely because they were carrying Bibles. Drummond is said to have burnt the Bibles in Old Kildonan House, using his sword as a poker to reduce them to ashes.[2] However, the phrasing of the grave inscription "for owning of King Jesus cause", the formula of Lin's epitaph and the fact that there was a continued pursuit as far as Craigmoddie may indicate that more than a merely passive martyrdom was involved here. Refusal of the Abjuration Oath is perhaps the most likely possibility. See *Craigmoddie*.

After the shootings two women, one of them Meiklewrick's fiancée, are said to have buried the bodies at night.[3] The same story is told of the shooting of Matthew Meiklewrath at Colmonell a few kilometres away. *Cf.* also *Wellwood*.

Inscriptions
(1) *Original (1787), as recorded by Thomson*

> Here lys John
> Murchie and
> Daniel MᶜJlurick
> martyrs By
> bloody
> Drummon
> they were
> shot 1685.

(reverse)

Renewed By
Gilbt McIurick
in Alticonnach
1787

When Thomson visited Barrhill in the last century he was able to obtain the complete inscription as above by piecing together three fragments of the 1787 stone. Only one of these fragments now survives in the nineteenth century grave enclosure, and its lettering has been picked out in white.

(2) *Verse epitaph*

> Here in this place two martyrs lie
> whose blood to heaven hath a loud cry;
> Murder'd contrary to devine laws,
> For owning of King Jesus cause
> By bloody Drummond they were shot,
> Without any trial near this spot.

(This epitaph, which appears on the 1825 gravestone, is probably contemporary with the original — possibly, according to Thomson, earlier than 1730.)[4]

Barrhill is about 6 km south of Pinwherry on the A714. The martyrs' tomb may be reached via a recently cleared woodland walk from the village west along the Cross Water.

[1] *Cloud* Appendix p384
[2] Thomson p320
[3] Thomson ib.
[4] Thomson p319

Bass Rock (NT 603 874)

This spectacular lump of granite off the north coast of Lothian opposite North Berwick served during Covenanting times as a penal colony. Many of the most persecuted and most illustrious of the Covenanters were imprisoned there, including Alexander Peden, John Blackader of Troqueer, James Mitchell the would-be assassin of Archbishop Sharp, Sir Hew Campbell of Cessnock and many others. Robert Louis Stevenson wrote a brilliant short ghost story about Covenanting days on the Bass called "The Tale of Tod Lapraik" (in his novel *Catriona*) and this incorporates some authentic shamanistic detail about Alexander Peden which is vouched for by John Howie of Lochgoin (in *Scots Worthies*) and by others.[1]

Those who wish to visit the Bass and its repellent old prison fortress should contact Mr Marr (North Berwick [01620] 892838), who possesses the landing rights. During the summer months he will take adults across for £10.50 per day and children for £5.50.

[1] Stevenson R L "The Tale of Tod Lapraik" in *Catriona*.
Cf Howie of Lochgoin pp509-510.

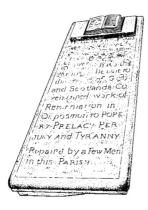

Bathgate (NS 994 680)

Bathgate Old Churchyard contains the tomb of one Covenanter, James Davie, shot during the dispersal of a conventicle at Blackdub Farm in 1673. This comparatively early martyrdom took place after the Second Indulgence (1672), during a time of renewed pressure on field conventicles.

Inscriptions
(1) *(Open book at head of tomb)*

THEY LOVED NOT
THEIR LIVES UNTO
THE DEATH
REV. XII 11

I SAW UNDER THE
ALTAR THE SOULS
OF THEM THAT WERE
SLAIN FOR THE WORD
GOD AND FOR THE
TESTIMONY WHICH
THEY HELD.
REV. VI 9

(2) (Main inscription)

> Here lies the Body
> of JAMES DAVIE
> who was Shot at
> Blackdub April
> 1673 by HERON
> for his adhering TO
> the Word of GOD
> and Scotlands Co
> venanted work of
> Reformation in
> Opposition TO POPE
> RY PRELACY PER
> JURY and TYRANNY
>
> Repair'd by a Few Men
> in this PARISH.

Bathgate Old Church is some way to the east of the town along the Edinburgh Road opposite the entrance to a large public park and adjacent to the railway. The stone will be found flat on the ground to the south-east of the ruined church, which is built on a small knoll like so many other churches of the same period.

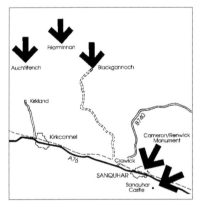

Upper Nithsdale: Auchtitench, Friarminnan, Blackgannoch and Sanquhar

Blackgannoch (also Blagannoch) (NS 775 177)

Blackgannoch is a remote farm nestling among the high hills overlooking Kirkconnel (Nithsdale) to the west. It lies at a strategic crossroads between the old hill road from Muirkirk to Sanquhar and the drove road to the south, and so it would have an important role in the upland communications network developed by the Society People from 1682. The mysterious site of Auchtitench and the farmhouse Friarminnan, which served as a safe house for James Renwick, are in the same general area. (See *Muirkirk*.)

In May 1685 Blackgannoch was the scene of a conference involving over 200 radical Covenanters including James Renwick who afterwards led them in a cavalcade down the steep and winding path into the valley to make the Sanquhar Protestation of 28th May from the Cross of Sanquhar. (See *Sanquhar* and Introduction p22-23.)

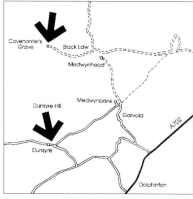

The Covenanter's Grave at Black Law

Black Law (Medwynhead) (NT 078 522)

After the Battle of Rullion Green in November 1666 an Ayrshire Covenanter, fleeing south-west and badly wounded, knocked on the door of a shepherd called Adam Sanderson at Black Law (east of Lanark). Sanderson refused him admission whereupon he said that if he were found dead in the morning he would like to be buried within sight of the hills of Ayrshire. Sure enough, his lifeless body was found the next morning in an oak thicket, and Sanderson buried him as requested. The grave is said to have been opened at the beginning of the nineteenth century, when the body was discovered in a miraculous state of preservation. (Cf. *Corsgellioch Hill*).

The grave, according to Thomson, was rededicated "about the time of the Disruption" (1843) and a monument was erected.

Inscription

SACRED
To the Memory of
A COVENANTER
who fought and was wounded
at Rullion Green,
Novr. 28th 1666,
and who died at Oaken Bush
the day after the Battle
and was buried here
BY ADAM SANDERSON
OF BLACK HILL.

This monument remains on site. Another stone, inscribed simply COVENTER DUNSYRE 1666, was discovered on the site and removed to Dunsyre Church where it may be seen inside the Church. This is a very primitive stone, simply a small irregular oblong rock with sprawling letters in two rough arcs above the date 1666, apparently enhanced in white. It seems to have been discovered in the vicinity of some oak trees.

The site of the Covenanter's grave at 1300 feet above sea-level on the Black Law may be reached by a rough track from Garvald (NT 100 490), which lies some way north-west of the A702 at Dolphinton (NT 108 466). Dunsyre (NT 072 481) is a little less than three kilometres to the west of Garvald, connected with it by an unlisted road. See map. Visitors are warned that the direct path from Garvald to Black Law is now vestigial at best, and although the track north to Medwynhead is better, there is still a deal of scrambling on the south contours of the Black Law.

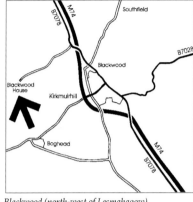

Blackwood (north-west of Lesmahagow)

Blackwood (NS 775 434)

A martyred Covenanter's tombstone stands in the private garden of the so-called "Dovecot House"[1] on the Blackwood Estate near Kirkmuirhill. Its subject, John Brown, bears the same name as at least two other Covenanting heroes but, as far as is known, this John Brown is not to be identified with any other. The execution took place in March 1685. There are few other details.

Inscription

HERE LYES THE CORPSE
OF . JOHN .
BROUN . VHO . VAS
SHOT . TO . DEATH
(*skull in relief*)
VITHOUT   SHADO
OF LAW . ANNO DOM
1685

(reverse)

MURRAY MIGHT MURDER
SUCH A GODLY BROUN
BOT COULD NOT ROB HIM
OF THAT GLORIOUS CROUN
HE NOU ENJOYES. HIS CREDIT
NOT HIS CRIME
WAS NONCOMPLYANCE
VITH A VICKED TIME.

Blackwood Estate has now been divided in two, and the visitor must approach Dovecot House from the east, crossing the M74 motorway by the bridge from the north end of Kirkmuirhill and immediately turning left. The drive is about 2 km. long.

[1]"Dovecot" here stands for Scottish "Doocot" but in fact this is not Scots for a dove-cot: it is the Gaelic *Dhu Chat*, "Black Wood". "Dovecot House" is the Blackwood Tower, an ancient Scottish stronghold now extensively altered. Cf. *Newmilns*.

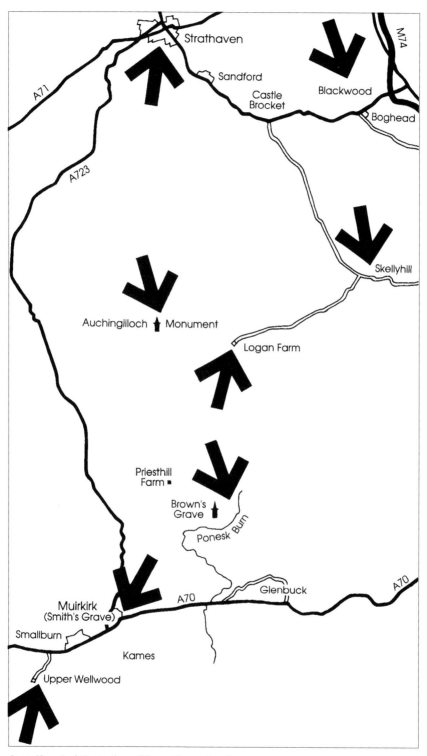

Logan House in elation to other well-known Covenanting sites.

Blair (NN 866 666)

The Church of St Bride at Old Blair is the burial place of John Graham of Claverhouse, Viscount Dundee ("Bonnie Dundee"), sometime Hammer of the Covenanters, killed just before his regiments scored a signal success over the forces of the usurper William of Orange at Killiecrankie on 27th July, 1689. A tablet on the wall of the ruined church was placed there by the Duke of Atholl in 1889.

Inscription

WITHIN THE VAULT BENEATH
ARE INTERRED THE REMAINS OF
JOHN GRAHAM OF CLAVERHOUSE
VISCOUNT DUNDEE
WHO FELL AT THE BATTLE OF KILLIECRANKIE
27TH JULY 1689, AGED 46

THIS MEMORIAL IS PLACED HERE BY
JOHN 7TH DUKE OF ATHOLE K.T.
1889

Old Blair is just to the west of Blair Atholl and the Pass of Killiecrankie itself on the A9 Perth-Pitlochry-Kingussie-Inverness road.

Bothwell Brig (NS 765 578)

The Battle of Bothwell Brig saw the end of the brief Covenanting revolt that had flared into life with the assassination of Archbishop Sharp on 3rd May, 1679, and reached its high point with the defeat of Claverhouse and his dragoons by an armed conventicle at Drumclog on 1st June, 1679. The disorganised Covenanting forces that came together after Drumclog marched north but were beset by fierce disagreement and poor generalship: they did not follow up their advantage at Glasgow, which they could have secured. (See *Glasgow*.) Instead they withdrew to an encampment near Hamilton at Bothwell Brig and started to waste valuable time, purging elements in their army whom they felt to be unworthy in the sight of God, and discovering that the differences between those who had accepted the Government's Indulgences in the past and those who had not were irreconcilable. In this, the radical Presbyterians of the West followed a lamentable precedent.

So it came about that on Sunday 22nd June 1679, four or five thousand ill-armed, under-officered and still squabbling Whigs found themselves facing 15,000 Government troops on the other (eastern) side of Bothwell Brig under a resolute team of officers headed by the Duke of Monmouth. Although there were isolated examples of bravery, and although Bothwell Brig could have been held against even a superior force for some time at least, the Whigs soon broke and fled, one of the first off the field being their general, Sir Robert Hamilton. Many were killed on the field, and 1400 were made prisoners. Morale among the Western Covenanters dropped to zero and, although there were sporadic acts of military resistance in later years, the Battle of Bothwell Brig represents the last coherent attempt by radical Covenanters to act as a national armed force.

A tall obelisk has been erected on the west bank of the River Clyde at Bothwell Bridge, which has been widened and modernized since the seventeenth century; a few hundred yards from the M74, it is now enmeshed in the tangle of major roads approaching Glasgow from the south-east.

Bothwell Bridge
(A nineteenth-century print taken from
Thomson's Martyr Graves of Scotland*)*

Caldons Wood (NX 396 788)

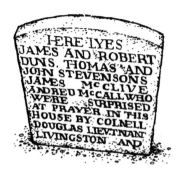

This monument is to be found in a small clearing about 100 metres from the Forestry Commission's Caldons campsite beyond Glentrool Village just short of the west end of Loch Trool. A stone enclosure contains a rather splendid modern tombstone replacing an original "Old Mortality" stone which was vandalised in 1983. The original has been repaired and is now in Newton Stewart museum. (For "Old Mortality", see *Balmaclellan*).

The entry in A *Cloud of Witnesses* (1741) read, "The said Colonel or Lieutenant General James Douglas, with Lieutenant Livingston and Coronet James Douglas, surprized six Men at Prayer at the Calduns in the parish of *Minigaf; viz.* James Dun, Robert Dun, Andrew Mackale, Thomas Stevenson, John Macklude, and John Stevenson, in *January*, 1685."[1] This appears to have been one of the operations mounted by Douglas, during the temporary disgrace of Claverhouse, within whose bailiwick Caldons fell.[2] The men were praying in the farmhouse of Caldons, now long gone. When, on 23rd January 1685, the dragoons came upon them, one man, a third brother Dun, managed to escape by diving into Loch Trool and standing up to his neck in water among reeds for hours. The rest were shot, probably for refusing the Abjuration Oath.

Inscription

HERE LYES
JAMES AND ROBERT
DUNS, THOMAS AND
JOHN STEVENSONS,
JAMES McCLIVE,
ANDREU McCALL, WHO
WERE SURPRISED
AT PRAYER IN THIS
HOUSE BY COLNELL
DOUGLAS, LIEVTENANT
LIVINGSTON AND

reverse

CORNET
JAMES DOUGLAS, AND
BY THEM MOST IMPIOUS
LY AND CRUELLY
MRTRED FOR THEIR
ADHERENCE TO SCOT
LANDS REFORMATION
COVENANTS NATIONAL
AND SOLEMN LEAGUE
1685

[1]*Cloud*, Appendix p383
[2]Terry *Claverhouse* p184

Cambusnethan (NS 767 540)

The Belhaven Mausoleum

NB This is not the present Cambusnethan, which is a district in the east of Wishaw. The churchyard here in question is to the west of the Netherton of Wishaw and to the north-west of Cambusnethan House itself, right down on the banks of the Clyde. It lies at the end of a precipitous and winding track. I suppose that the most conveniently identifiable feature is the Carbarns Sewage Works with its big tanks about 400 metres to the south-east.

To get to the site from the centre of Wishaw, drive south-west along the Caledonian Road (B7034) under the railway-bridge and turn north-west along Netherton Road (B754) beside the Netherton Industrial Estate. Fourth on the left is Kirkhill Avenue, which should be followed to a T-junction formed with Kirknethan Road and St Michael Road. Just at the junction a track plunges away south-west down the hill towards the river; this will lead the bold driver to the church; others will be advised to leave their cars and walk perhaps a kilometre down the rough track. Wet conditions will convert the site and its approaches into a quagmire.

The churchyard is a mere wreck, covered with the graffiti of vandals, and the Covenanting stones are no longer visible. The place is at least recognizable by a huge and ruinous mausoleum to the Belhaven family (apparently the monument indicated on the large-scale OS map), which was noted by Thomson in the last century.[1] The church itself is a sombre pile of rubble, and immediately to its side is— or was in1994 — a small railed enclosure totally overgrown by a huge tree or bush. The growth of the trunk has dislodged the tombstone within the enclosure from its base, and the stone now lies flat on its face on the ground. This may be the stone to Arthur Inglis but I could be wrong. It might be worth someone's while to find out — possibly through a local Youth Training Scheme or a similar enterprise — but they would have to bring tree-felling equipment and possibly heavy lifting gear, and having brought these there, it might not be so simple to retrieve them.

The church is probably the first of the parish churches of Cambusnethan, dating back to the eleventh century. The name of the patron is uncertain; St Patrick, St Michael and St Nechtan are all possible candidates, the first giving his name to an almost similarly ruined but slightly younger church about two kilometres away down river.

The episode which ended with the death of Arthur Inglis came during the aftermath of the Battle of Bothwell Brig not far away. The tradition is that some dragoons were scouring the countryside for fugitives the day after the battle, and saw Inglis reading a book — presumably a Bible — near Stockleton-dyke. From this simple observation they concluded that he must be a rebel, and took a shot at him. They missed, although startling Inglis so much that he threw his Bible in the air. This gave them a fresh mark, and one of them galloped up and split Inglis's skull with his sword.[2]

If this tale of a random killing is true, then this is a case in which the epitaph seems a little misleading, with its claim that Inglis was shot "for his adherance to the word of God" etc. Inglis would have no time to display his adherence or even to be identified. The month is wrong for Bothwell Brig and the mention of Claverhouse is suspect, at least because Claverhouse is recorded as being in Ayrshire the day after the battle. The epitaph, however, was not inscribed until 1733, 54 years after the event, and confusion may have arisen in that time.[3]

Inscription (as recorded by Thomson)

> HERE LYES
> ARTHUR INGLIS IN NETHERTON
> VHO UAS SHOT AT STOCKLTON
> DYKE BY BLOODY GRAHAM OF
> CLAVERSHOUSE JULY 1679
> FOR HIS ADHERANCE TO THE
> UORD OF GOD AND SCOTLANDS COVE
> NANTED WORK OF REFORMATION
>
> REV. 12 AND 11.

Erected in the year 1733.

(reverse)

> Memento mori
> When I did live such was the day
> Forsaking sin made men a prey
> Unto the rage and tyranny
> Of that throne of iniquity
> Who robbed Christ and killed his saints
> And brake and burn'd our covenants
> I at this time this honour got
> To die for Christ upon the spot.[4]

The graveyard is such a desolate wilderness, with most of the stones thrown down or partially overgrown, that I could not say whether the nineteenth-century cross to Arthur Inglis which Thomson noted is still there or not. It may well survive but will require more diligent search to find it than I was able to give. The inscription on the cross is as follows:

IN
MEMORY   OF
ARTHUR   INGLIS
1837

(reverse)

SOLEMN LEAGUE
AND
COVENANT

[1]Thomson p264
[2]Wodrow iii pp108-109; also Brown pp141-142
[3]Cf for various points of comparison *Galston, Barrhill, Wellwood* and
  Introduction p 21-22.
[4]Thomson p264

Campsie (NS 610 797)

The Clachan of Campsie is on the A891 about 10 kilometres from Kirkintilloch. In the churchyard lies a gravestone to William Boick (Bogue or Boag). He was one of the few victims of the circuit Court of Justiciary (in Stirling in June 1683) set up to enforce the taking of the Test Oath. He changed his mind about swearing too late, and was hanged in Glasgow on 14th June. Claverhouse, who had advised the King about setting up the Court, commented on the case

"I am as sorry to see a man day [die], even a whigue, as any of them selfs; but when on days [one dies] justly for his owen faults, and may saue a hondred to fall in the lyk, I have no scrupull."[1]

In fact Boick was executed in terrorem, in order to frighten like-minded dissenters into taking the Oath.

For inscription see over.

Inscription

ERECTED
IN
MEMORY OF
WILLIAM BOICK
Who Suffered at Glasgow
June XIV. MDCLXXXIII
For is Adherence to the
WORD OF GOD
AND SCOTLAND'S
COVENANTED WORK
OF
REFORMATION

Underneath this stone does lie
Dust sacrificed to tyranny
Yet precious in immanuel's sight
Since martyred for his kingly right.

REV. chap. 7 verse 14

[1]*Letters addressed to George, Earl of Aberdeen p121* quoted Terry *Claverhouse* p139

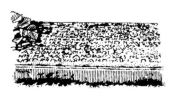

Cathcart (NS 583 606)

Old Cathcart churchyard is the burial place of three Covenanters, Thomas Cook, John Urie, and Robert Thom, shot by Major Balfour and his party at Polmadie on 11th May, 1685. This was the same day as the executions of Margaret MacLachlan and Margaret Wilson at Wigtown, and Andrew Hislop at Eskdalemuir (Craighaugh). It is the climax of the Killing Time in 1685. A series of questions is reported to have preceded the Polmadie shootings[1], and it may be that this is another case of refusal of the Abjuration Oath.

Inscription
(1) *(Left-hand side, at right angles to the main inscription)*

THIS : IS : THE : STONE : TOMB : OF : ROB-
ERT : THOM : THOMAS : COOK : AND :
JOHN : URIE : MARTYRS : FOR : OUNING
THE : COVENANTED : UORK OF : RE-
FORMATION : THE : 11TH : OF : MAY : 1685

(2) *(Main inscription)*

> THE : BLOODY : MURDERERS : OF : THESE : MEN :
> WERE : MAGOR : BALFOUR : AND : CAPTAIN : METLAND:
> AND : UITH : THEM : OTHERS : UERE : NOT : FREE :
> CAUSED : THEM : TO : SEARCH : IN : POLMADIE :
> AS : SOON : AS : THEY : HAD : THEM : OUT : FOUND :
> THEY : MURTHERED : THEM : UITH : SHOTS : OF : GUNS:
> SCARCE : TIME : DID : THEY : TO : THEM : ALLOU :
> BEFOR : THER : MAKER : THER : KNEES : TO : BOW :
> MANY : LIKE : IN : THIS : LAND : HAVE : BEEN :
> WHOS : BLOOD : FOR : WINGANCE : CRYES : TO : HEAVN
> THIS : CRUELL : WICKEDNESSE : YOW : SEE :
> WAS : DON : IN : LON : OF : POLMADIE :
> THIS : MAY : A : STANDING : WITNESS : BE :
> TUIXT : PRISBYTRIE : AND : PRELACIE :

The tower of Old Cathcart Church is easily spotted from the railway. Alas, this is the only part of the church still standing, and it is placarded DANGER: KEEP CLEAR. The tomb is within the shadow of the forbidding ruin, and is distinguished by a free-standing metal plate reproducing the whole of the above inscription.

[1]Defoe p282; Shields p37.

Claremont (NO 458 146)

Andrew Guilline's Monument

This is one of three monuments connected with Archbishop Sharp's assassination in 1679 in the immediate vicinity of Magus Muir, the others being the pyramid erected on the site of the assassination and the five martyrs' gravestone about 100 yards from that. (See *Magus Muir*). The gravestone at Claremont, however, is the only stone in the neighbourhood erected for a member of the actual party of murderers. Andrew Guilline or Gullin held the murderers' horses while they carried out the deed, and thus was held to be art and part of the crime. He escaped notice for a long time but was brought in from the fields on 11th June, 1683, on an unrelated charge, and and gave himself away under interrogation: when someone remarked how terrible it was for the Archbishop, an old man, to have been killed while on his knees praying, Gullin cried out, "O dreadful! He would not pray one word for all that could be said to him!"[1]

Inscription

The Grave Ston of
Andreu Gullin who Suffred
At the Gallowlee of Edinburgh
July 1683 & Afterwards was
hung upon a pol in Magus
Muir and lyeth hiar.

A FAITHFWL MARTYR HER DOTH LY
A WITNESS AGAINST PERJURY
WHO CRUELY WAS PUT TO DEATH
TO GRATIFY PROUD PRELATES WRATH
THEY CUT HIS HANDS ERE HE WAS DEAD
AND AFTER THAT STRUCK OFF HIS HEAD
TO MAGUS MUIR THEY DID HIM BRING
HIS BODY ON A POLE DID HING
HIS BLOOD UNDER THE ALTAR CRIES
FOR VENGEANCE ON CHRIST'S ENEMIES.

(The above version is not that on the present broken stone but the one given on p194 of Thomson's *Martyr Graves of Scotland*: it appears to be more authentic than the newer version, which dates from 1876. The later inscription is only partially successful in reproducing the characteristic spelling, and in this case I thought it better to give the original in full as attested by Thomson. One caveat is that Thomson's transcriptions themselves are quite often wrong; for instance, the word "MARTYR" is actually spelt "Martar" on the present stone, and one wonders if the 1876 carver was not more observant than Thomson after all in this case.)

Claremont Farm is about half-way between St Andrews and Cupar, on a side road off B939 (rejoining B939 just before Pitscottie). The stone is just to the west of the farmhouse across a small stream in the middle of a patch of woodland. Thomson believed that the spot had once been a garden, as witnessed by some gooseberry bushes growing wild. (See Map II on p. 74.)

[1]Wodrow iii p463; Hewison ii 404

Colmonell (NX 145 858)

Colmonell Parish Church, a very perfectly preserved old building with external access (now stopped up) to the Heritors' Gallery, stands on a small knoll at the west end of the village. Below the knoll to the south stands a blue-painted gravestone erected in the eighteenth century to the memory of James McCracken. On the reverse of this stone is a recut version of a verse epitaph commemorating the death of Matthew Meiklewrath (McIlwraith) who was shot in 1685 by Claverhouse's men; this is actually the grave of Meiklewrath, and McCracken's family were permitted to bury McCracken in the Covenanter's grave provided that they renewed the epitaph.

Inscription

> I Matthew McIlwraith in Parish of Colmonell
> By bloody Claverhouse I fell:
> Who did Command that I should die,
> For owning Covenanted presbytry;
> My Blood a Witness still doth stand,
> 'Gainst all defections in this land.

According to Daniel Defoe, in Colmonell "Claverhouse ... saw a Man run hastily cross the Street before his Troop, and as he might suppose did it to escape from or avoid them, tho' as the People of the Place related it, the poor Man had no Apprehensions of them, but as he [Claverhouse] took all occasions for his bloody design, he commanded his Men to shoot this Person, without so much as Examining him, or asking who he was, the poor Mans Name was Matthew Mekellwrat."[1]

On the face of it, Defoe's account confirms the arbitrary, despotic and "bloody" character of Claverhouse. If it is true, however, Meiklewrath would have had no time to "own Covenanted presbytery" as the epitaph has it, since he was not even identified. Arbitrary and even whimsical killing is, of course, not out of the question, but C S Terry reckoned that this was a case where the Abjuration Oath was offered and rejected.[2]

Colmonell is some way to the north-west of Barrhill, between Pinwherry and Ballantrae on the A765.

[1] Defoe p251
[2] Terry *Claverhouse* p210; cf Introduction p21.

Corsgellioch (Carsgailoch) Hill (NS 548 147)

This gravestone may have connections with others in the neighbour-hood. (*See Cumnock* [Dun and Paterson], *Waistland* and *Allan's Cairn*.) It is difficult to piece together a connected narrative, but it appears that these stones may be the visible relics of a dragnet operation extended over several days or weeks in 1685.

Originally, six or seven men were being sought near Wanlockhead some time that year. Two, Robert Morris and William Brown, were shot at Craignorth Hill (NS 813 165) at Corsebank on the B740, which runs beside the Crawick Water; no graves visible or recorded). Three other men, John Richmond, David Dun and Simon Paterson, were arrested but got away during a thunderstorm. Dun and Paterson later attended a conventicle held by James Renwick at Dalmellington, and were travelling away from that town when they were intercepted by a party of dragoons at Corsgellioch. One man, Alexander or James Jamieson got away; three — Joseph Wilson, John Jamieson and John Humphrey — were shot at Corsgellioch; David Dun and Simon Paterson were taken down to Cumnock where they were shot; and George Corson and John Hair were chased to the present Waistland Farm beyond Afton Bridgend (New Cumnock) where they were shot on the same day. Finally, it is said that Margaret, sister of David Dun, was shot on her way to Cumnock to find out what had become of her brother. No precise dating has survived.[1]

With regard to the last event mentioned, the shooting of a woman was a very rare occurrence indeed. This being so, it is remarkable that in the same locality — Dalgig Farm, on which Corsgellioch Hill stands— another woman, Marion Cameron, sister of Richard Cameron, is also reported to have been shot.[2] Even more remarkable is the existence of traditions, one of which at least is authentic, about the survival of buried relics; these traditions, although not parallel, exhibit oddly similar fea-tures:

(1) The monument at Corsgellioch was renewed in 1827, and when the foundations were being laid, the workmen uncovered at least one body in a very good state of preservation "so that anybody who had known the man alive would still have been able to recognize him". The farmer at Dalgig cut a lock of blond yellow hair from the body and took a fragment of knitted material from a mitten. These relics are still preserved by Mr Donald Smith of Skerrington Farm, Cumnock, and have recently (1992) been on display at the Baird Institute, Cumnock.

(2) The other tradition is recorded by Simpson: Marion Cameron was buried at Dalgig, and her body was partly uncovered "by the feet of

cattle"; a long yellow pin from the clothing was recovered and preserved by "a Mrs Gemmel of Catrine, a niece of Thomas Hutchison of Dalgig"[3]. I have been unable to confirm this story so far.

There are, however, elements in the two traditions that echo each other, and make the researcher wonder if Simpson's story is merely a garbled version of the discovery and preservation of the lock of yellow hair from the peat-bog corpse at Corsgellioch. More than that, although the hair belonged to a dead man and the pin to a dead woman, one wonders whether the relationship between the stories might not reflect a deeper confusion between the two female victims — whether the separate tales of the deaths of Margaret Dun and Marion Cameron are not distortions of one and the same event.

Considering this, one takes into account the otherwise mysterious event at Allan's Cairn — yet another woman, Margaret Gracie shot within 20 kilometres of Corsgellioch, the only such execution recorded on stone, and not another the length and breadth of Scotland.

David Dun, the brother whom Margaret Dun was coming to Cumnock to inquire after, was said to be the farmer of a property at Glass - or "Closs" or "Class". I have not traced a farm with any of these names in the Ochiltree / Cumnock / New Cumnock area[4]; a property named Glenglass is, however, recorded on the Euchan Water about eight kilometres west of Sanquhar and six north of Allan's Cairn. Simpson says that the Covenanters had a hiding-place at Glenglass, between the false walls of a double gable.[5] Is it possible that there was only one female victim of a dragoon's bullet in 1685, that in fact she was called Margaret, and that she would have gone to Cumnock to seek her brother David Dun of Glenglass, but that her married name was Margaret Gracie, and she met her end at the fawns of Altry high above Nithsdale? Unfortunately, it does not seem that reliable evidence can be uncovered.

Inscriptions at Corsgellioch
(1) *Original (as recorded by Thomson)*

HeRe . LyeS . IOSePH
WILSON . IOHN . IAMI
SON . AND IOHN WM
PHRAH . WHO . WAS
SHOT . IN . THIS . PLACe
By . A . PARTy . OF . HIGHL
ANDeRS . FOR

(reverse)
THeiR . ADHeRANCE
TO . THe . WORD . OF
GOD . AND . THe . COV
eNANTeD . WORK . OF
ReFORMATION . 1685

(2) *1868 inscription (Front only)*

HERE LIES
JOSEPH WILSON
JOHN JAMIESON
AND
JOHN HUMPHREY
WHO
WAS SHOT IN THIS PLACE BY
A PARTY OF HIGHLANDERS
FOR THEIR ADHERENCE
TO THE WORD OF
GOD
AND THE COVENANTED WORK OF
REFORMATION
1685
THIS STONE WAS RENEWED
1868

The monument at Corsgellioch lies in recently afforested moorland across rough terrain, and may be reached on foot either north of Dalgig Farm, which is about 3 km west of Afton Bridgend on an unlisted road, or south of Knockdunder Farm (B7046 at Skares).

[1]Cf Simpson *Traditions* pp129-135 and 150-153
[2]Simpson op cit pp117-120
[3]Simpson loc cit; Warrick p167; Thomson p337
[4]I am informed (1995) by Mr William Campbell a remote descendant of David Dun, that his ancestor did in fact farm Closs, now disappeared, on the lands of Auchlin near Ochiltree (NS 485 166).
[5]Simpson pp202-203.

Craighaugh (NY 249 985)

This is the tombstone of another martyr executed on or about 11th May, 1685. (For the significance of the dating, see Introduction p.20-23.) According to the sources, Andrew Hislop's mother had been guilty of "reset", i.e. of harbouring a Covenanting fugitive who in this case was dying and was later buried by the lady and her son.[1] When this came to the ears of Sir James Johnston of Westerhall, who had special powers of justiciary, he punished the family by destroying their house and turning them loose to wander in the countryside.[2]

On 10th May, 1685, Claverhouse came riding down from Priesthill and Mauchline, where he had just been dealing with John Brown and John Browning. (See named entries.) He came upon Andrew Hislop lurking in the fields and sent him back to Westerhall for examination. For reasons which are not clear, Westerhall condemned Hislop to death and called upon Claverhouse to execute the sentence. According to Wodrow, Claverhouse was unwilling to comply, and when Westerhall insisted, Claverhouse exclaimed, "The blood of this poor man be upon you, Westerhall; I am free of it."

He then ordered a captain of the Highland soldiers accompanying him to carry out the shooting, but the captain, "drawing of his Highlanders to a convenient Distance, sware, *that her nain Sell would fight Claverhouse and all his Dragoons first.*" So Claverhouse had to draw a firing-party from his own ranks and had Hislop shot.[2]

The *Cloud* then records, as it were in riposte, how Westerhall "died about the Revolution [1688], in great torture of body by the gravel, and horror and anguish of conscience, insomuch that his cries were heard at a great distance from the house, as a warning to all such apostates."

Inscription

> HERE LYES ANDR. HISLOP
> MARTYR SHOT DEAD UPON
> THIS PLACE BY SIR JAMES
> STE
> JOHNSTON OF WERHALL
> AND JOHN GRAHAM OF C
> LAVERHOUSE FOR ADHERI
> NG TO THE WORD OF GOD
> CHRIST'S KINGLY GOVERN-
> MENT IN HIS HOUSE AND
> YE COVENANTED WORK OF
> REFORMATION AGNST TYRAN
> NY, PERGURY AND PRELACY
> MAY 12 1685 REV 12. 11. HALT P

(reverse)

> ASSENGER, ONE WORD WI-
> TH THEE OR TWO WHY I LY
> E
> HERE WOULDST THOU TRU-
> LY KNOW BY WICKED HAN-
> DS, HANDS CRUEL AND UNJ-

UST WITHOUT ALL LAW
MY LIFE FR°M ME THEY
THRUST & BEING DEAD
THEY LEFT ME ON THIS S
POT, & FOR BURIAL THIS
SAME PLACE I GOT. TR-
UTHS FRIENDS IN ES
KDALE NOW TRIUMPH
THEN LET, VIZ THE FAITH-
FUL FOR MY SEAL [THAT]
GOT 1702

*Repaired by subscription. April
1825*

The monument lies in an open field 100 yards west of the B709 just north of Eskdalemuir.

[1]This unnamed man—and possibly a companion, also anonymous— are buried and commemorated at Mid-Windshiels "beside Boreland the Windshields Burn north of the Wamphray- Boreland Road: " possibly at or near NY 156 930: I have not myself visited the site.
[2]Wodrow iv p207 and p209
[3]*Cloud* Appendix p385; Shields p37; Terry *Claverhouse* pp207-209

Craigmoddie (NX 244 726)

*From a photograph by
K.M. Andrew*

Associated with the story of the execution of John Murchie and Daniel Meiklewrick at the Cross Water of Duisk (See *Barrhill*) is the tradition recorded in *A Cloud of Witnesses* that a man named Alexander Lin was shot dead "at the same time" by Drummond's soldiers. Lin(n)'s stone, which may be contemporaneous with the original Barrhill stone (now mostly lost), bears a more conventional epitaph. He seems to have been shot after being discovered in hiding by the soldiers; birds circling his place of concealment may have given him away.

Inscription

Memento Mori
HERE LYES
THE BODY OF ALEX-
ANDER LIN, WHO WAS

SURPRISED AND INSTAN-
TLY SHOT TO DEATH
ON THIS PLACE BY
LIUTENANT GENERAL
DRUMMOND FOR HIS
ADHERENCE TO SCOT-
LAND'S REFORMATION
COVENANTS NATION
AL AND SOLEMN LEAGUE
1685

The visitor may approach the tomb from the unfenced road that runs west from the windmill on B7027 about three km south of Loch Ochiltree; beyond the building marked Derry on the OS map there is a very rough track south-west from which the tomb may be reached across the open hillside, on the north-east contour of Craigmoddie Fell. A track from the south is marked on the OS map as far as the Standing Stones at Blood Moss, but I cannot say whether this is an easier access to the tomb.

Crossmichael (NX 729 670)

Crossmichael is a small village on the A713, on the east side of Loch Ken. It was a centre of Covenanting activity and bore a heavy weight of repression, but there is only one martyr's stone in the village graveyard, that to William Graham, who is said to have been shot while making his escape from his mother's house; in some versions of the tale Claverhouse is said to have ridden after him on the road and shot him dead with a pistol. It appears that there were two brothers, William and James Graham. William is buried in Crossmichael, having been shot on 15th March, 1684, not 1682 as stated on the tombstone; this dating error has led some scholars to suspect that the stone refers to James Graham, who was executed in Edinburgh on 9th December, 1684. The historian Wodrow makes it fairly clear, however, that there were two victims:

"The same day [9th December, 1684] James Graham, taylour in the parish of Crossmichael in Galloway, suffered. This good man was Brother to William Graham who was so barbarously cut of by the souldiers ye 15 of March this year [1684]."[1]

Claverhouse is not mentioned in this version: some killings are attributed to Claverhouse without adequate foundation.

Inscription

HERE LYES
WILLIAM GRAHAM
WHO MAKEING HIS
ESCAPE FROM HIS
MOTHERS HOUSE
WAS PURSUED AND
TAKEN AND INSTANT
LY SHOT DEAD BY
A PARTY OF CLAVER-
HOUSE'S TROOP FOR

(reverse)

(skull and crossbones)
HIS ADHERENCE
TO SCOTLANDS
REFORMATION CO
VENANTS NATION
AL AND SOLEMN
LEAGUE 1682

The stone has been broken and is now held together with iron clamps.

[1]Wodrow MSS xli. (4to, Rob. iii. 14) quoted Hewison ii 378

Cumnock (NS 571 203)

In the Old Cemetery on the Barony Hill, a group of covenanting tombstones and memorials has been gathered into one small railed enclosure fronting the road (A70). According to tradition, the cemetery itself used to be the local gallows ground, but after the dragoons had disinterred the body of Alexander Peden from its resting place in Auchinleck, hanged it on the Cumnock gibbet and then buried it at the gallows foot, the inhabitants of the town resolved to use this place as Cumnock's new burial ground.

Three monuments to Alexander Peden, who died of natural causes in 1686, may be seen in the enclosure. Also commemorated here are Thomas Richard, Simon Paterson and David Dun, all shot in 1685.

Alexander Peden is one of the better-known figures of the later Covenanting period.[1] Born in 1626 in Sorn Parish and initially a teacher in Tarbolton, he was ordained at New Luce in 1659 and was "outed" in 1662. As an illegal field preacher he developed a reputation for an earthy, homespun style of preaching, and also for foretelling the future, earning the title of *Prophet Peden*; no less than ten fatal prophecies are reputed to have been made by him. (See *Bass Rock* etc.) After a long and eventful career, including imprisonment, deportation and unexpected return, he ended his life in hiding within the parish of his birth, having first reconciled himself with James Renwick in a kind of farewell benediction to the younger generation of field preachers.

For detail on Dun and Paterson, see *Corsgellioch Hill*. Thomas Richard, an old man of 70 or 80, who farmed at Greenock Mains near Muirkirk, was trapped into revealing himself as a Covenanter, and taken to Cumnock to be shot on 5th April, 1685. Wodrow says that the provocateur in this case was Peter Inglis of Newmilns[2].

Inscriptions

(1) *Peden*
(*Only one of the three inscriptions is given here; the earliest is illegible, and the latest is inauthentic.*)

MR. ALEXANDER PEDEN
Faithful Minister of the
Gospel
sometime
at Glenluce
who departed this mortal life
the 26th of January 1686:
and was raised, after six weeks,
out of the Grawf
and buried here
out of
Contempt.

MEMENTO MORI

(2) *Richard*

HERE LIES
the Corpse of
THOMAS RICHARD

who was shot by Colonel James Douglas
for his adherence to
the Covenanted Work of Reformation
on the 5th Day of April
Anno 1685

Halt Passenger. This Stone doth show to thee
For what, by whom, and how I here did die
Because I always in my station
Adhered to Scotland's Reformation
And to our sacred Covenants and Laws
Establishing the same; which was the cause
In time of Prayer I was by Douglas shot.
Ah cruelty never to be forgot.

(3) Dun and Paterson (*as recorded by Thomson: now only partly legible*)

HeRe . LyeS . DAVID . DVN
AND . SIMON . PATeRS
ON . WHO . WAS . SHOT
IN . THIS . PLACE . BY .
A . PARTY . OF . HIGHL
ANDeRS . FOR . THEIR
(reverse) ADHeRANCE . TO . THe
WORD . OF . GOD . AND
THE COVeNANTeD
WORK OF ReFORMA
TION   1685. [3]

[1] Cf Howie of Lochgoin pp507-521
[2] Wodrow iv p252; Wodrow MSS xxxvii. 104:89
[3] Thomson pp328-329

Cupar (NO 375 146)

In the old graveyard in Cupar stands a martyrs' gravestone reflecting the consequences of the Battle of Airdsmoss and its Cargillite aftermath. At Airdsmoss, which took place on 22nd July, 1680, David Hackston of Rathillet was taken prisoner: he had participated in the murder of Archbishop Sharp on 3rd May, 1679, and he was executed for this on 30th July, 1680, in Edinburgh. His hands were cut off, and one was sent to St Andrews.

Meanwhile the principles of the Cameronian movement continued to be upheld by Donald Cargill, who excommunicated King Charles II and his brother James at Torwood before being captured on 12th July 1681, and executed on 27th July; three of Cargill's followers were executed in Edinburgh on 13th July, and the heads of two of them were sent to be displayed in Cupar, together with the hand of Hackston that had been sent to St Andrews. (Rathillet House [NO 357 207] is on the A914 north of Cupar). This collective gravestone commemorates the three.

Inscription

> (A head, an open right hand, another head)
> *Here lies Jnterred the Heads of LAUR^{CE} HAY*
> *and ANDREW PITULLOCH who*
> *Suffered martyrdom at EDIN^R July 13th 1681*
> *for adhering to the word of GOD, & Scotlands*
> *covenanted work of Reformation, and also*
> *one of the Hands of DAVID HACKSTON*
> *of Rathillot who was most cruelly murdered*
> *at EDIN^R July 30th 1680*
> *for the same cause.*

(reverse)

> 1680
> Our persecutors fill'd with rage
> Their brutish fury to aswage
> Took heads & hands of martyrs off
> That they might be the peoples scoff,
> They Hackstons body cutt asunder
> And set it up a worlds wonder
> In several places to proclaim
> These monsters gloryd in their shame.
>
> RE ERECTED
> July 13th 1792

Laurence Hay was a Fife weaver, and Andrew Pitulloch was a farm labourer from Largo.

Dalgarnock (NX 876 937)

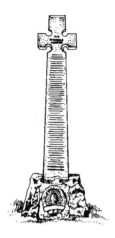

In Dalgarnock churchyard lies the gravestone of James Harkness, not a martyr, but a successful leader of the "Society People". Known as "Long Gun", Harkness, together with Black James McMichael[1] and others, organised the Enterkin Pass rescue in 1684, when perhaps as many as fourteen prisoners were set free, at least one soldier was killed and several rescuers were killed or wounded. Harkness had earlier been captured, but had broken out of the Canongate Tolbooth in Edinburgh with 24 others on 16th September, 1683.

After the Enterkin Pass rescue, John Graham of Claverhouse set out to track the rescuers down and came upon Harkness, his brother Thomas, and four other men sleeping in the open in the parish of Closeburn; he arrested them after a struggle during which some of the fugitives were wounded. Five of the men, including Thomas Harkness, were executed in Edinburgh after a very hasty trial in Edinburgh on 15th August, 1684, but James Harkness escaped, according to Hewison, probably out of the prison at Dumfries. He got clean away, and lived until 1723[2].

Inscription

Here Lyes the body of James
Harkness in Locherben who
died 6th Dec[r]. 1723 aged 72 yea[r]s
Belo this stone this dust doth ly
who indured 28 years
persecution by tirrany —
Did him persue with echo and cry
Through many a lonsome place
At last by Clavers he was tane —
Sentenced for to dy;
But God, who for his soul took car,
did him from prison bring
Because no other Cause they had
but that he cUld not give up
with Christ, his Glorious king,
and swear alligence to that beast
the duke of york, i mean,
In Spite of all there hellish rage
a naturel death he died
in full asurance of his rest
with Christ eternaly

Also to be found in Dalgarnock Churchyard are gravestones of other members of the Harkness family, and the Nithsdale Cross, a modern monument recording the names of all the Covenanting martyrs of Nithsdale.[3]

Dalgarnock Churchyard, where the church has been completely demolished, is south of Thornhill. A signpost directs the driver down the westernmost of two roads branching south from the B731: this (unlisted) road turns abruptly west along the course of the Cample Water for about half a kilometre; then it turns south over the Water by a small bridge and passes through Kirkbog Farm; south of the farm, at an eastward elbow of the track, the traveller may still encounter an electric fence and leave his car: beyond this fence the ancient churchyard lies in a small patch of woodland. *(See Map I on p74)*

[1]For Black McMichael, see *Auchencloy.*
[2]Hewison ii p433
[3]See Appendix IV

Dalry (St John's Clachan of Dalry, Kirkcudbright)) (NX 618 812)

Dalry Churchyard contains a gravestone commemorating two Covenanters who fell in the Auchencloy skirmish in which Black McMichael nearly killed Claverhouse. (See *Auchencloy*). McMichael and the others had been involved in the assassination of the Curate of Carsphairn on 11th December 1684, and in the Kirkcudbright prison break of 16th December. The Auchencloy "rencounter" took place on 18th December; five of the insurgents were killed, and perhaps three taken prisoner.

Inscription
(1) *(framing main inscription, round four edges of the flat rectangular gravestone)*

> HERE LYETH ROBERT STEWART SON TO MAJOR   }
> ROBERT STEWART OF ARDOCH AND JOHN GRIERSON } /
> WHO WERE MURTHERED BY GRAHAM OF CLAVER   }
> HOUSE ANNO 1684 FOR THEIR ADHERENCE   } /
> TO SCOTLANDS REFORMATION AND COVENANTS NATIONAL/
> AND SOLEMN LEAGUE.
>   MEMENTO MORI

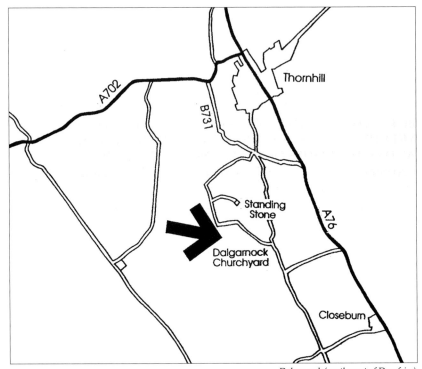

Dalgarnock (north-west of Dumfries)

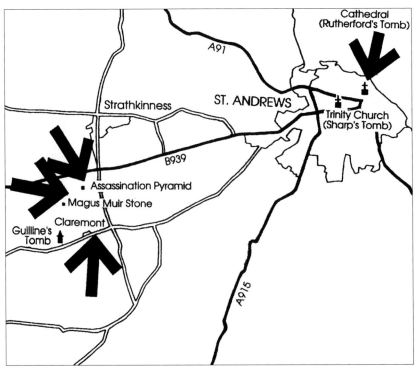

St Andrews showing site of assassination at Magus Muir

(2) *(main inscription)*

BEHOLD! BEHOLD! A STONE'S HERE FORC'D TO CRY
COME SEE TWO MARTYRS UNDER ME THAT LY!
AT WATER OF DEE WHO SLAIN WERE BY THE HAND,
OF CRUEL CLAVERHOUSE AND'S BLOODIE BAND.
NO SOONER HAD HE DONE THIS HORRID THING
BUT'S FORC'D TO CRY, STEWART'S SOUL IN HEAVEN DOTH SING
YET STRANGE! HIS RAGE PURSUED EVEN SUCH WHEN DEAD
AND IN THE TOMBS OF THEIR ANCESTORS LAID;
CAUSING THEIR CORPS BE RAIS'D OUT OF THE SAME
DISCHARGING IN CHURCH-YARD TO BURY THEM
ALL THIS THEY 'CAUSE THEY WOULD NOT PERJURE
OUR COVENANTS AND REFORMATION PURE
BECAUSE LIKE FAITHFUL MARTYRS FOR TO DY
THEY RATHER CHUS'D THEN TREACHEROUSLIE COMPLY
WITH CURSED PRELACIE THE NATIONS BANE
AND WITH INDULGENCIE OUR CHURCHES STAIN
PERJURED INTELLIGENCERS WERE SO RIFE
SHEW'D THEIR CURS'D LOYALTY TO TAKE THEIR LIFE

Dalry is also the scene of the incident which sparked off the Pentland Rising in 1666, when a party of soldiers maltreating a "recusant" because he had not paid his fine were set upon in their turn by a number of armed Covenanters under Maclellan of Barscobe. The house where the attack took place is said to have been still standing in the last century.

Dalveen (NS 885 070)

(Lower) Dalveen Farmhouse is the actual place where in January 1685 Daniel McMichael, brother of Black James McMichael, was shot when his captors discovered that he was too ill to travel. See *Durisdeer* for further details. The monument stands behind the farmhouse on a steep hillside. Close by is the path over to the Enterkin Pass.

Inscription

SACRED
To the Memory of
DANIEL M'MICHAEL
who suffered Martyrdom here
by Sir James Dalziel. A.D. 1685

Erected in 1836

Lower Dalveen lies at the end of a short unlisted road running north from the A702 at Pettylung.

Dron (NO 141 159)

John Welwood, who lies in Dron Churchyard, was an intercommuned preacher like, but much younger than Alexander Peden, with whom he seems to have shared a gift for edged prophecy; just before his own death in April 1679 he forecast the death of Archbishop Sharp— which may or may not indicate that the assassination was planned in advance. He is often bracketed with Cameron and Cargill, but like Peden again he died of natural causes (in Welwood's case, of tuberculosis). He stood against Erastianism — state interference with Church affairs — and the compromises which some ministers made with Erastianism in accepting the Government "Indulgences". Welwood held out against co-operation between Indulged and non-Indulged ministers in 1677[1].

When the Perth magistrates heard that an outlawed preacher had died in the town, they forbade his body to be buried within their boundaries, but could not prevent his friends taking it outside the limits for burial. According to Patrick Walker, the minister at Dron, Mr Pitcairn, "one of the old plagued Resolutioners", refused to hand over the keys of the graveyard; nothing daunted, "the honest men went over the churchyard dike, and digged the grave, where the corps were interr'd. Thus the churchyard of Drone is honoured with the precious dust of that pious and faithful preacher of the gospel."

Inscription

(An angel's head and wings)

17   31

HERE LYES THE REV
ERAND MᴿIOHN WEL
WOOD MINISTER OF
THE GOSPEL IN THE CHU
RCH OF SCOTLAND
WHO DYED AT PERTH
APRILE 1679 ABOUT
THE 30 YEAR OF HIS
AGE

(reverse)

HERE LYES

A FOLLOUER OF THE LAMB
THROU MANY TRIBULATIONS CAME
FOR LONG TIME OF HIS CHRISTIAN
RACE WAS PERSECUTE FROM
PLACE TO PLACE   A SCOTISH
PROPHET HERE BEHOLD
IUDGEMENT & MERCY WHO FORETOL[D]
THE GOSPEL BANNER DID DISPLAY
CONDEMND THE SINS OF THAT SAD
DAY   AND VALIENTLY FOR
TRUTH CONTENDED UNTIL[L]
BY DEATH HIS DAYS WERE ENDED

Dron is just out of sight, though within earshot, of the M90 south of Bridge of Earn. It can be approached from A912 on the east via Baigle and Newbigging, or on the west from Ecclesiamagirdle and Forgandenny through a network of small farm roads south and east of B935 and Bridge of Earn. The latter approach involves a spectacular crossing high above the M90. The village of Dron, which is near the historic Balmanno Castle, is idyllic, but the sound of the motorway is very intrusive. The church is a comparatively modern structure; Welwood's grave is in the south-east of the graveyard.

[1] Cowan p86

Drumclog (NS 625 397)

Here, on Sunday, 1st June, 1679, John Graham of Claverhouse, searching for a large conventicle reported in the neighbourhood, found it, and found that he had for once bitten off more than he could chew. Claverhouse's dragoons were outnumbered and outmanoeuvred on unfamiliar ground by the well-armed conventiclers. Hand-to-hand fighting led to the headlong flight of the Government forces, who were chased right through Strathaven. The inhabitants of the town tried to trap them as they fled through the streets, but Claverhouse fought them off and continued towards Glasgow, meeting a relief column on the way.

This, the first and last victory in battle of the post-Restoration Covenanters, followed directly from the Archbishop's murder on 3rd May, 1679, and led inevitably to the crushing defeat of the Western radical Whigs at the hands of the Duke of Monmouth on 22nd June, 1679, at Bothwell Brig. One of the murderers of Archbishop Sharp, William Dingwall, was killed at Drumclog and lies buried at Strathaven. See *Strathaven*, and also *Loudoun, Newmilns, Stonehouse* and *Lesmahagow* for the few other Whig victims. The grisly death of some dragoons cut off from the main body and trapped outside Strathaven is remembered in the name of the Trumpeter's Well.

The obelisk at Drumclog was not erected till 1839. It was struck by lightning a few years later and was rebuilt in 1867.

Inscription

IN COMMEMORATION
OF THE
VICTORY
OBTAINED ON THE
BATTLEFIELD
ON SABBATH THE 1ST OF JUNE 1679
BY OUR
COVENANTING FOREFATHERS
OVER GRAHAM OF CLAVERHOUSE
AND HIS DRAGOONS.

Close by, an inscribed stone from an earlier building now forms part of the wall of the present local authority centre at Drumclog:

1839
On the battle field of Drumlog, this Seminary of
Education was erected, in memory of those
Christian Heroes, who on Sabbath the 1st of June 1679.
nobly fought, in defence of Civil and Religious Liberty,
Dieu et mon Droit

(The names beneath this inscription are those of the committee which built the original school, and not those of the Christian Heroes referred to.)[1]

Drumclog is the first village east of Loudoun Hill, a conspicuous volcanic lump to the north of the A71. The battlefield itself is reached by driving west on the side road (unlisted) from the village and turning right (north) up the farm road to High Drumclog: the monument is a hundred metres west again of the farm.

[1] Thomson p23

Dumfries (NX 975 765)

Dumfries had a turbulent history throughout the Covenanting period and during the Civil Wars. At different times the town was invaded from Carlisle in the south and by Montrose from the north in 1645. It was a centre of Western radicalism, being vociferously anti-Engager in 1648; in 1650 it was the scene of a gathering of the so-called Western Association that produced the schismatic Remonstrance, practically splitting the Scottish Church into two wings until after the Restoration. Later, it was the headquarters of Sir James Turner when his soldiers provoked the Pentland Rising in November 1666, and the insurgents captured Sir James in his nightgown.[1]

After the collapse of the rebellion at Rullion Green on 19th November, 1666, and the authorities had taken their decision to execute many of the captured insurgents as traitors, local men were sent home to Dumfries to be hanged as a warning to their fellow-citizens. (*Cf. Ayr, Irvine* and *Glasgow.*)

The two Dumfries victims, William Grierson and William Welsh, were executed rather later than in the other towns, on 2nd January, 1667. Their gravestones are in the Old Parish Church yard, near a modern granite obelisk (1837).

A third gravestone in the churchyard is that of James Kirk or Kirko, of Sundaywell, Dunscore, who had been "out" at Rullion Green in 1666 and had been an intercommuned wanderer for nearly twenty years before being picked up by the agency of an informer and shot on 13th or 14th May, 1685, after refusing the Abjuration Oath. When being prepared for execution, the story goes, he begged for a little more time to "make up his peace with God". "Devil a peace ye get more made up," said Captain Andrew Bruce, and had him shot there and then.[2] (See Introduction p21.)

Inscriptions
(The present, deeply-incised epitaphs differ in certain respects from what is recorded by Thomson. In the end I have preferred Thomson's version as being more authentic, although he is not always to be trusted, in matters of spelling in particular).

(1) *Grierson*

(i) *(Framing main inscriptions along four edges of the flat stone)*

THIS AND THE NEIGHBOURING TOMBSTONE
WERE RE-ERECTED
AND REPAIRED [BY] VOLUNTARY SUBSCRIPTION
IN MARCH 1873

(ii) *(Main inscription)*

HERE LYES WILLIAM
GRIERSON PENTLAND
MARTYR FOR HIS
ADHERING TO THE
WORD OF GOD AND
APPEARING FOR CHRI
STS KINGLIE GOVERME
NT IN HIS HOUSE AND
THE COVENANTED WO
RK OF REFORMATION: A
GAINST PERJURY:
AND PRELACY EXECUTED -
JAN 2 1667: REV. 12 11.

(iii) *(At right angles to and beneath main inscription)*

UNDER THIS STONE LO HERE
DOTH LY
DUST SACRIFICED TO TYRANY
YET PRECIOUS IN IMMENULL
SIGHT   S
SINCE MARTYR'D FOR HIS
KINGLIE RIGHT
WHEN HE CONDEMNS
THESE HELLISH DRUGES
BY SUFFRAGE SAINTS
SHALL JUDGE THEIR JUDGES

(2) *Welsh* (i) *(Main inscription)*

HERE LYES WILLIAM
WELSH, PENTLAND
MARTYR, FOR HIS
ADHERING TO THE
WORD OF GOD AND
APPEARING FOR
CHRISTS KINGLY
GOVERMENT IN HIS
HOUSE AND THE CO
VENANTED WORK
OF REFORMATION

AGAINST PERJURY
AND PRELACIE EXE
CUTE JANR 2
1667 REV 12 11

(ii) *(At right angles to and beneath main inscription)*
STAY, PASSENGER, AND READ,
HERE INTERR'D DOTH LY
A WITNESS GAINST POOR
SCOTLANDS PERJURY,
WHOSE HEAD ONCE FIX'D UP
ON THE BRIDGE PORT STOOD
PROCLAIMING VENGEANCE
FOR HIS GUILTLESS BLOOD.

(3) Kirko (Kirk or Kirka)   (i) *(Main inscription)*
HERE LYES JAMES
KIRK A MARTYR
SHOT DEAD UPON
THE SANDS OF DR
UMFRIES: FOR HIS
ADHERING TO THE
WORD OF GOD CHR
ISTS KINGLY GOVE
RMENT IN HIS HO
USE: AND THE COV
ENANTED WORK OF
REFORMATION AG
AINTS TIRRANNIE
PERJURIE: AND PR
ELACIE 1685 REV
12 MAR

(ii) *At right angles to and beneath main inscription*
BY BLOODY BRUCE AND WRETCHED
WRIGHT
I LOST MY LIFE: IN GREAT DESPIGH
T
SHOT DEAD, WITHOUT DUE TIME
TO TRY,
AND FIT ME FOR ETERNITY,
A WITNESS OF PRELATICK RAGE
AS EVER WAS IN ANIE AGE

A cairn and saltire on the roadway on the roadway on the White Sands at Dumfries still marks the spot where Kirko was shot. Inscription:"James Kirko, martyr, of Sundaywell, was shot on the Sands, 13th May 1685."

Troqueeer, Dumfries (NX 975 751)

John Blackad(d)er, minister of Troqueer in Dumfries, was "outed" from his parish in 1662, to the clamorous dismay of his parishioners. The evicting officer in this case was none other than Sir James Turner, later famed for being captured in his nightgown by the Pentland rebels in 1666. He had an opprobrious nickname, and as the dispossessed Blackadders trudged disconsolately away from their manse — the infants apparently packed in creels — one of the children roared out: "I'm banish't, I'm banish't; Bite-the-Sheep has banish't me!"[3]

Blackadder, along with his near neighbour John Welsh of Irongray, soon rose to prominence among the field preachers, and did much to establish conventicling as an organised method of worship and resistance in succeeding years. Under his influence the conventicling movement grew into a virtual underground church, with a regular committee infrastructure, church courts, provision for students and so on. Blackadder ministered at some of the more spectacular conventicles of the late 1660s and 1670s — at Kinkell, East Nisbet, Eckford, Maybole, and, in 1678, Skeoch Hill near Irongray, where there was an attendance of 14,000 over a period of three days.

Blackadder also held house conventicles which, though necessarily smaller, were even more alarming to the authorities because they were less easily detected, could be held under their noses in the middle of cities, and so could draw influential people into their congregations.

Although a convinced anti-Erastian (opposed to state interference with the Church), Blackadder's influence was moderate, and he never shared in the excesses of men like Richard Cameron. After the Battle of Bothwell Brig, however, he was one of the ministers who encouraged the hard-core prisoners held in Greyfriars Churchyard, Edinburgh, not to sign the bond of good behaviour; so he may be said to have contributed indirectly to the tragedy of Mull Head of Deerness in Orkney, when the intransigence of these prisoners finally exasperated the Government into deporting them, and the ship carrying them to the Americas foundered off Orkney with the loss of hundreds of Covenanting lives (December 1679).

For all these reasons, the Government was glad when Blackadder fell into their hands in April 1681, and they lost no time in sending him off to the Bass Rock, where he died in late 1685.

A plaque was placed in the modern Troqueer Parish Church in 1902, and it reads as follows:

To the glory of God and in memory of
THE REVEREND JOHN BLACKADER
Born 1615
Ordained minister of the parish of Troqueer 1653.
Extruded 1662. Outlawed for preaching in the fields 1674.
Imprisoned on the Bass Rock 1681.
Died after cruel confinement 1685.
"Faithful unto death."
Erected A.D. 1902.

For an epitaph, see *North Berwick*. See also *Bass Rock*, *Irongray*, etc.

[1]Terry *Pentland* p11-13
[2]*Cloud* Appendix p384; Shields p36; Wodrow iv p251; Wodrow MSS xli p237
[3]Blackadder *Memoirs* pp85-87, 91, quoted Hewison ii p159

Dunnottar (NO 883 839)

This spectacular coastal fortress, south of Stonehaven, is where 167 Covenanting prisoners were confined on 24th May, 1685, after an exhausting march from Edinburgh starting on 18th May. The reason for the transfer is said by some authorities to have been the Government's alarm on hearing of the landing in Orkney on 6th May of the forces of the Earl of Argyll, bent on insurrection. Others state that Dunnottar was opened as a state prison merely to relieve overcrowding. Whatever the truth of the matter, in Dunnottar itself conditions were intolerable (in the "Whigs' Vault"), and many died before the rest were all marched back at the end of August to face transportation if they would not take the oath of allegiance. In the interval several managed to escape by clambering down the rock, though some fell and were killed, and others were recaptured and subjected to torture. (See next entry.)

Perhaps the best known of the prisoners was Patrick Walker, who subsequently wrote *Six Saints of the Covenants* and other works. Other prisoners left narratives, including Quintin Dick of Dalmellington in Ayrshire, whose story was published by Wodrow in his history.[1] One prisoner, Robert McLellan of Barmagechan, was imprisoned here under loathsome conditions and deported to America as a slave; he witnessed most of his fellow deportees dying on the voyage, was liberated in New

England, was captured by the French on his way back in 1689 and was imprisoned by them; was sent back via Genoa and Cadiz, and was driven by storms into a remote part of Ireland where he was held by the Irish peasantry for some time before being returned to Dublin; and came back to Barmagechan in Scotland on 31st October, 1691[2] McLellan's case was not unique.

Dunnottar may be easily reached by the A92.

[1] Cf Wodrow iv p322.
[2] Thomson pp226-227

Dunnottar Churchyard (NO 864 853)

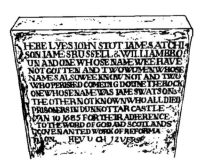

The churchyard of Dunnottar Parish lies some way inland from Dunnottar Castle, to the north-west across the A92. A collective gravestone stands to the east of the church.

Inscription

```
HERE . LYES . IOHN . STOT . IAMES . ATCHI
SON . IAMES . RUSSELL . & WILLIAM BRO
UN . AND . ONE . WHOSE . NAME . WEE . HAVE
NOT . GOTTEN . AND . TWO . WOMEN . WHOSE
NAMES . ALSO . WEE . KNOW . NOT . AND . TWO
WHO . PERISHED . COMEING . DOUNE . THE . ROCK
ONE . WHOSE . NAME . WAS . IAMES . WATSON
THE . OTHER . NOT . KNOWN . WHO . ALL . DIED
PRISONER . IN . DUNNOTTAR . CASTLE
    ANNO . 1685 . FOR . THEIR . ADHERENCE
TO . THE . WORD . OF . GOD . AND . SCOTLANDS
COVENANTED . WORK . OF . REFORMA
TION.                      REV . 11  CH . 12 VERSE
```

D Hay Fleming, in his Appendix to Thomson's *Martyr Graves of Scotland*, quotes James Anderson of Stonehaven as concluding from his lists "that

John Whyte, William Breadie, Mary Gibson, and Jean Muffet, were the four referred to on the tombstone whose names were unknown when it was erected."[1]

Dunnottar Churchyard is where Sir Walter Scott encountered Robert Paterson, "Old Mortality", the devoted Cameronian stonemason, at work on this stone.[2] It is a particularly fine stone of its kind, and shows to advantage the characteristic "Old Mortality" ligatures which enable the lettering to be densely packed on the surface of the stone. (For Paterson, see also *Balmaclellan*.)

[1]Thomson *Appendix* (D Hay Fleming) p497
[2]Scott *Old Mortality* Introduction

Dunscore (NX 926 833)

This is the burial-place of one of the most cherished monsters of Covenanting lore, Sir Robert Grierson of Lagg. He was the Government agent responsible for the drowning of the two women at Wigtown, the hangings at Hallhill (Irongray), the shootings at Kirkconnel Moor and Allan's Cairn and other misdeeds. He appears to have used deliberately coarse and stinging language, and this on one occasion was nearly the end of him when Viscount Kenmure, the father-in-law of one of his victims, attempted to run him through with this sword. (See *Anwoth*.)

Lagg is said to be the model for Scott's Sir Robert Redgauntlet; like the fictional character, Lagg lived for many years after the Glorious Revolution in reduced but still respected circumstances, in spite of (in Lagg's case) the attempt by some of his Covenanting enemies to have him prosecuted for clipping and coining, According to *A Cloud of Witnesses*, he was guilty of adultery and of "impenitent obstinacy"[1]; Hewison says he was "a smuggler, debtor, alleged debaser of the coin, a litigant put to the horn."[2] Nevertheless he remained a Justice of the Peace, and lived until 1736.

There is now a monument near Lagg's "neglected grave [which is] covered with rank weeds in a ruinous sepulchre."[3] The armorial bearings at the back of the grave enclosure may refer to Lagg's parents.

What seemingly was the original or at least earlier Dunscore Parish Churchyard lies in the angle of the A76 and the unlisted road which connects the major road with the B729 via Farthingwell and Milliganton. Not far away, on another unlisted road north of the modern Dunscore connecting B729 and A76, the ancestral tower of Lagg (NX 881 862) still stands adjacent to the farm of that name. (See Map on p.93.)

[1] *Cloud* Appendix p386
[2] Hewison ii p457; cf Walker i p330
[3] Hewison ib.

Durisdeer (NS 894 037)

Daniel McMichael was the brother of Black James McMichael who organized the Enterkin Pass rescue, killed the Curate of Carsphairn, and met his end in a skirmish after threatening the life of Claverhouse. (See *Auchencloy* for details.) Daniel, on the other hand, was a quiet man probably of frail health. He was participating in a house conventicle at Lurgfoot near Morton Castle when a party of dragoons under Sir John Dalziel and Lieutenant Straiton approached. McMichael was too ill to be moved and was left by his fellow worshippers concealed in a nearby cave. Unfortunately, the dragoons had tracker dogs that ran him to earth, and he was taken out and brought to Durisdeer[1]. He refused the oath of allegiance (not, apparently, the Abjuration Oath) and the dragoons prepared to take him to the garrison headquarters near Elvanfoot. On 31st January, 1685, however, while on the journey at Nether Dalveen, he again became too ill to go any further, and the soldiers feared another ambush in the Dalveen Pass similar to the earlier rescue at Enterkin. Daniel McMichael was accordingly shot there and then and his body was taken back to Durisdeer for burial. The flat raised stone is at the side of the church facing the entrance. See also *Dalveen*.

Inscription
(i) *(main inscription)*

HERE LYES DANIEL MC
MICHEL MARTYR SHOT
DEAD AT DALVEEN BY
SIR JOHN DALYEL FOR HIS
ADHEREING TO THE
WORD OF GOD CHRISTS
KINGLY GOVERMENT IN
HIS HOUSE AND THE

COVENANTED WORK OF
REFORMATION AGAINST
TYRANNY PERJURY AND
PRELACY 1685 REV 12 : 11

(ii) *(at foot of stone, at right angles to main inscription)*
AS DANIEL CAST WAS IN
LYONS DEN
FOR PRAYING UNTO GOD
AND NOT TO MEN
SO LYONS THUS CRUELY
DEVOURED ME
FOR BEAIRING WITNES TO
TRUTHS TESTIMONY -
I REST IN PEACE TILL
JESUS REND THE CLOUD
AND JUDGE TWIXT ME AND
THOSE WHO SHED ME BLOUD

Durisdeer is a very remote village with a magnificent church and a mausoleum for the Dukes of Queensberry. It is on a side road off the A702 Thornhill to Crawford Road.

[1] Wodrow iv p239; Simpson pp51-56; Thomson pp459-461; Shields p36

Eaglesham (NS 552 600)

Gabriel Thomson and Robert Lockhart were shot on 1st May, 1685, at two different places near Eaglesham: Cowplie, near Melowther Hill, and Sparrow Hill, about a mile further to the south-west, where the soldiers overtook the second man as he fled. Neither location can now be pinpointed, nor are either of these two men mentioned in the main source-book for the Killing Time, Wodrow's *History*. They seem to have been on their way back from a conventicle when they were chased and shot by a party of Highlanders under "Ardencaple". A Gabriel Thomson, apparently a different person, is mentioned by Hewison[1] as "a lad of eighteen years" of whom "nothing is known", but he was executed in November 1684, as part of the aftermath of the Swyne Abbey murders.

Inscription

PSA. CXII. & VI. THE RIGHTEOUS
SHALL BE IN EVERLASTING REME-
MBRANCE.
HERE LIE GABRIEL THOMSON
AND ROBERT LOCKHART
WHO WERE KILLED FOR OUNING THE COVEN-
ANTED TESTIMONY BY A PARTY OF HIGH-
LANDMEN AND DRAGOONS UNDER THE
COMMAND OF ARDENCAPLE 1ST MAY 1685.
THESE MEN DID SEARCH THROUGH MOOR AND MOSS
TO FIND OUT ALL THAT HAD NO PASS -
THESE FAITHFULL WITNESSES WERE FOUND
AND MURDERED UPON THE GROUND
THEIR BODIES IN THIS GRAVE DO LIE
THEIR BLOOD FOR VENGEANCE YET DOTH CRY
THIS MAY A STANDING WITNESS BE
FOR PRESBYTRY GAINST PRELACY -

Eaglesham lies at the junction of B767 and B764, not far from East Kilbride south of Glasgow.

[1] Hewison ii p443

Ecclesiamagirdle (also Ecclesmagirdle, locally Exmagirdle) (NO 107 164)

This Perthshire graveyard contains a Covenanting tombstone relating to the pre-Cromwellian period. Unfortunately, nothing is known of the person commemorated. From the date on the tombstone (1st September, 1645) it has been conjectured that he may have fallen defending the Covenants against the onslaught of Montrose, whose campaigns were just ending at that time.[1] The phraseology of the epitaph is typical of the period.

Inscription

HEIR . LYES . ANE . VER
TOVS . HVSBAND .
MAN . THOMAS . SMAL
WHO . DIED . FOR

<pre>
T   S
    [? Armorial
       design —
       effaced]
E   D
RELIGION . COVENA
NT . KING . AND . CO
VNTRIE . THE . 1 . OF .
SEPTEMBER . 1645 .
HIS . AGE . 58
</pre>

MEMENTO *[skull and crossbones]* MORI.

The ruined chapel at Ecclesiamagirdle is still accessible, but overgrown with ancient trees and bushes to such an extent that it is virtually invisible from the (farm) road at Glenearn steading; this road is marked as a no-through road where it branches west from the West Dron road south of Bridge of Earn. The chapel lies behind a stone wall to the north of the steading marking the boundary of the steading and the garden ground of Ecclesiamagirdle Castle. Visitors are advised to contact the occupants of Glenearn Farm or the nearby Glenearn House (Mrs McLaren).

The name *Ecclesiamagirdle* probably means the Church of St Adrian (Skene). The form *Exmagirdle* occurs as early as the fifteenth century; the first reference to the site comes in 1214 *(Eglesmagril)*. The whole area, which is very lovely, is overshadowed by the Ochil Hills.

> *The lasses o' Exmagirdle*
> *May very weel be dun,*
> *For frae Michaelmas till Whitsunday*
> *They never see the sun.*

[1] Thomson p215

Edinburgh (NT 255 730 etc.)

Much of the centre of the Scottish capital has Covenanting as well as other major historical associations: many of the most important events involving Covenanters were enacted and reached their climax in or around the High Kirk of St Giles, the Parliament House, the Cross, Edinburgh Castle, the West Bow, the Grassmarket, the Canongate Tolbooth, Greyfriars Church and other sites. A list of Covenanters executed in Edinburgh, together with their origins if from outside the city, will be found in Appendix Ia.

(1) *Greyfriars Churchyard*
(i) *Burials*
Several of the most important Covenanting figures of the seventeenth century are reputedly buried here, but few of them are identifiable. Alexander Henderson, the partner of Johnston of Wariston in drawing up the National Covenant in 1638, is buried in the western part of the graveyard just adjacent to the Covenanter's Prison, and his monument is still recognizable, topped by an urn. The inscriptions on the stone were erased after the Restoration by order of the Earl of Middleton, whose soldiers fired bullets at it, and the marks can still be seen; the inscriptions, however, were restored after 1689.

Inscription (English only)

> Reader, bedew thine eyes
> Not for the dust here lyes -
> It quicken shall again.
> And aye in joy remain
> But for thyself, the Church and States
> Whose woes this dust prognosticates.

(ii) *Covenanters' Prison*
Also in Greyfriars Churchyard, at the south-west corner, there is a walled enclosure open to the air but barred by an iron gate; this is now labelled "Covenanters' Prison". After the Battle of Bothwell Brig on 22nd July, 1679, several hundred captured Whigs were confined in this "concentration camp", rather to the embarrassment of the Government.

Some prisoners, indeed, were picked off as sacrificial victims. (See *Magus Muir*). The authorities, however, did not know what to do with the vast majority; after some time they began to whittle down their numbers by arranging for the more pliable to give bonds of good behaviour against release. Others simply escaped, since the wall was not difficult to scale and the guards were bribable. The remaining prisoners fell out among themselves after someone pointed out that signing the bond meant admitting that the rising had been sinful and thus defecting from the cause.[1]

At this point, the Government lost patience and decided to deport them *en masse* to the Barbados. 246 Bothwell prisoners were taken down to Leith and put on board *The Crown of London*, which left on 27th November, 1679. It was a bad time of year for a long sea-voyage, and the ship foundered off Mule (Muil, Mull) Head in the Orkney Islands on 10th December, 1679. It is alleged that the captain of the vessel refused to open the hatches, and all but 49 prisoners drowned. (See *Orkney*.) The compilers of the martyrology called *A Cloud of Witnesses* listed the victims by parishes. This list is reproduced in Appendix lc.

Edinburgh, Greyfriars

(iii) *The Signing of the Covenant*

Near the south-east corner of Greyfriars Church lies a flat stone enclosed in railings on which the National Covenant is said to have been signed on 28th February, 1638, by a large number of people who had waited outside the church until the then leaders of the Covenanters had signed it inside the church. According to the Earl of Rothes, who was among the first signatories, the subscription in the churchyard went on until eight at night, and torches had to be lit. Thereafter copies were made and another mass signing took place on 2nd March. What is said to be the original Covenant is now preserved in an effective glass display showing both closely inscribed sides in Huntly House Museum in the Canongate.

(iv) *The Martyrs' Monument*

On 29th October, 1701, at Crawfordjohn, a meeting of the Societies took a resolution for the erection of suitable monuments over all martyr graves in Scotland[2] and, in 1706, in pursuance of this resolution, the Edinburgh authorities put up a collective memorial in Greyfriars Churchyard overlooking the gallows site in the Grassmarket. Most of those hanged in the Grassmarket were buried anonymously in a "Thieves' Hole" in Greyfriars Churchyard; or at least, this was the intention of the Government, but it is said that the grave diggers secretly interred the Covenanters in a part of the graveyard unpolluted by criminal corpses.

The original monumental slab, as carved by James Currie in 1706, will now be found (HH59) next to the gravestone of James Currie himself (*d* 1736) at the bottom of the small garden annexed to Huntly House Museum in the Canongate. It is well-preserved and finely carved, with beautiful, regular lettering (except for the last line, which may have been added at a later date). By contrast the present Greyfriars monument, whose inscription seems to have been subject to inauthentic alteration, is beginning to deteriorate with quite bad weathering in the centre. The following is the 1706 inscription:

> *Halt passenger take heed Qt thou dost see*
> *This tomb doth show for Qt some men did die*
> *Here lyes interr'd ye dust of these who stood*
> *Gainst perjury resisting unto blood*
> *Adhering to the Covenant's and Law's*
> *Establishing the same which was the Cause:-*

Their lives were sacrific'd unto the Lust
Of Prelatist's abjured though here their dust
Ly's mixt with murderers and other crew
Whom justice did justly to death pursue.
But as for thir in them no cause was found
Worthy of death but only they were sound
Constant and stedfast Zealous wittnessing
For the prerogatives of CHRIST their king
Which truth's were seal'd by famous Guthri's head
And all along to Master Ranwick's blood
They did endure the wrath of enemies
Reproaches torments deaths and injuries
But yet they're these who from such trobls came
And now triumph in glory with the LAMB.

From may 27ᵗʰ 1661 that the noble Marquess of
Argyle suffered to the 17ᵗʰ of febr. 1688 that Mᴿ
Iames Ranwick suffereᵈ were execut at Edin
burg about an hundered of Noblemen Gent
lmen Ministers & others noble martyres for
JESUS CHRIST . the most part of them ly
                             here.
This Tomb was Erected Anno 1706.

(2) *The Canongate Tolbooth*
This building, notable for its modern external clock (nearly opposite Huntly House in the Canongate), was used as a prison for Covenanters throughout the Restoration period, and was the scene of jailbreaks so frequently that, after the escape of 25 prisoners on 16th September, 1683, the magistrates of Edinburgh were charged with passive complicity, although acquitted later.[32] Among the 25 who got away was James "Long Gun" Harkness, later a leader in the Enterkin Pass rescue and other feats. (See *Dalgarnock* and *Enterkin*.)

[1] The ringleader of the intransigents was Robert Garnock,
a blacksmith or hammerman from Stirling. He was encouraged by letter by the Rev. John Blackadder. (See *Dumfries - Troqueer*). Wodrow MSS xxxvi p17; Walker i pp53-54. Garnock was later hanged. (See Appendix 1a 48).
[2] Thomson p64; Hewison ii Appendix II p550
[3] Fountainhall *Historical Notices* i p454

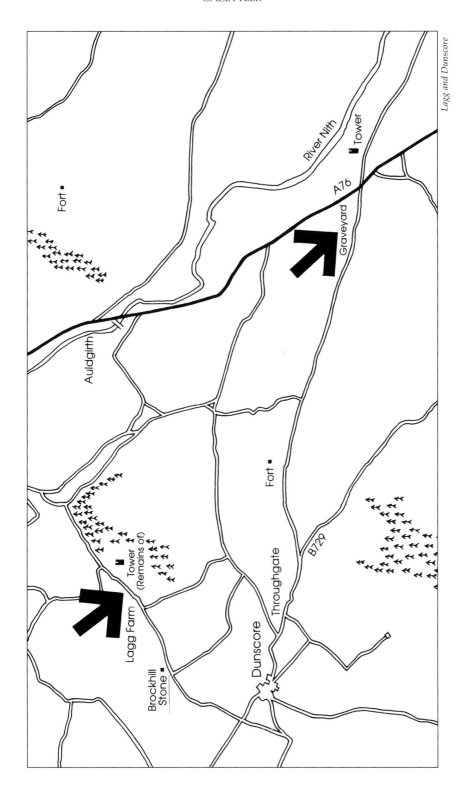

Lagg and Dunscore

Enterkin Pass (Wanlockhead to Glenvalentine etc) (NX 876 127 - 878 078)

The Enterkin Pass is a wild and gloomy footpath between Wanlockhead and the A702, along the Enterkin Burn part of the way to the River Nith, under the shadow of the Green Lowther, Thirstane Hill and Steygail. Nowadays it intersects with the Southern Upland Way. In the 17th century it was part of the route from the south-west to Edinburgh, and troops and their prisoners often marched along it. On 29th July, 1684, soldiers escorting a party of prisoners to Edinburgh were set upon by a three-pronged ambuscade at the very difficult point of Glenvalentine; the ambush was well organised by James "Long Gun" Harkness, his brother Thomas "White Hose" Harkness, "Black" James McMichael and others. (See *Auchencloy, Durisdeer, Dalveen, Dalgarnock* etc.) There was a fusillade and several on either side were killed. With his first shot Black McMichael is said to have "tumbled dead Sergeant Kelt into the linn which tradition has named after him."(Hewison) The majority of the prisoners were rescued.

It was after this major incident that Claverhouse, whose troops had been involved on the Government side, personally ran five of the rescuers to earth, arrested them, and hurried them to Edinburgh, where they were tried and executed with peremptory speed on 15th August, 1684. James Harkness was among the captured men, but he succeeded in escaping; his brother Thomas was hanged with the others in the Grassmarket.

Fenwick (NS 465 435)

This village was an important centre of Covenanting activity in the 17th century in spite of the proximity of garrisons at Kilmarnock and Newmilns. Repeated dragoon raids seem to have been normal, to judge by the testimony of the inhabitants of Lochgoin and other farms, and there are more Covenanting gravestones and memorials here than in any other single locality in Scotland. No less than seven victims of the Killing Time and of earlier persecutions are recorded on five tombstones in the parish churchyard.

The church in whose graveyard these stones stand was virtually destroyed by fire in 1929 but has been lovingly restored. It now houses two important relics - the Bible used by Captain Paton on the scaffold in

Edinburgh in 1684 and handed by him to his wife before execution, and
a Covenanting flag inscribed

PHINIGK FOR GOD C^oVVNTRY
AND COVENANTED VVORK OF REFORMATIONS

Graveyard Inscriptions

(1) *Paton*

SACRED
TO THE MEMORY
OF
CAPTAIN JOHN PATON
LATE IN MEADOWHEAD
OF THIS PARISH
WHO SUFFERED MARTYRDOM
IN THE GRASSMARKET
EDINBURGH, MAY 9TH, 1684.

HE WAS AN HONOUR TO HIS COUNTRY: ON
THE CONTINENT, AT PENTLAND, DRUMCLOG
AND BOTHWELL, HIS HEROIC CONDUCT TRULY
EVINCED THE GALLANT OFFICER, BRAVE
SOLDIER AND TRUE PATRIOT. IN SOCIAL AND
DOMESTIC LIFE HE WAS AN ORNAMENT,
A PIOUS CHRISTIAN, AND A FAITHFUL
WITNESS FOR TRUTH IN OPPOSITION TO THE
ENCROACHMENTS OF TYRANNICAL AND
DESPOTIC POWER IN CHURCH AND STATE.

THE MORTAL REMAINS OF
CAPTAIN PATON
SLEEP AMID THE DUST OF
KINDRED MARTYRS IN THE
GREYFRIARS CHURCHYARD
EDINBURGH

NEAR THIS IS THE
BURYING PLACE OF HIS FAMILY
AND DESCENDANTS.

Who Antichrist do thus oppose
And for truth's cause their lives lay down
Will get the victory o'er their foes
And gain life's everlasting crown.

For further details about Captain Paton, see Introduction p17.

(2) *White*

HERE LIES THE BODY
OF
JAMES WHITE
WHO WAS SHOT TO DEATH
AT LITTLE BLACKWOOD
BY PETER INGLES AND
HIS PARTY 1685
RENEWED
BY
SUBSCRIPTION
1822

(reverse)

This Martyr was By PETER
INGLES Shot
By birth a Tyger rather
(t)han a Scot
Who that his monstrous
Extract might be Seen
Cut off his head & Kick't it
o'er the Green.
Thus was that head which
was to wear a Crown
a football made by a profane
Dragoun.

For further details on the James White episode, see Newmilns and Priesthill.

---

(3) *Gemmel*

Here lies
the Corps of peter
Gemmel who was Shot to death
by Nisbet and his party, 1685 for
bearing his faithful Testimony to the
Cause of Christ, aged 21 years.

This man like holy Anchorits of old
For conscience sake was thrust from house
               and hold.
Bloodthirsty Redcoats cut his prayer short
And ev'n his dying groans were made their sport
Ah Scotland breach of solemn vows repent
Or blood thy crime will be thy punishment

Gemmel, like Fergushill and Woodburn, was shot in a gunfight at Midland in November 1685, when John Nisbet of Hardhill was arrested by Lieutenant Nisbet, in fact a cousin of Hardhill. All four were "Society People", and Captain John Nisbet was a veteran of the Covenanting campaigns not unlike Captain Paton; he was hanged in Edinburgh on 4th December, 1685.

(4) *Fergushill and Woodburn*

> HERE LIES
> The dust of JOHN FERGUSHILL
> and GEORGE WOODBURN who
> were shot at MIDLAND by
> NISBET and his party 1685
> When bloody prelates
> Once these nations pest
> Contrived that cursed
> Self-contradicting test
> These men for Christ
> Did suffer Martyrdom
> And here their dust lies
> Waiting till he come
>
> RENEWED by SUBSCRIPTION
> 1820

For brief comment, see under Gemmel above.

(5) *Buntine and Blackwood*

> ERECTED
> IN MEMORY OF
> ROBERT BUNTINE
> WHO WAS EXECUTED AT GLASGOW
> 19TH DECEMBER 1666
> AND
> JAMES BLACKWOOD
> WHO WAS EXECUTED AT IRVINE
> 31ST DECEMBER 1666
> (BOTH NATIVES OF FENWICK)
> FOR THEIR ATTACHMENT
> TO THE COVENANTED WORK OF REFORMATION
> AND THEIR SHARE
> IN THE STRUGGLE AT PENTLAND
> IN NOVEMBER OF THE SAME YEAR

These two Pentland martyrs, who were treated as traitors after the defeat at Rullion Green, were executed in Glasgow and Irvine as stated. See *Glasgow* and *Irvine*, and compare *Ayr, Dumfries, Newmilns, Kilmarnock* and *Hamilton*.

(6) *Guthrie*

IN MEMORY
OF
THE REV. WILLIAM GUTHRIE
FIRST
MINISTER OF THIS PARISH
AND AUTHOR OF
"THE
CHRISTIAN'S GREAT INTEREST".
BORN, 1620; ORDAINED 1644.
EJECTED BY
PRELATIC PERSECUTION 1664;
WORN OUT BY
LABOURS AND SUFFERINGS,
HE DIED, 1665;
AND WAS INTERRED
IN THE CHURCH OF BRECHIN.
HIS ACTIVE AND
SELF-DENIED MINISTRY
THROUGH THE DIVINE BLESSING
PRODUCED A DEEP AND
LASTING IMPRESSION.
THIS STONE IS ERECTED 1854
AS A TOKEN OF GRATITUDE
BY
THE CHRISTIAN PUBLIC.

With heavnly weapons I have fought
The battles of the Lord:
Finish'd my course, and kept the faith
Depending on his word.

William Guthrie of Fenwick was a cousin of the great James Guthrie who was marked out for King Charles's special displeasure after the Restoration in 1660 and was hanged in 1661. The Fenwick Guthrie was a gentle, witty, clever man who produced one very well-known book and was lucky to be punished only with internal exile in Brechin in 1664.

(7) *Howie*

> The dust here lies under this stone
> Of James Howie and his son John;
> These two both lived at Lochgoin,
> And by Death's pow'r were called to join
> This place. The first, November twenty-one
> Years sixteen hundred and ninety-one.
> The second, aged ninety years,
> The first of July was brought here,
> Years seventeen hundred and fifty-five
> For owning truth made fugitive;
> Their house twelve times, and cattle all,
> Once robb'd and fam'ly brought to thrall,
> All these, before the Revolution
> Outliv'd Zion's friends 'gainst opposition.

And he said unto me, these are they which came out of great tribulation.
- Rev vii. 14.

> The voice said cry. What shall I cry?
> All flesh is grass and so must he ly;
> As flow'r in field withereth away,
> So the goodliness of men decay.
> ISA. xl. 6-7

> John Howie of Lochgoin in FENWICK:
> Also of his son JOHN,
> who lived at Lochgoin, author of the
> *Scots Worthies* and other publications.
> who died Jan. 5, A.D. 1793, aged 57 years.

The last-named above was in the nineteenth century one of the most popular historians of the Scottish Covenanters.[1]The tales with which he grew up and which fired his imagination are hinted at in the narrative verse of the first epitaph above.

Fenwick is a small village to the north of Kilmarnock just off the main route to Glasgow. A77 for B751.

[1]Howie's principal work is *The Scots Worthies: Biographia Scoticana*. See Bibliography for details.

Forgandenny (NO 087 184)

Forgandenny is a small village south of Perth on B935 not far from Ecclesiamagirdle. The single martyr's stone here used to stand in the churchyard south of the church but in 1926 it was removed to the church porch (key with Mr Bob Robertson in the cottage forming part of the Primary School). This is an isolated tombstone, the case not being mentioned in *A Cloud of Witnesses*. The shooting took place during a renewed drive against conventicles in 1678, while tension was increasing towards the assassination of Archbishop Sharp.

Inscription

HERE LYES
ANDREW BRODIE WRIG
HT IN FORGUNDENNY WHO
AT THE BREAK OF A MEETING
OCBR 1678 WAS SHOT BY A
PARTY OF HIGHLAND MEN
COMMANDED BY BALLECH
EN AT A CAVES MOUTH FLY
ING THITHER FOR HIS LIFE &
THAT FOR HIS ADHERENCE
TO THE WORD OF GOD & SCO
TLANDS COVENANTED
WORK OF REFORMATION
REV 12C VII

A tradition recorded by the Statistical Account is that after the shooting Brodie's wife covered the body with a scarlet cloak, whereupon one of the soldiers came up and asked her what she now thought of her husband. She replied, "I think more of him than ever." Almost the same exchange is recorded as taking place between John Graham of Claverhouse and John Brown's widow after Brown's execution at Priesthill on 1st May, 1685. (See *Priesthill*.)

Friarminnan
(also Friarminnion and Freminnan) (NS 739 190)

This remote farmhouse, half-way between Auchtitench and Blackgannoch on the former Sanquhar-Muirkirk hill road was James Renwick's refuge while he wrote and edited the 1684 Apologetical Declaration and other pronunciamentos. It has recently been suggested that Friarminnan was identical with the fabled Covenanting hide-out known as the"Miny", as Auchtitench might also be with the so-called "Auchty".[1] If so, the very remoteness of both these sites would serve as cover. (Auchtitench is now buried deep in the Penbreck Forest area).

Friarminnan is now (1988) merely a forbidding heap of stones and two gable-ends in the centre of a dangerous boghole in a high, windswept valley. Visitors are counselled to avail themselves of the OS Pathfinder map NS/61/71. If they do, they may find a rockface inscribed with the name *Peden* and a date (?1684), somewhere on the higher ground nearer the forest road:

[1] Finlay p6

Galston (NS 560 367)

Resistance to episcopacy goes back a long way in Galston and its surroundings. When the Lollards of Kyle were reported to King James IV in 1494 for denying the authority of the bishops and the Pope, among their number was a Campbell of Cessnock[1] — and 190 years later we find Sir Hew Campbell of Cessnock involved in the Argyll conspiracy of 1684-85 and prosecuted for encouraging the rebels at Bothwell Brig.

Six names from the later Covenanting period appear on gravestones in the Parish Churchyard.

Inscriptions
(1) *Richmond*

Carving: a man levelling a musket at another whose arms are raised in an attitude not of surrender but of benediction.

HERE LIES
ANDREW RICHMOND
WHO WAS KILLED BY
BLOODY GRAHAM OF CLAVERHOUSE
IN JUNE 1679
IN HIS ADHERENCE TI THE WORD OF GOD
AND SCOTLAND'S COVENANTED REFORMATION

(reverse)

WHEN BLOODY TYRANTS HERE DID RAGE
OVER THE LORD'S OWN HERITAGE
TO PERSECUTE HIS NOBLE CAUSE
BY MISCHIEF FORMED INTO LAWS
CAUSE I THE GOSPEL DID DEFEND
BY MARTYRDOM MY LIFE DID END.
(Renewed in 1940)

Richmond, whose name is otherwise unrecorded, appears to have been shot by Claverhouse when the latter was pursuing defeated Covenanters as far as Ayr after the Battle of Bothwell Brig in 1679[2].

(2) *Richmond/Smith et al.*
(Gravestone flat with grass at right of main entrance stairway)

IN MEMORY
of
JOHN RICHMOND
Younger of Know
Who was Executed at the Cross of Glasgow
March 19th 1684 and interred in
The high Church Yard there
AND
JAMES SMITH
East Threepwood
Who was shot near Bank on Burn Ann 1685
By CAPT. INGLIS and his Dragoons
And buried there
ALSO
JAMES YOUNG & GEORGE CAMPBELL
who were banished in 1679
AND
THE REV[D]. ALEXANDER BLAIR
who suffered imprisonment 1673.

For Richmond of Know(e), see *Glasgow*. James Smith of East Threepwood is discussed below. James Young and George Campbell were captured at the Battle of Bothwell Brig in 1679 and sentenced to transportation: the ship they were being deported in went down off Orkney and both perished along with many hundreds of Bothwell prisoners. See *Edinburgh (Greyfriars)*, *Orkney* and Appendix 1c. The Rev. Alexander Blair was imprisoned "for disowning the king and council's power and authority" in July 1673 and actually died in January 1674[3].

James Smith of Wee or East Threepwood is rather mysterious. He appears to have been caught up in the aftermath of the prison break at the Ducat Tower. (See *Newmilns, Priesthill, Mauchline*. The tradition is that he was shot on his own doorstep for having given food to the escapees[4]. Yet this stone says that he was shot "near Bank on Burn Ann ... and buried there". Bank is some distance away from Wee Threepwood[5]. Another tradition is that his tombstone was dislodged and thrown into the Burn Ann by a frolicsome herdboy, and that it was broken into several pieces. One fragment, marked JS 1684 (or 1685) was recovered and built into the steading at Wee Threepwood.

No such stone is evident nowadays at Wee Threepwood which for about two hundred years has been merely a pile of rubble on the lands of

Threepwood Mains[6]. A much later tombstone, unconnected with Smith, is discoverable in thick grass under a large tree just beside the site. A tombstone to Smith might yet turn up there.

A tombstone to James Smith does exist at Mauchline (*q.v.*) The epitaph on that stone states that he was "wounded by Captain Ingles, and his Dragoons, at the Burn of Ann in kyle, and there after died of his wounds in Mauchline prison." This tombstone looks authentic. The fact that five men, one of whom at least is known to have participated in the Newmilns prison break in April 1685, were hanged at Mauchline on 6th May, 1685, seems to indicate that Mauchline was the centre to which all the suspects implicated in the affair at Newmilns were transferred. It looks as if James Smith, grievously wounded, was carried to Mauchline perhaps for interrogation, but died before he could be hanged.

The Mauchline tombstone is dated 1684, and we know that the Newmilns attack took place in April 1685, but this need not invalidate our surmise, since tombstone dating can be very unreliable; some of the epitaphs were not composed until nearly forty years after the events they commemorate; this date may have been derived from that published in *A Cloud of Witnesses*, which is full of printing errors.

If, however, this is what happened to James Smith, how do we explain the tradition of the vanished tombstone at Bank or Wee Threepwood? Yet another tradition states that in his rage after the escape of his prisoners, Captain Ingles had two innocent men shot. If James Smith was one, who was the other? Could there have been two James Smiths of Wee Threepwood (perhaps father and son)? Martyrs with the same name were not uncommon. (*Cf.* the two David Hallidays buried in the same grave at Balmaghie.)

In November 1926 a group of miners decided to erect a memorial to James Smith near Burn Ann, since all trace of the original had disappeared. They built the present large marker on the Gallows Hill overlooking Burn Ann and Threepwood, incorporating pieces of glass to reflect the sun's rays. This is also dated 1684, deriving probably from the same sources. It will now be found on the lands of Hillend Farm. (Please follow the farmer's directions fixed on the wooden gate leading from the side road.)

[1]Knox vol i p8
[2]Terry *Claverhouse* p83 n5; Hendrie pp83-84
[3]Wodrow ii p267
[4]Macleod NSA v p838 (Loudoun Parish)
[5]Hendrie pp84-85
[6]Hendrie pp82-83

Girthon (NX 605 535)

The Covenanting tombstone in Girthon Old Churchyard commemorates Robert Lennox of Irelandton, one of five men shot by Lagg on Kirkconnel Moore on 21st February, 1685. For details see *Kirkconnel Moor* and *Anwoth*, *Balmaghie* and *Twynholm*. The stone will be found hard against the east wall of the ruined church, which is built on a high knoll.

Inscription

WITHIN THIS TOMB
LYES THE CORPS OF
ROBERT LENNOX SOME
TIME IN IRELAND TOUN
WHO WAS SHOT TO
DEATH BY GRIER OF
LAGG IN THE PAROCH
OF TOUNGLAND FOR
HIS ADHERENCE TO
SCOTLANDS REFORMATION
COVENANTS NATIONAL
AND SOLEMN LEAGUE
1685

Girthon is just south of the Fleet Forest and may be reached from Gatehouse of Fleet by an unlisted road running south-west from the A75 towards Sandgreen.

Glasgow (NS 605 656)

Glasgow was an important cathedral city before the Reformation, and afterwards it had its share of exciting events and famous men. Archibald Johnston of Wariston, the principal draftsman of the 1638 National Covenant, was a scholar at Glasgow University; in November 1638, also, he took a leading part in the Glasgow Assembly in the Cathedral, when the Church of Scotland finally broke with King and bishops. On that occasion, when the Marquis of Hamilton, the King's Commissioner, found that his authority has been rejected by the Assembly, he tried to make a dignified withdrawal—but lo! the Cathedral door had been locked and the key "mislaid"; the Marquis had to wait in fuming dudgeon until the door was broken down.[1]

In 1679, after the Battle of Drumclog, Sir Robert Hamilton and the victorious Whigs thought to repeat their triumph by taking Glasgow, but the commander of the town, Lord Ross, set up road-blocks on all the approaches and concentrated troops at strategic points. The Whigs, their brief valour already evaporating, split into two bodies, one attacking the Gallowgate area and the other making for the Cathedral and the College. Hamilton committed a basic error of timing in not synchronizing the attacks; the defenders were able to deal with the Gallowgate party first and then regroup at their leisure to reinforce the resistance at the Cathedral.[2] At both points the Whigs were easily driven off by a withering fire: seven Whigs are reputed to have died, and no defenders at all.[3] Thus ended the battle for Glasgow. (See also *Drumclog* and *Bothwell Brig*).

One Covenanting monument is in Glasgow Cathedral and another has now found a haven at Sighthill Cemetery. The stone at the Cathedral has been built into the wall of the staircase descending to the crypt and is normally very poorly lit.

Inscriptions
(1) *Cathedral*

> Here lies the corps of
> ROBERT BUNTON, JOHN HART,
> ROBERT SCOTT,
> MATTHEW PATOUN,
> JOHN RICHMOND,
> JAMES JOHNSTOUN,
> ARCHIBALD STEWART,
> JAMES WINNING,
> JOHN MAIN.
>
> Who suffered at the cross of Glasgow
> For their testimony to the covenants
>   And work of reformation,
> Because they durst not own the
> Authority of the then tyrants
>   Destroying the same,
> Betwixt 1666 and 1688.
> YEARS sixty-six and eighty four
> Did send their souls home into glore,
> Whose bodies here interred ly
> Then sacrificed to tyranny
> To covenants and reformation
> Cause they adheared in their station.
> These nine, with others in this yard
> Whose heads and bodies were not spar'd

Their testimonies, foes, to bury
Caus'd beat the drums then in great fury.
They'll know at resurrection day
To murder saints was no sweet play.

The original Stone and Inscription
Repaired and new lettered
MDCCCCXXVII
At the expense of a few FRIENDS of the CAUSE
For which the MARTYRS SUFFERED.

Bunton (Buntine), Scott, Hart, and Paton were all Pentland martyrs who were executed on 19th December, 1666. (Cf. *Ayr, Irvine* and *Dumfries,* as well as *Rullion Green*; for Buntine and Paton, see *Fenwick* and *Newmilns* respectively.)

The other five were tried on 17th March, 1684, and hanged two days later at Glasgow Cross. This multiple execution was part of the general hardening of Government attitudes following James Renwick's return to Scotland in September 1683, and the growing fear of rebellion with the revival of conventicling. Richmond is also commemorated at Galston (*q.v.*). Stewart came from Lesmahagow and the other three from the Glasgow area — Winning from Glasgow itself, Johnston from Calder and Main from Old Monkland.

It is related of John Richmond the younger of Knowe that "in November 1683 he was walking in Glasgow, when Major Balfour endeavoured to seize him. He tried to escape, but was speedily captured, and was cruelly used, although it was not known who he was; and the only charge that could be brought against him was, that he did what he could to flee when it was sought to lay hold of him."[4]

Thus Thomson; Major Balfour's version of the arrest has not come down to us; at least, who he thought he was laying by the heels and why, do not now seem to be known. Yet charges were brought against Richmond and the others, and Hewison says that "the scaffold made these sufferers rapturous"[5]; in *A Cloud of Witnesses* Richmond is reported to have exclaimed, "Scare not at the Cross of Christ; for, O! if ye knew what I have met with since I came to Prison! what Love! What matchless love from my sweet and lovely Lord! ye would long to be with him, and would count it nought to go through a Sea of Blood for him."[6]

The strain of incredulous indignation that we might expect from the innocent victim of a tyrannical whim appears to be absent, and Richmond was a big enough fish for his friend James Nisbet to risk attending his funeral.

(2) Sighthill Cemetery

THE DEAD YET SPEAKETH
BEHIND THIS STONE LYES
JAMES NISBET
Who suffered Martyrdom at this Place
JUNE 5th 1684
ALSO JAMES LAWSON
AND ALEXANDER WOOD
Who suffered Martyrdom October 24th 1684
for their adherence to the Word of God and
Scotland's covenanted work of the reformation

Here lyes martyrs three
Of memory
Who for the Covenant did die
And witness is
Against all the nation's perjury
Gainst the Covenanted cause
Of CHRIST their royal king
The BRITISH rulers made such laws
Declared 'twas satan's reign.
As BRITAIN lyes in guilt, you see,
Tis ask'd, o' reader art thou free
THIS STONE WAS RENEWED BY
the proprietors of
THE MONKLAND NAVIGATION
APRIL 1818
AND AGAIN IN GRANITE BY
THE CITIZENS IN 1862
DRINK AND THINK
THE MARTYRS MONUMENT

James Nisbet of Highside in Loudoun Parish seems to have been a member of a large Covenanting family that included John Nisbet of Hardhill and John Nisbet the younger of Glen or Know. (See *Fenwick*, *Newmilns* and *Kilmarnock*). Nisbet of Highside was apprehended at John Richmond of Know's funeral by (it is said) his own cousin, Lieutenant Nisbet, who was responsible for the arrest of Nisbet of Hardhill — yet another cousin.[7] John Nisbet the younger of Know, on the other hand, was arrested outside Kilmarnock by Major Balfour — the same man who picked John Richmond of Know off the street in Glasgow, and was responsible for the shooting of three men at Polmadie. (See *Cathcart*.)

Nothing seems to be known about Lawson and Wood. They share a "joint testimony" in *A Cloud of Witnesses*.

As will be seen from the inscription, the 1862 version of the Nisbet/Lawson/Wood memorial is in the shape of a drinking fountain, first put up as a replacement for the original stone by the proprietors of the Monkland Canal in 1818. When the motorway came to be built, the granite plaque was set in the structure of the motorway underpass near Glasgow Royal Infirmary. Then it began to receive the attentions of vandals, and so it was transported again to a place of safety in Sighthill Cemetery. This is an enormous burying ground, and visitors would be advised to contact the Cemeteries Office of the City of Glasgow Council Parks and Recreation Department at 302 Buchanan Street, Glasgow G3 (0141 332 0800 or 0141 552 3145) and arrange for an appointment with a guide.

[1] Burnet *Memoires* p106; Hewison ii p303
[2] Creichton pp32-33; Wodrow iii p7
[3] Creichton p33; Wodrow loc cit
[4] Thomson p139
[5] Hewison ii p421
[6] Cloud p260
[7] Hewison ii p422

Glassford (West Quarter) (NS 734 471)

Glassford is a small village between Strathaven and Stonehouse, on a by-road north of the A71. The ruins of the old church and the surrounding grave-yard are in a section of the village known as West Quarter, some way away from the present Glassford Church. Here lies buried William Gordon of Earlstoun, a returned exile and former conventicler who was going to the Battle of Bothwell Bridge when he was captured and shot by soldiers. His son, Sir Alexander Gordon, seems to have been involved in the preparations for the Argyle Rising of 1685 and was condemned to death but reprieved and survived until the Revolution.[1] William Gordon's epitaph, composed in the flowery style of the late 18th century, is almost unique.

Inscription

To the Memory of the very *Worthy Pillar* of the
*Church. M*ʳ *W*ᵐ *Gordon of Earlston in Gallo*
    way. Shot by a partie of Dragoons. on his
    way to *Bothwell Bridge*. 22d June 1679.
    Aged 65. Inscrib'd by his Great Grand
    Son. *Sir J. Gordon, Bar*ᵗ. 11ᵗʰ June 1772.
    Silent till now, full ninety years hath Stood,
    This humble Monument, of Guiltless Blood.
    Tyrranick Sway, forbad his Fate to name
    Least his known Worth, shou'd prove the Tyrant's
                shame.
    On *Bothwell* road, with love of *Freedom* fir'd,
    The Tyrant's minons, boldly him requir'd.
    To stop, and yield, or it, his life wou'd cost.
    This he disdain'd, not knowing all was lost:
    On which they fir'd. Heaven so decreed His doom.
    Far from his own, laid in this silent Tomb.
    How leagu'd with Patriots, to maintain the Cause
    Of true RELIGION, LIBERTY, and Laws
    How learn'd, how soft his manner, free from Pride,
    How clear his Judgement, and how he liv'd and dy'd
    They well cou'd tell, who, weeping round him stood
    On *Strevan* plains that drank his Patriot Blood.

REPAIRED
By Sir John Gordon Bart.
of Earlston.
His Representative.
1842.

[1] Hewison ii pp405-407; Simpson p346

Glencairn (Kirkland) (NX 810 905)

This churchyard is one of a cluster of memorial sites around Moniaive near the River Nith. It is the burial place of four of the five men who were surprised hiding in a cave at Ingliston about a mile away and shot by a party of soldiers under Colonel James Douglas (the Duke of Queensberry's brother) and Lieutenant Livingston. The fifth man, Robert Grierson, lies buried in Balmaclellan (*q.v.*). From the Balmaclellan epitaph it seems that their hiding place was betrayed by an informer, "knavish Watson". The brief account of *A Cloud of Witnesses* says that "one John Ferguson, sometime a profest Friend, thrust one of them through supposing he was not dead."[1] A tradition has it that one of the men, Robert Edgar, had fled from his home after refusing the Abjuration Oath. Grierson was implicated in the Enterkin pass rescue.[2] For the significance of the date, 28th April, 1685, *cf.* Introduction p21.

Inscriptions
(1) *Gibson*

HERE LYES JOHN GIBS
ON MARTYR SHOT
TO DEATH BY COL: DO
UGLAS AND LIVINGS
TON'S DRAGOONS AT
ENGLESTON IN GLEN
CAIRN FOR ADHERING
TO THE WORD OF GOD
CHRIST'S KINGLY GOV-
ERMENT IN HIS HOU
SE AND THE COVENA
NTED WORK OF REFO-
RMATION AGAINST
TYRANY, PERJURY AND
PRELACY. APRIL 28
1685 REV 12 11

(ii) *At right angles to and beneath main inscription*

MY SOULS IN HEAVEN
HERE'S MY DUST
BY WICKED SENTANCE
AND UNJUST
SHOT DEAD CONVICTED
OF NO CRIME
BUT NON COMPLYANCE
WITH THE TIME
WHEN BABELS BASTARD
HAD COMMAND
AND MONSTEROUS TYRA
NTS RUL'D THE LAND

(2) *Edgar/Mitchell*   (i) *Main inscription*

> HERE LYES ROBERT EDGAR
> AND ROBERT MITCHELL MAR-
> TYRS SHOT TO DEATH BY
> COL DUGLAS AND LIVING-
> STONS DRAGOONS AT ENG-
> LISTON FOR ADHERING TO
> THE WORD OF GOD CHR
> ISTS KINGLY GOVERMENT
> IN HIS HOUSE AND THE COVE-
> NANTED WORK OF REFOR
> MATION AGAINST TYRANY
> PERJURY AND PRELACY APRYL
> 28 1685 REV- 12-11

(ii) *At right angles to and beneath main inscription*

> HALT PASSENGER TELL IF
> THOU EVER SAW
> MEN SHOT TO DEATH
> WITHOUT PROCESS OF LAW
> WE TWO OF FOUR WHO IN
> THIS CHURCHYARD LY
> THUS FELT THE RAGE OF
> POPISH TYRANNY.

(3) *Bennoch*   (i) **Main inscription**

> HERE LYES JAMES
> BENNOCH SHOT DE
> AD BY COL DUGLAS
> AND LIVINGSTONS
> DRAGOONS AT ENG
> LESTON FOR ADHE
> REING TO THE WORD
> OF GOD CHRISTS KI
> NGLY GOVERMENT
> IN HIS HOUSE AND
> THE COVENTED WO
> RK OF REFORMATION
> AGAINST TYRANNY
> PERJURY AND PRELA
> CY APR 28 1685 REV
> 12 11

(ii) *At right angles to and beneath main inscription*

HERE LYES A MONUMENT
OF POPISH WRATH
BECAUSE I'M NOT PERJUR
D I'M SHOT TO DEATH
BY CHRUEL HANDS MEN
GODLES AND UNJUST
DID SACRIFICE MY BLOOD
TO BABELSS LUST

NB All three stones are becoming badly weathered and are now scarcely legible. In the last example in particular the lower right hand corner has been broken off, and the letters Y BLOOD and LUST have been lost. (1991).

Glencairn Church, adjacent to Kirkland on OS sheet 78, lies on the A702 about three kilometres from Moniaive, beside the Cairn Water. See p.114.

[1] *Cloud* Appendix p383
[2] Thomson p387; Hewison ii p432 n.2

Hamilton (NS 765 578)

In the aftermath of the Battle of Dunbar (3rd September, 1650), when Cromwell defeated the Scots Army, the covenanting government of Scotland began to crumble, and various smaller military and political groupings tried to influence the course of events. One of these was the Army of the Western Association representing the radical covenanters ("Remonstrants") of the southwest. At Hamilton, on 1st December, 1650, this army unwisely took on a strong force of the English Army under General Lambert, Oliver Cromwell's second-in-command. The Scots were cut to pieces at the Battle of Heiton — a skirmish commemorated by a plaque at the bridge on Cadzow Street.

Also in Hamilton is the Cameronian Museum, next to the Burgh Museum in Muir Street. Strictly speaking, the title of the museum does not refer to the followers of Cameron, at least directly, but to the regiment raised after the Revolution of 1688, a body of soldiers that preserved customs originating with the need to have armed guards at conventicles. The museum has many interesting relics. (Tel [01698] 235382)

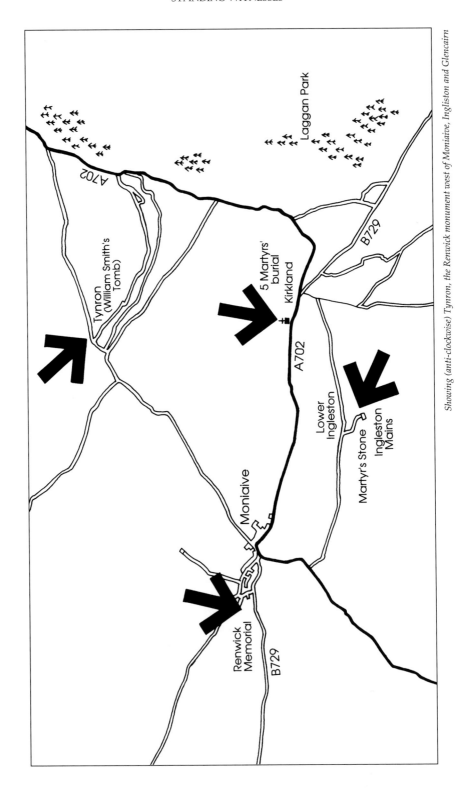

Showing (anti-clockwise) Tynron, the Renwick monument west of Moniaive, Ingliston and Glencairn

In 1666 the severed heads of four covenanters executed after the Battle of Rullion Green were sent to Hamilton from Edinburgh for display in order to terrify the locals into keeping the peace. (*cf. Kilmarnock* and *Cupar*.) The Heads Memorial — a gravestone set into the eastern wall of the Old Parish Churchyard — consists of a frieze depicting the four severed heads.

Inscription

At Hamilton
lie the heads of
JOHN PARKER, GAVIN HAMILTON,
JAMES HAMILTON
and
CHRISTOPHER STRANG;
who suffered at
EDINBURGH
Dec[r] 7th 1666
(*Four heads as a sculptured frieze*)
Stay, passenger, take notice
what thou reads:
At Edinburgh lie our bodies,
here our heads.
Our right hands stood at Lanark,
these we want,
Because with them we sware
the Covenant.

RENEWED
MDCCCXXVI

Inchbelly (NS 669 748)

Rescuing prisoners under military escort was not unusual in the 1680s.[1] On 8th June, 1683, at Inchbelly Bridge, a prisoner named Alexander Smith, who had escaped on at least one occasion before, was being taken to Edinburgh for trial when seven Covenanters set upon the escort of five men, killing one and releasing Smith, who got clean away. During the following search the soldiers came upon John Wharry and James Smith "sitting on the ground, without arms".[2] The sources state that there was no evidence that they were concerned in the rescue but the soldiers took them away to Glasgow where they were tried on 13th June and executed on 14th June—the same day as William Boick. (See *Campsie*). Their bodies were subsequently taken to Inchbelly Bridge and hanged in chains.

There are two stones by the side of the A803, and the one flat on the ground appears to be the older, with the more authentic epitaph.

Inscription

> (HERE) LIES THE CORPS OF
> (JOHN WHA)RRIE AND JAMES
> (SMI)TH WHO SUFFERED AT
> (G)LASGOW 13th JUNE 1683 FOR
> (th)eir Adherance to the Word of GOD And
> (S)cotlands Covenanted Work of Reformation
>   Rev 1 [ ]

> EPITAPH

> (Ha)lt Courtious passenger And look on
> Our bodies dead hang under this stone
> Altho We did Commit no deed nor fact
> That Was Against the Bridegrooms Contrac(t)
> Yet We to Glasgow Were As prisoners brough(t)
> And against us false Witnesses they sought
> There Sentence cruel & unjust they past
> And then Our Corps on Scaffold they do (?w)
> There We Our lives & right hands also lost
> The pain Was Ours but theirs shall be the Cost
> From Glasgow We Were brought to this place
> In Chains of iron hung up for Certain space
> Then taken down interred here We ly
> From 'neath this stone Our blood to Heaven doth cry

> Had foreign foes, Turks or Mahometans,
> Had Scythians, Tartars, Arabain Caravans
> Had Cruel Spaniards, the popes bloody seed
> Commenc'd the same less strange had been the (deed)
> But protestants profest Once Covenanted too
> Our Countrymen this Cruel deed Could do
> Yet notwithstanding of their hellish rage
> The Noble Wharrie stepping on the Stage
> With Courage bold and with a heart not faint
> Exclaimd this blood now seals our Covenant
> Ending, they Who Would follow Christ should take
> Their cross upon their back, the world forsake.

As Thomson points out, this differs from the inscription as given in *A Cloud of Witnesses*; in the interests of space, however, we shall not follow Thomson in quoting the *Cloud* version also; the differences are comparatively small.

The Inchbelly Bridge monuments will be found at the side of the A803 about half-way between Kirkintilloch and Kilsyth.

[1] See *Enterkin, Stonepark, Dalgarnock* etc. for other examples.
[2] Thomson p240

Ingliston (NX 797 896)

For burials of the five men shot at this farmhouse, see *Glencairn* and *Balmaclellan*. An informer named Andrew Watson led a party of soldiers under Colonel James Douglas to a secret cave in the neighbourhood. Within were five "fugitives"; precisely what they were in flight from is not known, but one, Robert Grierson, had been implicated in the Enterkin Pass rescue, and another, Robert Edgar, had lately refused the Abjuration Oath and had fled from his home. Douglas had them brought out and shot in the yard of Lower Ingliston, now a part of Ingliston Farm itself.

Inscription

> In this yard were Shot John Gibson
> James Bennoch Robert Edgar
> Robert Mitchell & Robert Grier
> Son April 28: 1685 by Colonell
> DouglaSs and Livingstouns Dra
> goons for adhereing to Christs King
> ly Government in his Church against
> Tyrannie perjurie & prelacie

In 1991 the old enclosure in which this monument stands was heavily overgrown; towards the road end (away from the farmhouse, which lies round a bend) it was being used as a stand for a caravan; to the rear of the caravan against the lane-side wall, under a very large bush, the stone will be found.

See map on p114. For the significance of the date (28th April, 1685) see Introduction p21.

Irongray (NX 915 796)

Irongray, a small parish north-west of Dumfries, is famed in Covenanting annals for its minister, John Welch or Welsh, a great-grandson of the reformer John Knox and grandson of the famous anti-episcopalian John Welch of Ayr. John Welch of Irongray was outed in 1662 and became involved in the Pentland Rising of 1666. (Irongray was the rallying point for the rebels before their descent on Dumfries and capture of Sir James Turner). Welch put new heart into the rebels at Dalmellington, and accompanied them to Rullion Green, where he urged them on with Old Testament fervour, crying out "See the Lord of Hosts fighting for us!"

After making his escape, however, Welch's pious intransigence cooled a little, and although he became a leading field preacher with a price on his head, he was a leader of the moderate party which was so disastrously pitted against Robert Hamilton's "honest" party in the squabblings before Bothwell Brig. After the battle, in 1679, he escaped to England where he died in 1681.

Irongray is also celebrated for the closing act of the Lochenkit tragedy: here, in the words of *A Cloud of Witnesses*.

> "Bruce ... carried ... *Edward Gordon* and *Alexander M'Cubine*, prisoners, and next Day he and monstruous *Lag* without any Trial caused hang them upon a growing Tree, near the Kirk of *Irongray*, and left them there hanging, *February* 1685."[1]

The monument to these martyrs is at Hallhill, about a kilometre to the west of Irongray Kirk itself.

The conventicle site and monument at Skeoch, with the so-called "Communion Stones", are further west again, in the hills. An enormous conventicle was held there in 1678, with an attendance of over 14,000, and four ministers, including Welch and Blackadder. The Communion Stones served as Communion-table, pulpit and seating for the congregation.

Hallhill inscription

HERE LYES EDWARD GO
RDON AND ALEXANDER
M'CUBINE MARTYRES
HANGED WITHOUT

LAW BY LAGG AND CAP.
BRUCE FOR ADHEREING
TO THE WORD OF GOD
CHRISTS KINGLY GOVE
RMENT IN HIS HOUS
AND THE COVENANTED
WORK OF REFORMATION
AGAINST TYRANNY
PERJURY AND PRELACY
REV xii. 12 11 MAR 3 1685

AS LAGG AND BLOODIE
BRUCE COMMAND
WE WERE HUNG UP BY
HELLISH HAND
AND THUS THER FURO
US RAGE TO STAY
WE DIED NEAR KIRK
OF IRON-GRAY
HERE NOW IN PEACE
SWEET REST WE TAKE
ONCE MURDER'D FOR
RELIGEON'S SAKE.

Irongray may be reached along an unlisted road running to the north-west from the A76 at Lincluden.

[1] *Cloud* Appendix p384; see *Lochenkit* for further details.

Irvine (NS 322 386)

After the defeat of the Pentland Rising at Rullion Green on 28th November, 1666, many of the prisoners were executed as rebels, some in their home towns as a warning to local malcontents. (See *Ayr, Glasgow* and *Dumfries*, as well as *Fenwick*.) Blackwood and McCoul were hanged on 31st December, 1666, in Irvine. William Sutherland, the Irvine hangman who would not execute Covenanters in Ayr, made the same refusal in the case of these two, and the wretched weakling Cornelius Anderson, who had been bribed to hang his friends at Ayr, also executed the Irvine victims.[1]

The tombstone, at the south-east corner of Irvine Old Parish Churchyard, is inscribed as follows:

STOP, PASSENGER:
THOU TREADEST NEAR TWO MARTYRS:
JAMES BLACKWOOD & JOHN McCOUL
who suffered at *IRVINE*
on the 31st. of December 1666
REV. XII, 11*th*

These honest country men whose bones here lie
Both victims Fell to Prelates' cruelty:
Condemn'd by Bloody and unrighteous Laws,
They died Martyrs for the good old Cause
Which Balamn's wicked race in vain assail
For no enchantments aginist Israel prevail.
Life and this evil world they did contemn
And died for Christ who died first for them.

They liv'd unknown
Till Persecution dragged them into Fame
And chased them up to Heaven

Erected by Friends to Religious Liberty
31st Dec. 1823

[1] Wodrow ii p54

Kells (NX 632 786)

Kells is a small church just north of New Galloway on the A762. (See Map on p.36) Its churchyard contains two martyr's tombs, one of them (Adam MacWhan's) forming part of the April-May cluster of summary executions in 1685 from which the Killing Time derives its name. Nothing is known of Adam MacQwhan or MacWhan beyond what is inscribed in his epitaph; it is not known whether the remote feature called McWhann's Stone (NX 492 804; between Clatteringshaws Loch and Loch Dee) has anything to do with the martyrdom recorded here, but for a suggestive, if tenuous, comparison, see *Straiton* (Thomas McHaffie).

The other stone in Kells Churchyard is that of a Pentland Martyr — not, however, executed, but dying of wounds received at the Battle of Rullion Green. (Cf. *Black Law* and *Kirk o' Shotts*.)

Inscriptions   *(reverse)*

(1) *MacQwhan*
    HERE LYES
    ADAM MACQWHAN
    WHO BEING SICK
    OF A FEVER WAS
    TAKEN OUT OF HIS
    BED AND CARRIED
    TO NEUTOUN OF
    GALLOWAY AND THE
    NEXT DAY MOST
    CRUELLY AND UN-
    JUSTLY SHOT TO
    DEATH BY THE COM-
    MAND OF LIEVTENANT

(MEMENTO
[*Skull and Crossbones*] MORI)

GENERAL IAMES
DOUGLAS, BROTHER
TO THE DUKE OF
QUEENSBERRY FOR
HIS ADHERENCE
TO SCOTLANDS
REFORMATION CO
VENANTS NATION
L AND SOLEMN
LEAGUE. 1685.

(The stone to Adam MacQwhan was set in a granite frame in 1832)

(2) *Gordon*

    HERE LYES THE CORPS OF RO
    GER GORDON OF LARGMORE
    WHO DIED MARCH 2ND 1662
    AGED 72 YEARS AND OF JOHN
    GORDON OF LARGMORE HIS
    GRANDCHILD WHO DIED JAN
    UARY 6 1667 OF HIS WOUNDS
    GOT AT PENTLAND IN DEFENS
    OF THE COVENANTED REFOR-
    ATION.

Kilmarnock (NS 428 380)

Kilmarnock was garrisoned by General Dalyell and his troops after the collapse of the Pentland Rising in 1666, and Dean Castle remained a headquarters for the army until after the Revolution of 1688. Many Covenanters were imprisoned there, including Jasper Tough, a local apothecary who gave first aid to the Ducat Tower fugitives. (See *Newmilns*). Dean Castle is now a museum (12—5 on weekdays) and contains the walking-stick used by Alexander Peden, the Prophet of the Covenant. (See *Cumnock*. Peden's wig and face-mask are held in the Royal Museum of Scotland, Queen Street, Edinburgh.)

Only three Covenanting monuments now survive in Kilmarnock.

Inscriptions
(1) *Laigh Kirkyard (Bank Street)*
(i) *Ross and Shields*

HERE LIE
the
Heads of JOHN ROSS and JOHN
SHIELDS Who Suffered at
Edinburgh
Dec[r] 27th 1666 and had their
Heads set up at
Kilmarnock

Our Persecutors mad with wrath & Ire
In Edin[b] members Some do lie Some here
Yet instantly united they Shall be
& witness 'gainst this Nation's perjury.
(see Cloud of Witnesses)

These two men were captured a week before the Battle of Rullion Green in 1666; they had been on an intelligence-gathering mission for the rebels near Kilmarnock. Ross came from Mauchline and Shields was a native of The Mearns in Renfrewshire. According to Thomson, the date is in error: it should be Dec[r] 7th, 1666, and the "[r]" became corrupted to "2".[1] (Cf. *Hamilton*).

(ii) *Nisbet*
(Carving: crossed swords, a flag inscribed *God & our Country*, and a scroll inscribed *Solemn League & Covenant*).

HERE LIES
JOHN NISBET
Who was Taken by
Major Balfour's Party &
Suffered at Kilmarnock
14th April 1683 for Adhereing
to the Word of GOD & our
Covenants. Rev[n] XII & 11

Renewed by Public
Contribution
A.D. 1823

(reverse)

Come Reader see here pleasant NISBET lies
Whose blood doth pierce the high & lofty Skies
Kilmarnock did his latter hour perceive
& CHRIST his Soul to Heaven did receive
Yet bloody Torrence did his body raise
& buried it into another Place
Saying shall rebel lie in grave with me
We'll bury him where evil doers be
see Cloud of Witnesses

John Nisbet of Know was captured and executed in April 1683. John Richmond of Know was captured in November 1683 and hanged in March 1684. The arresting officer in both cases was Major Balfour. James Nisbet of Highside was arrested at Richmond's funeral by Lieutenant Nisbet, a cousin, and hanged in June 1684. The same Lieutenant Nisbet was responsible for the capture in November 1685 of John Nisbet of Hardhill, another cousin, who was hanged in Edinburgh in December 1685. See *Glasgow, Fenwick* and *Newmilns.*

In the case of the execution of John Nisbet of Know, some confusion exists as to the precise date. Thomson transcribes it as 4th April, but in the present version it is 14th April. The same date is given in the second monument to John Nisbet of Know in Kilmarnock, at what used to be

(2) *King Street*

This monument, at the site of the actual execution, now takes the form of a granite plug cemented into an ornamental circular seat in Kilmarnock (Burns) Shopping Precinct adjacent to the bus station and perhaps a hundred metres away from the far more dignified and peaceful surroundings of the Laigh Kirkyard. Thomson records it as two letters, J.N., formed by white stones, where the gallows stood. The present inscription reads

JOHN NISBET
WAS EXECUTED HERE
14TH APRIL 1683

A fourth Kilmarnock stone, in the Laigh Kirkyard, was vandalised some years ago and is no longer to be seen. It was put up in 1823 at the same time as the renewal of the Nisbet stone. Its inscription read as follows:

SACRED
TO THE MEMORY OF
THOMAS FINLAY
JOHN CUTHBERTSON
WILLIAM BROWN, ROBERT & JAMES
ANDERSON
Natives of this parish
Who were taken Prisoners at Bothwell 22nd
June 1679, sentenced to Transportation for
Life, & drowned on their passage near
the Orkney Isles.
ALSO JOHN FINLAY
who suffered martyrdom 15 Dec. 1682
in the Grassmarket, Edinburgh

Peace to the Church, her peace no friends invade;
Peace to each Noble Martyr's honour'd shade;
They, with undaunted courage, truth and zeal
Contended for the Church and Country's weal,
We share the fruits, we drop the grateful tear
And peaceful altars o'er their ashes rear.[2]

Finlay was a Cargillite who was executed with two others, Robertson and Cochran. Finlay had been arrested and held in Dean Castle, and Robertson was detained when he visited him there. For the five deportees, see *Edinburgh (Greyfriars)* and Appendix 1c.

[1] Thomson pp287-289
[2] Thomson pp290-291

Kirkandrews (NX 602 482)

The martyr buried in this charming little churchyard, a few metres from the Solway coast, is completely unknown. A local tradition states that he was shot in his own garden in the parish of Borgue. The soldier responsible, Captain Douglas, appears in other monumental inscriptions.

Inscription

MEMENTO   MORI
(*Skull & Crossbones*)
HERE LYES
ROBERT M'WHAE

WHO WAS BARBAROUSLY
SHOT TO DEATH BY
CAPTAINE DOUGLASH IN
THIS PAROCH FOR HIS
ADHERENCE TO SCOTLANDS
REFORMATION COVENANTS
NATIONAL AND SOLEMN
LEAGUE   1685

Kirkandrews lies on the eastern short of Wigtown Bay, not far from Gatehouse of Fleet. Other Covenanting memorial sites in the neighbourhood include Girthon and Anwoth. Kirkandrews may be reached along an unlisted road from the B727 at Borgue.

Kirkconnel Moor (Kirkcudbright) (NX 672 599)

This site is at Kirkconnel north of Kirkcudbright, not Kirkconnel in Nithsdale. It is where, on 21st February, 1685, Sir Robert Grierson of Lagg came upon five men in hiding and shot them out of hand. For the circumstances, compare *Ingliston/Glencairn*. In this case, too, the men were fugitives, but it is not known what they were hiding from. Bell of Whiteside had been on the run since 1679. He was the victim who begged for a little more time for prayer, and Lagg furiously asked, "What the devil have you been doing? Have you not prayed enough these many years in the hills?" Clement is the only victim buried where he fell; see *Anwoth, Balmaghie, Girthon* and *Twynholm* for the others.

Inscriptions
(1) *Clement*
(i) *Surface top edge:*   Rend. by J.G.

(ii) *Main inscription :*

HERE LYES
IAMES CLEMET
WHO W SURPRIS
ED AND SHOT TO
DEATH ON THIS
PLACE BY GRIER
OF LAGG FOR HIS
ADHERENCE TO

(reverse)

MEMEN (Skull and crossbones) TO MORI
SCOTLANDS REFOR
MATION COVENANTS
NATIONAL AND SO
LEMN LEAGUE 1685

(2) *(Obelisk 1832)* *(Main inscription only)*
Halliday, Bell, Lennox, M'Robert, Clement

SACRED
TO THE MEMORY OF
DAVID HALLIDAY OF MAYFIELD
JOHN BELL OF WHITESIDE
ROBERT LENNOX
OF IRLANDTON
ANDREW M'ROBERT AND
JAMES CLEMENT
WHO SUFFERED MARTYRDOM
ON THIS SPOT AD 1685
FOR THEIR
ADHERENCE TO THE COVENANTS
AND TRUE PRESBYTERIAN
PRINCIPLES BY THAT WICKED
PERSECUTOR GRIER OF LAG.

The Kirkconnel monuments are about a kilometre west of the A762 at Waterside, between two hills half-way to Loch Mannoch. There is a signposted track from the road.

Kirkcudbright (NX 684 510)

Two later victims of the Auchencloy skirmish are buried in Old St Cuthbert's churchyard. As related in the entry for Auchencloy, Claverhouse and his men had been on the track of Covenanters who had carried out a large-scale prison rescue at Kirkcudbright on 16th December, 1684. The soldiers had caught up with some of the Covenanters two days later near the headwaters of the River Dee, and chased them to Auchencloy, where they had a battle. Five Covenanters were killed at Auchencloy, one being buried there, two at St John's Clachan of Dalry, and two at unrecorded sites. Another two, Smith and

Hunter, were taken back down to Kirkcudbright. Claverhouse had been appointed Bailie of the Regality of Tongland in 1682, and in that capacity presided over a Court which sentenced them to be hanged.

Little is known of John Hallume or Hallam, who also lies buried here. He is reported to have been only eighteen years old; he ran away when challenged by a party of soldiers who opened fire, wounded him and brought him to Kirkcudbright. Here he paid the penalty for refusing the Abjuration Oath.

Inscriptions
(1) *Smith, Hunter*
(i) *At side of stone, at right angles to main inscription*

WILLIAM HOUNTURE
ROBERT SMITH   1684

(ii) *Main Inscription*

THIS MONUMENT SHALL SHEW POSTERITY
TWO HEADLES MARTYRES UNDER IT DOTH LIE
BY BLOODY GRHAME WERE TAKEN AND SURPRISED
BROUGHT TO THIS TOUN AND AFTERWARDS WERE SAIZ'D
BY UNJUST LAW WERE SENTENCED TO DIE
THEM FIRST THEY HANGED THEN HEADED CRUELY
CAPTANS DOUGLAS BRUCE GRAHAME OF CLEVERHOUS
WERE THESE THAT CAUSED THEM TO BE HANDLED THUS
AND WHEN THEY WERE UNTO THE GIBBET COME
TO STOPE THEIR SPEECH THEY DID BEAT UP THE DRUM
AND ALL BECAUS THAT THEY WOULD NOT COMPLY
WITH INDULGENCE AND BLOODIE PRELACIE
IN FACE OF CRUEL BRUCE DOUGLAS AND GRAHAME
THEY DID MANTAINE THAT CHRIST WAS LORD SUPREAM
AND BOLDLY OUNED BOTH THE COVENANTS
AT KIRKCUDBRIGHT THUS ENDED THESE TWO SANTS.

(2) *Hallam*

HERE LYES JOHN
HALLUME WHO
WAS WOUNDED
IN HIS TAKEING
AND BY UNJUST
LAW SENTENCED
TO BE HANGED
ALL THIS DONE
BY CAPTANE

(reverse)

(Death's head)
MEMENTO MORI

DOUGLAS FOR
HIS ADHERENCE
TO SCOTLANDS
REFORMATION,
COVENANTS NATION
AL AND SOLEMN
LEAGUE   1685

Old St Cuthbert's Churchyard is a large burying-ground high above the town of Kirkcudbright to the east; the B727 runs past the entrance. Smith and Hunters' grave is west of the tall knoll in the centre of the cemetery, and Hallam's is further west again, near the wall overlooking the town. Neither is very distinguishable from the other stones, but Smith/Hunter's is a flat table stone, and Hallam's is a small upright stone.

Kirkmichael (NS 346 099)

In the beautiful churchyard of Kirkmichael stands a small square monument with a high, heavily-ornamented pyramidal roof. On one side is displayed an original stone commemorating Gilbert McAdam, a returned deportee who was shot during a raid on suspected premises by two lairds, Sir Alexander Kennedy of Culzean, and the Laird of Ballochmyle (presumably in command of a detachment of troops). There is some dubiety about the date, but if we follow the stone itself it is July 1685. Wodrow states it was June 1685, and another source gives it as 1684. Partisans of the two lairds deleted their names from the inscription, but Old Mortality is said to have recut it, making the present clearly visible depression in the face of the stone.

Inscription

HERE . LYES . GIL^LBERT .
M^CADAM . UHO . UAS .
SHOT . IN . THIS . PARISH
BY . THE . LAIRD . OF . CO
LZEAN . AND . BAL^LOCHMIL
FOR . HIS . ADHERANCE . TO

```
THE . UORD . OF . GOD . AND
SCOTLANDS . COVENAN
TED . UORK . OF . REFORM[*]
1685                    ATION
```

[*] *Vertical, at right angles to the beginning of the two last lines but one, the word*
JULY

Kirkmichael is about 4 kilometres east of Maybole on the B7045.

[1] Thomson p494

Kirk O'Shotts (NS843 629)

It is not certain whether William Smith, who is buried here, a returning fugitive from the Battle of Rullion Green in 1666, was a martyr for the Good Old Cause, or merely the victim of a private assassination.

Inscription

(Surface of top edge)

Repaired from the proceeds of a sermon
preached here 1836 by the Rev. Mr Graham

(Main inscription)

```
HERE . LYES . THE . BON
ES . OF . WILLIAM . SMITH
WHO . LIVED . AT . MOREMELL
EN . WHO . WITH . OTHE
RS . APPEARED IN A
RMS AT PENTLAND
HILLS IN DEFENCE OF SCOT-
LANDS COVENANTED W
ORK OF REFORMATION IN
ANNO 1666 AGREEABLE TO
THE WORD OF GOD IN O
PPOSITION TO POPERY
PRELACY AND PERJURY
AND WAS MURDERED IN HS
HIS RETURN HOME NEAR
        THIS PLACE.
```

Kirk o'Shotts is on the B7066 (parallel with the M8) and some distance from Shotts itself. The nearest large town is Wishaw.

Lanark (NS 885 435)

Lanark is closely associated with the last years of radical Covenanting and in particular with the "Society People", the largely anonymous bearers of the Cameronian torch who banded together in a "Union or General Correspondence" after the death of Cameron himself in 1680 and the execution of Cargill in 1681. It was the Society People, including James Renwick, who published a fiery "Act and Apologetic Declaration of the true Presbyterians of the Church of Scotland" on 12th January 1682, at the Cross of Lanark, which they broke with forehammers, after burning copies of the "professedly Popish" statutes of which they disapproved. For taking part in this public act William Harvey was laid by the heels and hanged on 2nd March, 1682. His well-preserved stone will be found in the churchyard of the beautiful ruined St Kentigern's Church in Lanark. Also to be found there is a collective memorial to various Lanark Covenanters.

Inscription (*Harvey only*)
(i) *(Upper edge of stone)*

> HEIR . LYES . WILLI
> AM . HERVI . WHO

(ii) *(Side)*

> SWFERED . AT
> THE . CROS . OF
> LANERK . THE
> 2 OF . MARCH
> 1682 AGE 38
> FOR HIS ADHERENC
> TO THE WORD OF
> GOD AND SCOTLANDS
> COVENANTED WORK
> OF REFORMATION.

Lesmahagow (NS 814 398)

There are three Covenanting monuments in Lesmahagow churchyard. One relates to the Battle of Drumclog in 1679, and another to a very late and isolated martyrdom, of David Steel, in 1686. There is also a red granite memorial to Archibald Stewart of Underbank, executed at Glasgow Cross in 1684. (See *Glasgow*.)

Weir, the Drumclog hero, was a standard bearer whose horse ran away with him. He was wounded during the pursuit of the dragoons and died after three days, one of the few Whig victims of Drumclog.

With regard to the Steel martyrdom, two different stories exist. The traditional account from the Covenanting side asserts that after having been arrested at Meadow beyond Yonderton on a promise of fair trial, Steel was hustled back to his own farm at Nether Skellyhill, where he was brutally shot in the presence of his wife and child by Highlanders under Lieutenant John Creichton, a party of dragoons also led by Creichton refusing to do the deed.[1]

Creichton's own version is that Steel was killed resisting arrest in a farmhouse by dragoons with swords. After an exchange of shots, Steel made a break for it down a flight of stairs but was overwhelmed by superior numbers and cut down.[2]

The first version is supported by the existence of a monument at Skellyhill (NS 789 375) inscribed *Exact spot of martyrdom about 27 feet to the west.* However, this was not erected until 1858, and the story itself has curious echoes of the John Brown story (*Priesthill*), and also that of Hislop at Craighaugh. It may be that we should give credence to Creichton's story as being the more straightforward. Creichton's version also gives a reason for the arrest: Steel had succeeded David Hackston of Rathillet as leader of the Cameronians after the latter's execution following the Battle of Airdsmoss. (If this is so, however, Steel remained leader for a very long time.)

Inscriptions *(Weir and Steel only)*
(1) *Weir*

Here lies
THOMAS WEIR
who was shot in a rencounter
at Drumclog June 1st 1679

by bloody Graham of
Claverhouse for his
adherence to the Word of
God and Scotlands
Covenanted work of
Reformation Rev. xii. 2
As also Gavin Weir
in Waterside who departed
this life. July 25 1732
Aged 79

Repaired by a few
friends to the
    Covenanted Cause
        1833

(Gavin Weir was Thomas Weir's son, and was placed on the wanted list
in 1684 but was not arrested.)

(2) Steel

HERE LIES
the Body of DAVID STEEL Martyr
who was Murdered by Chrichton for his
Testimony to the Covenants and Work
of Reformation and because he durst
not own the Authority of the
Tyrant destroying the same. He was
shot at SKELLYHILL the 20th of Dec[r]
1686 in the 33[d] year of his age

Be thou faithful unto Death and
I will give thee a Crown of Life

David a Shepherd first and then
Advanced to be King of Men
Had of his Graces in this Quarter
This Heir, a Wand'rer now a Martyr
Who for his Constancy and Zeal
Still to the Back did prove true Steel
Who for Christ's Royal Truth and Laws
And for the Covenanted Cause
Of *SCOTLANDS* famous Reformation
Declining Tyrant's Usurpation
By Cruel Chrichton Murder'd lies
Whose Blood to Heaven for Vengeance cries.

Lesmahagow lies on the A74, south-west of Lanark.

[1] Thomson pp274-278 [2] Creichton pp58-59

Lochenkit (NX 812 752 and 810 751)

Here, in early 1685, eight men, most of them on the wanted list, were discovered by a party of soldiers under Captain Bruce. The Abjuration Oath was proferred and refused. Four of the men were shot on the spot and are buried here. The other four were marched to Old Bridge of Urr, south of Kirkpatrick Durham (now a crossroads on the B794). Here they were interviewed by the notorious Sir Robert Grierson of Lagg, who proferred them the oath again. Again they refused. Lagg then marched them across country to Irongray, where he hanged another two of them on a tree as a warning to the congregation of the parish, who had lately insulted their "curate". The remaining two were deported, and one of these, also called Robert Grierson, who farmed Lochenkit, returned after the 1688 Revolution, to be recognized first by his dog, like Odysseus after his wanderings.[1] One source gives late February, 1685, as the date of the executions[2], but the tombstone and memorial here give 2nd March, 1685. (See also *Irongray*).

Inscriptions
(1) *(gravestone: original, as given in* A Cloud of Witnesses; *the existing stone has been renewed and altered several times.)*

HERE LYES

Four Martyrs, John Wallace, William
Heron, John Gordon, and William
Stewart, found out and shot dead
upon this place by Captain *Bruce*
and Captain *Lag* for their adhearing
to the Word of GOD, CHRIST'S Kingly
Government in his house, and the
Covenanted work of reformation
against Tyranny, Perjury, Prelacy
2 March MDCLXXXV
Rev. chap. XII. ver. 11:
Behold
Here in this wilderness we lie
Four witnesses of hellish cruelty

Our lives and blood could not their ire assuage
But when we're dead, they did against us rage,
That match the like, we think, ye scarcely can
Except the *Turk* or Duke de *Alva's* men.

Repaired by the friends of civil and
religious liberty

(From the above, it may appear that Lagg himself was present at the initial arrest at Lochenkit— but there is a trace of ambiguity about these words.)

(2) *(obelisk)*
(a hand pointing heavenwards)

> YONDER LIE
> WILLIAM HERON FROM GLENCAIRN
> JOHN GORDON   }
> WILLIAM STEWART }   GALLOWAY
> JOHN WALLACE   }
>
> MEN WHO WERE FOUND OUT AND SHOT
> DEAD HERE 2nd MARCH 1685
> BY CAPTAIN BRUCE FOR THEIR
> ADHERENCE TO SCOTLANDS
> COVENANTED REFORMATION.
> TO COMMEMORATE THE
> PRINCIPLES FOR WHICH THESE
> MARTYRS SUFFERED THIS
> MONUMENT IS ERECTED BY
> SUBSCRIPTION AFTER SERMONS
> 1843

Lochenkit is near Crocketford west of Dumfries. An unlisted road runs north from the A712, rounding the shoulder of Brookland Hill and passing to the south of Bloodmire Moss. The monument and martyrs' grave, which are some distance apart, are north of Bloodmire Moss, about a kilometre south-east of Lockenkit Loch itself.

They are now (1992) in the midst of a rapidly enveloping sea of conifers, and may soon be completely invisible. The monument is on top of a small hill and is still visible from the A712. The gravestone itself will be found in an ancient small grove on the other side of the forestry road which is the only means of access.

[1] Wodrow iv p240 [2] *Cloud* Appendix p384

Lochgoin (NS 530 469)

In the seventeenth century this isolated farm was a safe house for fugitive Covenanters, although it seems to have been the subject of repeated dragoon raids. (See the Howie tombstone at Fenwick.) It was later the home of John Howie, who became one of the more popular historians of the Covenanters and to whose memory the adjacent obelisk was erected.[1] Lochgoin is now in the ownership of a Trust which has set up a museum inside the farmhouse for the purpose of exhibiting relics of Covenanting times and publicising the Covenanters. A considerable collection of Howie's books and papers is held in the museum. Among the relics is a sword which once belonged to Captain Paton and a Covenanting drum belonging to the village of Fenwick.

Lochgoin is near the Lochgoin Reservoir, south of the B764. Intending visitors should contact Mr James Barr (Loganswell 249).

[1] See Bibliography herein.

Logan House (NS 740 354)

This farmhouse, at the end of a long and winding path leading west from Lesmahagow via Auchlochan, Whiteside and Birkenhead, might be considered as remote as it could well be in Southern Scotland, but its significance derives from its close links with its neighbours. It is roughly equidistant from Muirkirk, Strathaven, Lesmahagow and Douglas; it is only about four kilometres north of John Brown's grave at Priesthill, five kilometres west of the alleged scene of David Steel's death at Skellyhill, and only two kilometres east across the hill from the conventicle monument at Auchingilloch (Kype Water). The geographical centrality of Logan House in a sense becomes spiritual pre-eminence in Covenanting history; this isolated point was the conference site chosen by the Cameronians after the loss of Cameron in 1680 and of Cargill in 1681 for the launching of the "Union or General Correspondence" — a correspondence union in fact — of the largely anonymous Societies of the radical western Presbyterians who had by then been persecuted for more than twenty years. Their first meeting took place at Logan House on 15th December, 1681, and was followed by the Lanark Declaration of 12th January, 1682.[1] (See *Lanark* and *Lesmahagow*.) Various locations for subsequent meetings included Priesthill and Friarminnan, where James Renwick, a founder member of the correspondence union, was to hide.

See map on p.51 for the relationship of Logan House to some other well-known Covenanting sites. Besides the locations shown, Priesthill, Muirkirk, Upper Wellwood and Airds Moss are just off the map to the south-west, Drumclog to the north-west, Lesmahagow due east and Douglas south-east.

[1] Cf. Cowan p110

Loudoun (NS 493 375)

This is a charming pre-Reformation ruin, left to fall into decay when the original congregation migrated to Newmilns in the eighteenth century. One of the early ministers was John Nevoy or Nevay. He has been identified as the instigator of the Massacre of Dunaverty (south of Campbeltown in Kintyre) in 1647, when, after days of Nevoy's exhortation, General Leslie allowed himself to be persuaded into killing several hundred Irish soldiers who had surrendered to his army. Nevoy appears to have based his argument upon the fate of Agag and the Amalekites in I Sam. xv, a precedent that appears with sinister regularity in Covenanting sermons until quite late:

> "What meaneth this bleating of the sheep in mine
> ears, and the lowing of the oxen which I hear?"

Nevoy was perhaps the principal agitator if not leader of the ill-organized Covenanting forces at the Battle of Mauchline Muir in 1648.(See *Mauchline* and Introduction p 5-6.) He was chaplain to the Earl of Loudoun. In 1662 he was exiled and died in the Netherlands.[1]

Against the north-eastern interior wall of the ruined church stands the gravestone of Thomas Flem(m)ing, one of the very few Whigs who fell at Drumclog fighting against Claverhouse's men.

Inscription

HERE LIES
THOMAS FLEMMING OF
LOUDOUN HILL
Who for His appearing in *ARMS*

In his Own Defence & in Defence
OF THE GOSPEL
According to the Obligations of
Our National Covenants and
Agreeable to the *WORD*

OF **GOD**

(clog
was Shot in a Rencounter at Drum
June 1st, 1679, by bloody *GRAHAM*
of Claverhouse.

Loudoun Church is north-west of Galston, across the A71 and west of the A719 on an unlisted road running directly from the ruined Loudoun Castle.

[1] Stevenson D 1975

Magus Muir (NO 557 152)

After the assassination of Archbishop James Sharp on 3rd May, 1679, and the subsequent battles of Drumclog and Bothwell Brig, the Government felt that they had to"expiate and appease the Archbishop's ghost" by executing *someone* at least near the site of the murder.[1] They were singularly unsuccessful in laying the real assassins by the heels, and they cast around for suitable substitutes. Among the prisoners captured after Bothwell Brig, there were several who refused to sign the bond to be of good behaviour and some of these were put on trial. Some of these again refused to call the killing of the Archbishop murder, and that was good enough for the authorities' purpose. They declared that these five men were accessories to murder after the fact and hanged them in chains at this site on Magus Muir (near a long-vanished village) on 18th or 25th November, 1679. It has never been proved that any of them had anything at all to do with the murder of Archbishop Sharp.

Inscription (original, as given in *A Cloud of Witnesses* [1741]: the present stone is the latest of several renewals).

(*"Upon the Grave-stone of* Thomas Brown, James Wood, Andrew Sword, John Waddel, and John Clyd, *who suffered Martyrdom at* Magus-Muir, Nov. 25, 1679, *and ly buried in a Corn-field near* Magus-Muir, *is this inscription:-"*)

> 'Cause we at Bothwel did appear
> Perjurious Oaths refus'd to swear
> 'Cause we Christ's Cause would not condemn

We were sentenc'd to Death by Men
Who Rag'd against us in such Fury
Our dead Bodies they did not bury;
But upon Poles did hing us high
Triumphs of Babel's Victory.
Our Lives we fear'd not to the Death
But constant prov'd to the last breath.

(reverse)

Here lies Thos Brown
James Wood Andrew Sword
John Weddell & John Clyde
who suffered martyrdom on Magus Muir
for their adherence to the Word of God
and Scotland's Covenanted Work of Reformation.
Nov. 25th, 1679

The B939 from St Andrews to Pitscottie and Cupar is bisected at right angles by an unlisted road running from Strathkiness south to the neighbourhood of Claremont Farm. About 200 metres to the south of a junction a path with signposts leads west to the edge of a patch of woodland; in the cornfield beyond, a small path has been kept open leading to a railed enclosure containing the stone described above. The main path continues northward through a thicker part of the wood, and at a bend in the path stands a large stone pyramid commemorating the assassination of Archbishop Sharp. This bears a Latin inscription from which someone seems to have tried to delete the name Sharp. (Cf *St Andrews*).

Inscription

HUNC PROPE LOCUM
JACOBUS SHARP
ARCHIEPISCOPUS SANCTI ANDRAE
A SALVIS INIMICIS
ADSTANTE FILIA SUA ET
DEPRECANTE
TRUCIDATUS EST
A.D. MDCLXXIX

(Near this place James Sharp, Archbishop of St Andrews, was murdered by savage enemies in the presence and despite the prayers of his daughter A.D. 1679.)

Map II on page 74 shows the two monuments at Magus Muir and Andrew Guilline's tombstone, which is in a little patch of woodland just west of a small stream at the side of Claremont Farm.

[1] Fountainhall *Decisions* i p63

Mauchline (NS 496 273)

Mauchline is mentioned frequently in the annals of the Scottish Reformation. George Wishart and John Knox both preached on the Town Muir in the sixteenth century, and in the seventeenth the Muir was also the scene of a brief engagement between radical Covenanters and Government soldiers (12th June, 1648). The Covenanters were led by ministers, John Nevay and William Adair among others. (See *Loudoun* and *Ayr.*) They were scattered by the future Earl of Middleton, who later became Charles II's first Commissioner in the Restoration period.

Next to the Parish Church stands Mauchline Castle, still frowning over the old centre of the town. This was the headquarters of Sir William Drummond of Cromlix, to whom Claverhouse consigned John Browning of Lanfine after arresting him along with John Brown at Priesthill on 1st May, 1685.

John Brown was shot the same day; Drummond hanged Browning and four other prisoners in Mauchline on 6th May, 1685. A sixth man, James Smith of Wee Threepwood, who had been arrested at Burn Ann near Galston by Captain John Inglis's dragoons, died in Mauchline Prison of the wounds he had sustained during the arrest.

It is known that Browning, and probably Smith, had been involved in the spectacular prison break at Newmilns in April 1685, when sixty men led by Browning had broken into the Ducat Tower and released prisoners under sentence of death. It is not unlikely that the other four Mauchline victims were also implicated in the affair.

They were hanged, it is said, from the windows of a white-painted building now serving as a dental surgery near the Burns Museum and not far from the old castle. The five are commemorated in three successively-erected monuments on the Loan Green near the present Primary School. Smith's gravestone will be found in the Parish Churchyard. For further details, see especially *Newmilns* and *Priesthill*, besides *Galston*, and *Fenwick*.

Inscriptions
(1) *Loan Green (early inscription)*

> Here lies the Bodies of Peter
> Gillies john Bryce Thomas
> Young William Fiddison & john
> Beuning Who Were Apprehen
> ded & Hanged Without Trial
> at Mauchline Anno 1685 acc
> ording to the then Wickeds
> Laus for their Adherance to
> the Covenanted Works of
> Reformation Rev XII & XI
>
> Bloody Dumbarton Douglass &
>   Dundee
> Moved by the Devil & the Laird
>   of Lee
> Draggd these Five Men to Death
>   With Gun & Sword
> Not Suffering them to Pray
>   nor Read God's Word
> Ouning the Work of God Was All
>   their Crime
> The Eighty Five was a Saint
>   Killing Time.

The earliest inscription, presumably that transcribed by Thomson in *Martyr Graves*, is to be seen on stones collected within the enclosure of the 1885 monument and is now almost completely illegible. The above inscription will be found on a stone built into the wall of the Primary School just opposite the monument.

(2) *Parish Chuchyard: Smith*

> HERE LIES
> intered the corpse of JAMES
> SMITH who was wounded by
> Captain Ingles, and his Drag-
> oons, at the Burn of Ann in kyle,
> and there after died of his wounds
> in Mauchline prison for his adhe
> arance to the word of GOD and
> scotland's Covenanted Work
> of reformation, A.D. 1684

If this is the same James Smith who was shot as described in the aftermath of the prison break at Newmilns, the date should read 1685; the source of the error is perhaps the hagiography *A Cloud of Witnesses*, whose first edition may antedate this gravestone.

In the Parish Church at Mauchline there hangs a Covenanting flag. Whether it was carried at the Battle of Mauchline Muir I cannot tell. Its inscription is as follows:

(St Andrew's Cross)
MACHLIN

FOR GOD
COVENANTED REFORMATION
PRESBETORY GOVERNMENT
AND CROUN

Mauchline is on the A76 south of Kilmarnock.

Minnyhive or Moniaive (NX 772 911)

Although Moniaive was the birthplace of the last famous martyr of the Cameronians, James Renwick, and many martyrdoms are recorded in the neighbourhood, there is no martyr's stone in Moniaive itself. (See *Glencairn, Ingliston, Tynron, Dalgarnock* etc). A monument just outside the village was erected to James Renwick in 1828.

Inscription

IN MEMORY OF
the late
REV^D JAMES RENWICK
the last who
Suffered to Death
for
Attachment to the Covenanted Cause
of CHRIST
in SCOTLAND;
Born
Near this Spot
15th Feby 1662;
and Executed
at the Grassmarket Edinburgh
17th Feby 1688,
"The Righteous shall be in

Everlasting Remembrance."
Psal. CXII:6
Erected by Subscription
A: D. MDCCCXXVIII

The monument is to the north of the road, at the top of an incline west of Moniaive on the B729. (See Map on p. 114)

Muirkirk (NS 702 278)

Muirkirk was one of the stages through which the army of the Pentland Rising marched on their way to Edinburgh in November 1666. In the 1680s Covenanting activity in the neighbourhood was intense, and numerous important sites and monuments are to be found in the surrounding countryside. Airds Moss and Upper Wellwood are a short distance away to the west, and to the north and east are Newmilns, Drumclog, Priesthill, Auchingilloch, Logan House, Lesmahagow and Blackwood. South of Muirkirk an old hill road bypassing the great hill of Cairntable connects the village with Auchtitench, Friarminnan, Blackgannoch and Sanquhar. In Muirkirk itself a stone commemorating a Covenanter named John Smith will be found in the Parish Churchyard.[1]

Inscription

> HERE LYES JOHN SMITH
> WHO WAS SHOT BY COL
> BUCHAN AND THE LAIRD
> OF LEE   FEB 1685
> FOR HIS ADHERENCE TO THE
> WORD OF GOD AND SCOT
> LANDS COVENANTED W
> ORK OF REFORMATION
> REV. 12. 11. ERECTED IN THE
> YEAR 1731

(reverse)

> EPITAPH
> WHEN PROUD APOSTA
> DID ABJURE SCOTLAND'S
> REFORMATION PURE AND
> FILLd WITH PERJ

URY AND ALL SORTS OF IN
IqUITY SUCH AS WOUD NOT
WITH THEM COMPLY THEY PE
RSECUTE WITH HUE AND
CRY. I IN THE FLIGHT
WAS OVERTANE AND FO
R THE TRUTH BY THEM
WAS SLAIN.

Little is known of John Smith, although Hewison seems to think that is was John Smith, and not James Smith of Wee Threepwood, who was shot at "Croonan" (? = Burn Ann) after giving food to the escapers from the Ducat Tower in April 1685. Compare *Newmilns, Mauchline* and *Galston*; John Smith might have been the second man shot after the prison break. If this is so, however, the date on the tombstone, February 1685, is wrong. In the Mauchline memorial to the five hanged on 6th May, 1685, complicity in arresting and condemning the five to death is attributed to the Laird of Lee (Cromwell Lockhart)mentioned in the epitaph above.

Muirkirk is on the A70. (See map on p.51.)

[1] The Laird of Glenbuck put up a memorial to all local Covenanters in the modern Muirkirk Cemetery, and a plaque on the external wall of Glenbuck Parish Church (now partly ruined and used for storing farm machinery). Glenbuck is a tiny, much-decayed village on an unlisted loop road north of the A70 five kilometres east of Muirkirk.

Newmilns (NS 535 374)

The vignette shows the Ducat Tower[1], a grim little stronghold still standing in the centre of Newmilns and recently — 1994— the subject of restoration and conservation. The Tower forms the setting for the central part of one of the most remarkable episodes of the Killing Time — that ending in the execution of John Brown at Priesthill on 1st May, 1685. The story will be found in the section of the following entry dealing with John Law's tombstone at the Ducat Tower.

Besides that stone, several tombstones and monuments survive in Newmilns (Loudoun) Parish Churchyard close to the Ducat Tower. Two of the men commemorated fell at Drumclog in 1679.

Inscriptions
(1) *Parish churchyard*
(i) *Gebbie*

Here lies *JOHN GEBBIE*
in Feoch
Who for his appearing
in arms in his own Defence
and in Defence of the Gospel
according to the obligations
of our National Covenants &
Agreeable ^{to} the Word of GOD
was Shot in a Rencounter at
Drumclog June 1st 1679 by
Bloody Graham of Clavers
hous

RESTORED 1929

(ii) *Morton*

HERE LIES
JOHN MORTON
IN BROOMHILL
who for His appearing in *ARMS*
in His Own Defence
And in Defence of the *GOSPEL*
According to the Obligations
of our
NATIONAL COVENANTS
And Agreeable to the WORD of

GOD

Was Shot in a Rencounter at
Drumclog June 1st 1679 by bloody
Graham of *Clavers House*

RESTORED 1920

For the other Covenanter victims of Drumclog and for details of the battle itself, see *Strathaven, Stonehouse, Loudoun, Lesmahagow,* and *Drumclog.*

(iii) *Nisbet*

To the memory of
JOHN NISBET of HARDHILL
who suffered martyrdom at the Grassmarket
Edinburgh. 4th December, 1685
Animated by Spirit
To which Genuine Religion alone could give birth
the pure flame of civil & Religious Liberty
alone could keep alive,
He manfully struggled for a Series of years
To stem the tide of National Degeneracy,
And liberate his Country from the tyrannical
aggressions of the perjured House of
Stuart
His conduct in war at Pentland, Drumclog And Bothwell Bridge
In opposition to Prelatic Encroachment &
In Defence of Scotlands Covenanted Reformation
Is recorded in the annals of
these oppressive times.

His remains lies at EDINBURGH
But the inhabitants of this his Native Parish
And friends to the cause for which he fought and died
Have caused this stone to be Erected.

The above inscription is not dated, but it is obviously 19th-century, probably contemporary with the collective memorial in the next entry (1829). For further detail on John Nesbit of Hardhill, see *Fenwick* (Gemmel, Fergushill, Woodburn), *Glasgow*, and *Kilmarnock* .

(iv) *Collective*

ERECTED SEP^t 1829
by the
Parishioners of Loudoun in testimony
of their deep admiration of the
noble struggle in defence of the
civil and Religious Liberties of their
Country against the despotic and
persecuting measures of the House
of Stuart maintained by the under
named Martyrs belonging to this
Parish who suffered and died for
their devotedness to the covenanted
work of Reformation.

Matthew Paton Shoemaker in
Newmilns who was taken in the
Rencounter at Pentland & executed
at Glasgow Dec 19th, 1666
David Findlay who was Shot at
Newmilns by order of Dalziel 1666
James Wood taken at the Battle
of Bothwell Bridge & executed at
Magusmuir Nov. 25th 1679
John Nisbet in Glen executed at
Kilmarnock April 14th 1683
and James Nisbet in Highside executed
at Glasgow June 11th 1684

These are they who came out of great tribulation
Rev. vii 14

RESTORED [date illegible]

The story goes that David Findlay, second named in the inscription above, was shot on the orders of Tam Dalyell of the Binns because he was unable to name the rebels who had been in Lanark on their way to Rullion Green on the same day when Findlay himself had been visiting Lanark. Another David Findlay or Finlay was shot out of hand while being taken captive to the Ducat Tower in April 1685 after being wounded during Peter Ingles's operation against Little Blackwood. The burial of that David Findlay does not seem to have been recorded.

For Matthew Paton, see *Glasgow*; for James Wood, see *Magus Muir*; for the two Nisbets— Glen (Know) and Highside—see *Glasgow* and *Kilmarnock*. (These Nisbets are easily confused with John Nisbet of Hardhill.)

Also, in a prominent position in the churchyard near the roadside, a modern monument has been erected naming Matthew Paton 1666, David Findlay 1666, James Wood 1679, John Morton 1679, John Gebbie 1679, Thomas Fleming 1679 [See *Loudoun*.], John Nisbet Junr. 1683, James Nisbet 1684, John Nisbet Senr. 1685 and John Law 1685. A plaque has been placed on the external church wall reproducing part of Law's inscription at the Ducat Tower.

(2) *Law*

(external western precinct wall of the Ducat Tower; now fronting a lane giving rear access to a number of premises)

> HERE LIES JOHN LAW
> Who was shot at Newmilns AT
> The relieving of 8 of Christ's
> Prisoners, Who were taken at A meet[g]
> For Prayer at Little Blackwood, in the
> Parish of Kilm[k] in April 1685, By Cap[t]
> INGLIS and his Party, For Their
> Adherance to the Word of God
> And Scotland's Covenanted Work
> of Reformation
> Cause I Christ's Prisoners relieved
> I of my life was soon beriev'd
> By cruel Enemies with rage
> In that Rencounter did engage
> The Martyr's honour and his Crown
> Restow'd on me, O high Renown
> That I Should not only believe
> But For *Christ's* cause my Life
> should give.
>
> RENEWED
> in 1822 and 1930

The above inscription is now very badly weathered, in spite of frequent renewals, and is almost illegible.

The story behind this singular epitaph is long, tangled and dramatic. As mentioned above, it ends with the execution of John Brown at Priesthill — and with that of John Browning and four others at Mauchline. Law's part, and that of the Ducat Tower, comes in the middle.

The episode starts at James Paton's farm at Little Blackwood (now no longer existing as a separate unit) on the Grougar Estate south of Fenwick. There, in April 1685, twelve Covenanters met "for religious purposes"[2] — probably a house conventicle. The farmhouse was raided by a party of soldiers led by Peter or Patrick Ingles, son of Captain John Ingles, Commandant of the Ducat Tower, Newmilns.

When the soldiers closed in, James White seized the only gun in the house and fired but missed; the light of the shot gave him away and the soldiers shot him dead. The other Covenanters fled in different directions, nine to the "spence" (inner room of the house), and two — John Gemmell and the farmer James Paton — to the byre. Gemmell and Paton were attacked in the byre. Gemmell wrested the bayonet from a soldier and stabbed him with it, thereafter making his escape. Paton was arrested. Two of the spence party succeeded in making a hole in the thatch and breaking out, but the other seven were cornered, and Ingles started negotiations for their surrender. According to M'Kay, this was at the prayers of Mrs Paton, a young woman with a babe at her breast.[3] Peter Ingles granted her wish, it is said, because he had known her while he was on garrison duty at her father's house at Darwhilling just north of Little Blackwood.

The terms of the surrender were that the seven should emerge from the spence one by one on their knees. The arrangement was clearly insecure to begin with, since the first to surrender, an old man named David Findlay, was stabbed in the thigh with a bayonet by a nervous soldier who was well cursed for his pains — and those of Findlay — by Ingles. The remaining six were arrested without incident.

The farm was then plundered and the cattle and horses driven off, trampling the dead body of James White, which still lay where it had fallen. Peter Ingles— or, according to Wodrow, "ane soldier in partic-ular" [4] — cut off White's head with an axe, and brought it to Newmilns, where they played football with it the next day. One source states that the soldier who cut the head off was later found with his neck broken at the foot of the Ducat Tower.[5]

White was buried at Fenwick where, as mentioned in the entry for that village, the reverse of his tombstone bears the following verse:

> This Martyr was By PETER INGLES Shot
> By birth a Tyger rather than a Scot
> Who that his monstrous Extract might be Seen
> Cut off his head & Kick't it o'er the Green
> Thus was that head which was to wear a Crown
> A foot ball made by a profane Dragoun

Ingles's party, then, took their prisoners to the Ducat Tower, shooting Findlay out of hand on the way because his wound immobilised him. When they arrived, however, instead of shooting the survivors on the spot, old Captain Ingles discovered some doubts about his powers to inflict summary execution, and Peter Ingles was sent off to Edinburgh to obtain proper authority.

According to the sources Peter Ingles returned from Edinburgh with a flea in his ear, having been told that there was no need to refer the matter to higher authority. He spent the night, however, at a tavern some distance from the Tower, before delivering his message. The same night most of the Government troop "was absent on one of its bloody raids"[6], leaving only a few on guard duty.

In the meantime one John Browning from Lanfine "with others who had been with him at Airds Moss"[7] raided the smithy at Darvel close at hand, stole the forehammers, and broke down the door of the Ducat Tower. Perhaps sixty men took part in the attack. Two soldiers were killed, as was one of the attackers, John Law, whose epitaph is given above; the tombstone is built into the small precinct wall of the Tower, probably just where he was killed. The prisoners got clean away.

When the troopers got back, Captain Ingles was beside himself with fury. (Thomson says that he was in the Tower throughout the raid, hiding beneath his bed for fear. Other sources reveal that he was dismissed from his command as a result of this fiasco.) During the subsequent search the dragoons are said to have shot two innocent men, one of whom was James Smith of Wee Threepwood. (For further detail about this man and his fate, see below and *Galston* and *Mauchline*). A Kilmarnock doctor named Jasper Tough, who had treated some of the fugitives for gunshot wounds sustained during the escape, was thrown into a dungeon beneath Dean Castle in Kilmarnock.[8]

Meanwhile, according to MacLeod, "the dragoons soon went in pursuit of the prisoners, but they had reached the heather, and there no cavalry could pursue them." This, however, is not strictly true, as it was at this point that Claverhouse with his specially-trained rough-riders was called in.

John Graham of Claverhouse,
Viscount Dundee (by David Paton).
Courtesy of the National Galleries
of Scotland.

(In the interests of narrative, the rest of the story is given here; other details bearing on the case, including some traditionary material, will be found under *Priesthill* and *Mauchline*.)

On 1st May, 1685, Claverhouse and his dragoons caught up with "tuo fellous ... amongst the hilles betuixt Douglas and the Plellands".[9] Claverhouse writes from Galston (3rd May, 1685) that they pursued them "a great way through the mosses" and in the end caught them just at the elder man's house at Priesthill or Priestsheil above Glenbuck. (For the full text of this letter, see Appendix III.) The two men turned out to be John Browning and his uncle John Brown "the Christian Carrier", who had been on the wanted list since Bothwell Brig in 1679.

Brown had been excluded from the Indemnity published on 2nd March, 1685, since he had "refused the allegiance"[10]. As a carrier, he seems to have been one of the key, if shadowy, personnel of the "Society People" whose Union or General Correspondence was formed not far away at Logan House on 15th December, 1681 (see *Logan House*) and who held a quarterly meeting at Priesthill on 15th March, 1682.

Claverhouse, who was a skilled interrogator, started to question the prisoners. While this was going on the dragoons were searching the house and discovered arms and ammunition and "treasonable peapers". Claverhouse pressed the Abjuration Oath upon Brown, but he refused it, "nor would he swear not to ryse in armes against the King but said he kneu no King." This was more than sufficient for the purposes of Claverhouse and, in his own words, "I caused shoot him dead, which he suffered very inconcernedly."[11]

As intended, the execution, and preparations for his own, broke the nerve of the younger man, John Browning, and "he confessed that he was at that attake of Neumilles."[12] He went further, and named men from Galston and Newmilns who had taken part in recent, highly illegal manoeuvres, marching and drilling in the Cairntable region above Muirkirk to the south. He confirmed that James Renwick had been present at these exercises, which had been combined with conventicling. Finally, he offered to take the Abjuration Oath.

In the meantime, the dragoons had continued their search and discovered an underground "vault" or chamber roomy enough for twelve men and containing swords and pistols. John Brown had been using this dug-out as a hiding-place for six years.

Claverhouse sent John Browning down to Mauchline for further interrogation by Lieutenant-General William Drummond of Cromlix, whose headquarters were there. On 6th May, 1685, Browning was hanged at Mauchline with four other men. No evidence seems to survive to connect the other four men with either the Little Blackwood episode or the Newmilns rescue, but such a connection cannot be unlikely.

A sixth man, James Smith, died of his wounds in Mauchline prison: he was probably the same James Smith of Wee Threepwood who was shot by Captain Ingles's dragoons during the aftermath of the Newmilns raid. If so, it looks as if Mauchline had become an interrogation and disposal centre to which all suspects connected with the affair were sent after their arrest. The date on James Smith's stone at Mauchline, 1684, is probably in error, deriving from the account in *A Cloud of Witnesses*, which is full of printing and other errors.

Such was the famous episode involving the "Christian Carrier". For further discussion of its significance and timing, see Introduction p21. (See also map on next page.)

[1] The name "Ducat" does not have anything to do with the former European gold coin — or the Scottish word for a pigeon-loft, "Doo-cot"; it is the Gaelic Dhu-chat, black wood, bearing testimony to the density and gloom of the primaeval Scottish forest around Newmilns in past centuries. Peter Inglis made his arrest at a farm called Little Blackwood. Blackwood Farm is still on the map southeast of Fenwick, and Blackwood is a well-known personal name in Ayrshire to this day. Compare also the separate entry for Blackwood (NS 775 434).

[2] M'Kay p63

[3] M'Kay p64

[4] M'Kay pp63-65

[5] M'Kay ib. Paterson II p318

[6] Paterson II ib. (quoting Wodrow)

[7] MacLeod *NSA* v.838

[8] McKay pp53-55; Wodrow iii p426

[9] Claverhouse to Queensberry 3rd May, 1685; quoted Terry *Claverhouse* pp 197-198

[10] Wodrow iv p216; Terry *Claverhouse* p200

[11] *Claverhouse* loc. cit.

[12] *Claverhouse* ib.

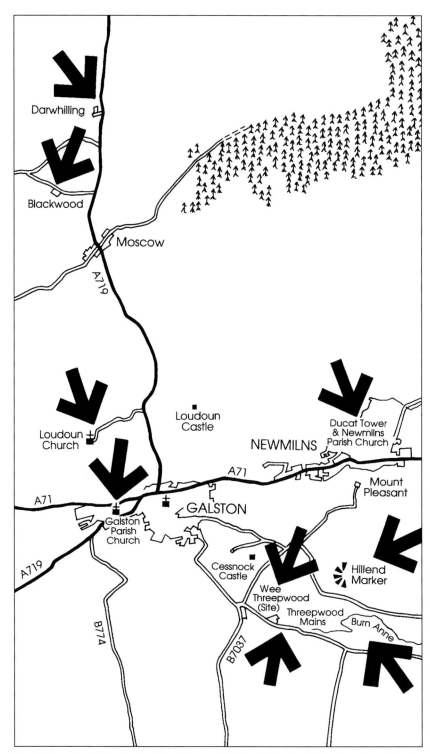

Showing Newmilns, Galston, Loudoun Church, the present Blackwood Farm, Darwhilling Farm, Cessnock Castle, Burn Ann, Threepwood Mains, the site of Wee Threepwood and the miner's marker at Gallows Hill (Hillend).

North Berwick (NT 552 853)

John Blackad(d)er, who lies buried here, became famous as a field preacher after being "outed" from his parish in 1662. (For details see *Dumfries* [*Troqueer*]; cf. also *Bass Rock*). The tombstone is flat, raised on short legs.

Inscription
(Vertical at top of table: carved angel and bible)

Here lies the body of
Mr. JOHN BLACKADER minister of the
gospel at Troqueer in Galloway, who
died on the Bass after five years impri-
sonment Anno Dom: 1685 and of his age
63 years.
Blest John for Jesus sake in Patmos bound
His prison Bethel, Patmos Pisgah found;
So the bless'd John on yonder rock confin'd,
His body suffer'd, but no chains could bind
His heaven-aspiring soul; while day by day
As from mount Pisgah's top he did survey
The promised land, & viewed the Crown by faith
Laid up for those who faithful are till death,
Grace form'd him in the Christian Hero's mould,
Meek in his own concerns, in's master's bold,
Passions to reason chain'd Prudence did lead,
Zeal warm'd his breast & reason cool'd his head.
Five years on the bare rock yet sweet abode
He Enoch like enjoy'd & walk'd with God,
Till by long living on this heavenly food
His soul by love grew up too great too good
To be confin'd in jail, or flesh & blood;
Death broke his fetters off, then swift he fled,
From sin and sorrow & by angels led
Enter'd the mansions of eternal joy.
Blest soul thy warfare's done, praise, love, enjoy,
His dust here rests till Jesus come again;
Ev'n so bless'd Jesus come, come Lord Amen.

Renewed
by private Subscription
July A.D. 1821
J. Grieve fecit

(Vertical at bottom of table: MEMENTO MORI [Skull & crossbones])

Old Dailly

Old Dailly Churchyard, a short distance inland from Girvan, is raised, circular, surrounded by trees, and very beautiful. The ruined church, unusually, has two belfries. Six covenanters are commemorated here.

Inscriptions
(1) Semple/McClorgan

HERE LIES
The corpse of JOHN
SEMPLE who was
shot by Kilkerran
at command of
Cornet James Douglas.
Also here lies
THOMAS M[c]CLORGAN
who was shot
uncertain by whom
for their adherance
to the Word of GOD
and the covenanted
work of Reformation.

1685

(This version of the monument was put up in 1825).

Nothing is known of McClorgan. Semple was shot trying to escape through a window at Eldington Farm. According to Wodrow this took place in April 1685 when a party of soldiers was about to arrest Semple probably on a charge of reset. (" .... being given to hospitality, and of a compassionate temper, he did sometimes harbour those poor people who were then hunted for their lives."[1])

(2) Stevenson/Martin et al.

IN HONOUR OF
JOHN STEVENSON OF CAMREGAN
A MAN OF FAITH AND PRAYER
WHO SUFFERED MUCH
FOR HIS CONSCIENTIOUS ADHERENCE TO
SCOTLANDS COVENANTED WORK
OF REFORMATION,
BORN 1656, DIED 1729.
ERECTED BY
THE PEOPLE OF THIS DISTRICT
AUGUST 1886

(reverse)

ALSO
IN MEMORY OF
GEORGE MARTIN, SCHOOLMASTER,
OLD DAILLY,
WHO AFTER AN IMPRISONMENT OF
FOUR YEARS AND FOUR MONTHS
SUFFERED IN THE GRASSMARKET, EDINBURGH,
ON 22ND FEBRUARY, 1684,
FOR HIS ADHERENCE TO THE COVENANT:
ALSO
OF OTHER TWO COVENANTERS
ONE OF WHOM, ACCORDING TO TRADITION,
WAS SHOIT DEAD, WHILE HERDING HIS COW
AT KILLOUP;
AND THE OTHER WAS STRUCK DOWN ON HIS
OWN HEARTH, AT BLACK CLAUCHRIE, BARR,
AND IS BURIED NEAR THIS SPOT.

The first Covenanter commemorated on this modern monument, John Stevenson, came from Camregan Farm, which is about one kilometre from Old Dailly on the Girvan side. After hearing the preachers at the great Craigdow conventicle of 1678, he took up arms in the cause and fought in the battle of Bothwell Brig. He managed to get away after the battle and had many adventures which he described in a small manuscript book collected and published by the historian Wodrow.[2]

George Martin, the only well-known martyr in this churchyard, was not only a schoolteacher but also a notary and a church reader. Hanged in early 1684, he was a victim of a Government clampdown on those unwilling to acknowledge the King's authority, i.e the anti-Erastians. Martin had been in jail for four years, and his execution along with others demonstrates the hardening of Government attitudes towards religious dissent following the return of James Renwick to Scotland in September 1683. As ever, the religious intolerance of the authorities went hand in hand with their fear of insurrection.

It is said that the anonymous Black Clauchrie victim mentioned in the epitaph above is buried here beneath the very hearth-stone on which he was shot. I was not able to identify this burial.

Old Dailly is four kilometres east of Girvan on the B734.

[1] Wodrow iv p244   [2] See Bibliography under Stevenson J

(Orkney (Mull Head of Deerness) (HY 571 087)

After the battle of Bothwell Brig on 22nd July, 1679, disposal of the many hundreds of Whig prisoners confined in Greyfriars churchyard in Edinburgh became an acute problem for the Government. Some few, indeed, were executed (cf. *Magus Muir*), and many simply escaped or bribed the guards to let them go; a large number were induced to sign a bond for their future good behaviour and were released immediately. A hard core, however, refused to sign on the grounds that to do so would be to admit that the purpose of the Bothwell rising was wrong. At last the authorities decided that the only thing to do with these intransigents was to "transport" them to the American colonies, and arranged a passage for about 250 prisoners in the *The Crown of London* from Leith to the Barbados on 27th November, 1679.

The usual route for the Americas from the East Coast of Scotland involved sailing round the North of Scotland, and on 10th December, 1679, when they had reached the Orkneys, a winter storm drove *The Crown of London* on to the rocks at Mull Head of Deerness. The captain, one Paterson, is alleged to have refused to open the hatches, and all the prisoners, save about fifty, drowned there and then.

The bodies are said to be buried at Scarva Taing, just beneath the memorial. A list of those who perished and those who survived is given in Appendix Ic, taken from *A Cloud of Witnesses*; the names are divided by parishes. See also *Edinburgh , Greyfriars* . The memorial here is late nineteenth century.

Inscription

FOR CHRIST HIS CROWN & COVENANT

(design)

ERECTED

BY

PUBLIC SUBSCRIPTION
AUG 1888
TO

THE MEMORY OF

200 COVENANTERS
WHO WERE TAKEN PRISONERS
AT BOTHWELL BRIDGE, AND
SENTENCED TO TRANSPORTATION
FOR LIFE BUT WHO PERISHED BY
SHIPWRECK NEAR THIS SPOT
ON 10TH DECEMBER 1679

Paisley (NS 485 640)

In February 1685 John Park and James Algie were informed against in revenge for having given up the joint tenancy of a farm at Kennishead. They had stopped going to church. Under interrogation they said that they were willing to take the Abjuration Oath, i.e. to renounce James Renwick's Apologetical Declaration of November 1684, but not to take the Test Oath, which would have involved them more directly in acknowledging the ecclesiastical authority of the King. (Their epitaph gives the reason for their execution as refusal to take the Abjuration Oath, but other authorities, including Wodrow, state otherwise.) Their hanging at Paisley Tolbooth, carried out within four hours of their sentence, was used to terrorise one of their neighbours, the miller Robert King, into taking the Test.[1]

The nineteenth-century obelisk, erected above the original stone transferred from the Gallowgreen in 1779, will be found at the rear of the old Martyr's Memorial Church in Broomlands Street. This churchyard is adjacent to Woodside Cemetery. The original stone is almost completely illegible.

Inscription
(Main Panel only)

HERE LIE THE CORPSES OF
JAMES ALGIE AND JOHN PARK
WHO SUFFERED AT THE CROSS OF PAISLEY
FOR REFUSING THE OATH OF ABJURATION
FEBRUARY 3 1685

Stay, passenger, as thou goest by
And take a look where these do lie
Who for the love they bore to truth

Were deprived of their life and youth
Though laws made then caused many die
Judgers and 'sizers were not free
He that to them did these delate
The greater count he hath to make
Yet no excuse to them can be
At ten condemned, at two to die
So cruel did their rage become
To stop their speech caused beat the drum
This may a standing witness be
'Twixt Presbytry and Prelacy.

The above episode took place in the early part of the Killing Time, which reached its crescendo in April and May 1685. The Killing Time had erupted in November 1684, after a long build-up of tension in the south-west of Scotland. One of the most important stages in this build-up began on 10th June, 1684, when a wildly improbable alliance was being sealed in Paisley Abbey — the marriage between John Graham of Claverhouse and Jean Cochrane.

Claverhouse, the hammer of the Covenanters, was not a man to act without consideration, and this applied to his marriage as to other things.

He was ambitious, and had already tried to ally himself with an aristocratic family (leading to the Earldom of Menteith). He now successfully wooed and won the Honourable Jean Cochrane of the Cochranes of Paisley and of Dundonald in Ayrshire.

Jean Viscountess of Dundee (by a imitator of Lely). Courtesy of McManus Galleries, Dundee.

What makes this extraordinary was that the Cochranes were deeply involved in Covenanting, and were allied to the Earl of Cassillis, one of the few Scottish magnates after 1660 to identify himself whole-heartedly with the Covenanting cause. Jean's uncle, Sir John Cochrane of Ochiltree, was implicated in treasonable activities along with Sir Hew Campbell of Cessnock and, having fled to Holland, was actually being investigated by Claverhouse at the time of the latter's marriage.[2]

Claverhouse, who had thought deeply about the roots of and possible remedies for the Covenanting problem, perceived that one of the keys to the situation was family relationships, and he may even have felt that bringing non-Whig blood into a Whig family might, as it were, begin to dissipate and disentangle the tight-knit Whig genes. He wrote, "For my owen part I look on myself as a cleanger. I may cur people guilty of that plaigue of presbitry be conversing with them, but can not be infected, and I see very litle of that amongst those persons but may be easily rubed of." At least he thought that it was an advantage to have a foot in the other camp: "I must say the neu alleyance that I am lyk to mak is not unusfull to me in the shyr of Air and Ranfrou. They [the Cochranes] have the guyding of those shyrs and they do strenthen my hands in the Kings service."[3]

In spite of this astonishing degree of premeditation, the marriage appears to have been happy, if short, and Jean helped in fund-raising in 1689 before the Battle of Killiecrankie.[4]

On 10th June, 1684, the happy pair were joined in marriage in Paisley Abbey. During the service a message was brought to Claverhouse that fugitives from a conventicle at Blackloch near Slamannan had been pursued out of a neighbouring military command area into the Ayrshire/ Renfrewshire region. More than a hundred men and women, "under" (as the sources state) "the spiritual leadership of Renwick"[5] were on the run southward.

No sooner was the knot tied at Paisley Abbey, then, than Claverhouse was into the saddle and off in hot pursuit of the conventiclers. He galloped to Newmilns in Ayrshire, where Colonel Thomas Buchan from Dalmellington rendezvoused with him and with Captain John Ingles, Commandant of Newmilns Castle (the Ducat Tower). Up and down Ayrshire, Clydesdale and Upper Nithsdale ranged Claverhouse and his men in fruitless search of the conventiclers. Baffled, he returned to Paisley and the interrupted wedding celebrations on 12th June, but on 13th June news reached him that contact with the conventiclers had been made and shots exchanged, possibly near Muirkirk. Off he rode again, this time to Cumnock via Kilmarnock and Mauchline, and got word of the fugitives near Airdsmoss, "barefooted many of them and taking horses in some places to help them forward."[6]

On 14th June, 1684, then, Claverhouse organised a vast search of the whole of south-eastern Ayrshire and south-western Lanarkshire. He wrote, "We were at the head of Douglas. We were round and over Cairntable. We were at Greenock-head [Greenock near Muirkirk], Cummer-head, and through all the moors, mosses, hills, glens, woods; and spread in small parties, and ranged as if we had been at hunting and down to Blackwood, but could learn nothing of those rogues ... We traced them from the Boghead near Airdsmoss to the Hakhill, within two miles of Cumnock town, and from that to Gap, towards Cairntable, but could never hear more of them. They are separated, as most believe, and gone towards the hills of Moffat."[7]

The conventiclers vanished into thin air, possibly in the remote fastnesses above Kirkconnel (Nithsdale) to the east, where there appear to have been carefully prepared hideouts and safe houses. Claverhouse returned once more to his Covenanter bride and Paisley.[8] However, as mentioned in the Introduction, captured conventiclers from the Blackloch conventicle may have been involved in the Enterkin Pass incident in July 1684, the ambush of an armed party from Claverhouse's troop taking prisoners from Dumfries to Edinburgh. In this incident there were several deaths, and Claverhouse personally tracked down and arrested a number of those concerned. (See *Enterkin, Dalgarnock, Durisdeer* etc.)

All these incidents materially contributed to a heightening of tension in south-west Scotland in 1684; a process that began on a summer morning in Paisley Abbey may, through Claverhouse's tenacity of purpose and devotion to duty, have led to the explosion of violence known as the Killing Time in late 1684 and 1685.

[1] Wodrow iv pp189-191
[2] Terry *Claverhouse* p155
[3] Claverhouse to Queensberry
[4] Terry *Claverhouse* p160 n1
[5] Hewison ii p426 (quoting Erskine *Journal* p65)
[6] Terry *Claverhouse* p163
[7] Claverhouse to the Archbishop, quoted Terry *Claverhouse* pp 163-164
[8] Terry *Claverhouse* loc. cit.

Priesthill (also Priestshiel and Priestfield) (NS 731 316)

Here, on 1st May, 1685, John Brown, the "Christian Carrier", refused the Abjuration Oath. Claverhouse reported, "I caused shoot him dead, which he suffered very inconcernedly."[1] Weapons and "treasonable peapers" had been found in Brown's house, and along with him was arrested John Browning, suspected of organising a rescue of prisoners at Newmilns a few days before. Browning was a nephew of John Brown, and the sight of his uncle being shot broke Browning's nerve: he confessed to participating in the Newmilns rescue and other things as well.[2]

According to the Covenanting writers, the execution was witnessed also by Brown's wife and children. Isabel Brown had been married to John in 1682 by Alexander Peden, who, says Howie of Lochgoin, had made one of his celebrated fatal prophecies after the ceremony:

"You [Isabel] have got a good man to be your husband, but you will not enjoy him long; prize his company, and keep linen by you to be his winding sheet, for you will need it when ye are not looking for it, and it will be a bloody one."[3]

According to some sources, Peden had spent the night in Brown's house and only left on the approach of Claverhouse and his dragoons.[4] Now, when Brown was being prepared for execution, he is reported (by Patrick Walker) to have recalled Peden's prophecy, and said to his wife, "Now, Isabel, the day is come that I told you would come when I spake first to you of marrying me." She replied, "Indeed, John, I can willingly part with you." He rejoined, "That is all I desire; I have no more to do but die; I have been in case to meet death for so many years."[5] (He was, according to his tombstone, 58 years old.)

Claverhouse then gave the order to fire, but the soldiers, Wodrow states, had been so moved by Brown's valediction and earlier prayers, that they refused to obey orders. Claverhouse, according to this source, "was forced to turn executioner himself, and in a fret, shot him with his own hand."[6] He is then reported to have said to Isabel Brown, "What thinkest thou of thy husband now, woman?" "As much now as ever," she replied.[7]

Much controversy has been generated by this episode, and the Convenanters have been accused of surreptitious pathetic embroidery of the tale designed to blacken Claverhouse's name and heighten the suffering of the Browns. It is not, perhaps, irrelevant to note that certain elements of the above sad story are paralleled in other locations: see Craighaugh, immediately following the Priesthill event, on 10th May, 1685, where a Highland captain is said to have refused Claverhouse's order to shoot Andrew Hislop, so that Claverhouse had to select a firing party from among his own ranks;[8] and Skellyhill (Lesmahagow) where on 20th December, 1686, Lieutenant Creichton is said to have had David Steel brutally shot in the presence of his wife and child[9]; Creichton's own dragoons refused to do the deed, so that in this case Creichton had to call upon a party of Highlanders.[10] (Compare also *Forgandenny*.)

It is to be noted that in the case of the Skellyhill shooting Creichton's own narrative makes no mention of these circumstances[11] and neither does Claverhouse himself in his version of the Priesthill event. (See Appendix III.) Skellyhill is only a few kilometres across the moors from Priesthill.

To note these parallels is not to impugn the stories: all of them could have happened — and Claverhouse had a very ugly temper. Nevertheless the caution with which we treat such stories ought to be proportional to the propaganda advantage they confer on either side. In this case Claverhouse's letter, which was written from Galston (Appendix III) only two days after the Priesthill shooting, is frank to the point of ingenuousness and perhaps should be given more credit for that reason.

With the execution of Brown, Claverhouse had forced a confession about Newmilns from John Browning, and it may be that this was the entire purpose of the shooting. Browning was sent down to Mauchline, where he was hanged with four other men on 6th May. (For further details see *Newmilns, Galston, Mauchline, and Fenwick*.)

Priesthill was an important place for the "Society People", who held their first quarterly meeting there on 15th March, 1682, after the formation of their "Union or General Correspondence" in December 1681. (See *Logan House*.) John Brown did not live at the farm itself — he was a "carrier", not a farmer — but in a small dwelling about a mile away. This has now completely vanished, although its foundations were excavated in the 1920s, and some relics are held in the Royal Scottish Museum in Edinburgh. Claverhouse reported that while he was interrogating John Browning after the execution of John Brown, "the soldiers found out a house in the hill under ground, that could hold a dozen of men, and there wer swordes and pistolles in it: and this fellou [Browning] declared that they belonged to his uncle, and that he had lurked in that place ever since Bothwell, where he was in armes."[12] This discovery must have represented a signal success for Claverhouse's policy of gathering intelligence under pressure, and it would be interesting to find out if any trace of this underground hide now survives.

The inscription on John Brown's tomb, which is very early, is as follows:

(i) *(along the four edges of the flat stone, forming a rectangular "frame line"):*

> Here lies the body of JOHN
> BROWN martyr who was murdered in this place by
> GRAHAM of Claverhouse for his testi
> mony to the Covenanted work of Reformation Because

(ii) *(inside the "frame line" at the head of the stone, at right angles to the verse inscription):*

> he durst not own the
> authority of the then
> Tyrant destroying the
> Same, who died the first
> day of May A D 1685 and
> of his age 58.

(iii) *(verse inscription with acrostic)*

> In deaths cold bed the dusty part here lies
> Of one who did the earth as dust despise
> Here in this place from earth he took departure
> Now he has got the garland of the martyr
> Butchered by Clavers and his bloody band
> Raging most ravenously over all the land
> Only for owning Christ's supremacy
> Wickedly wronged by encroaching Tyranny
> Nothing now near soever he to good
> Esteemed, nor dear for any truth his blood.

The site of the tomb, north-east of Muirkirk, can be reached from the A73 (Muirkirk to Strathaven) road; north of Greenock Bridge a turn-off to the east leads past Blackside Farm to Priesthill. Beyond Priesthill white markers lead for about a mile across open moorland to the martyr's grave. (see also Map on p.51.)

[1] Claverhouse quoted Terry *Claverhouse* p201; see Appendix III herein.
[2] Terry op. cit. pp 197-202
[3] Howie of Lochgoin p511
[4] Walker i p484
[5] Walker i p84
[6] Wodrow iv p245
[7] Walker i p86
[8] *Cloud*, Appendix p385
[9] Hewison ii p497; Thomson p274-275
[10] Thomson loc. cit.
[11] Creichton pp58-59
[12] Claverhouse to the Archbishop

Rullion Green (NT 219 625)

On 27th November, 1666, the depleted forces of the Pentland Rising reached their point furthest east, at Colinton on the outskirts of Edinburgh. They had started their insurrection almost by mistake, as a gut reaction against the mistreatment of a poor old farmer at St John's Clachan of Dalry in Kirkcudbrightshire by a handful of Sir James Turner's brutal soldiery. Having rescued the farmer and shot and wounded one of the soldiers, M'Lellan of Barscobe and his three companions realised that they were now in a state of rebellion. That was on 13th November, and on 14th November they repeated their performance at Balmaclellan, making sixteen soldiers prisoners and killing one who resisted. They then rallied at Irongray Kirk, and in the grey early morning of 15th November about 250 rebels entered Dumfries and took Sir James Turner prisoner in his nightgown.

The rebels had no very clear idea what to do next, but they set off on a trek through the south-west of Scotland, passing through Dalmellington, Ayr, Tarbolton and Muirkirk before pushing on to Lanark and Edinburgh. They may have had no more hostile intent than presenting a petition to the authorities against abuses in the south-west. Some may have remembered the Whiggamore Raid of eighteen years before, when the radical Covenanters of the west marched on Edinburgh and took it over after the Battle of Preston in 1648.

At their high point the insurrectionary forces may have numbered about 1,500 men, but by the time they approached Edinburgh morale was slipping badly and they were down to about 900 men. In the meantime, Thomas Dalziel of the Binns, the commander of the Government forces, had paced them along a slightly different route to the northward, and was preparing to make an attack. After a night at Colinton the rebels made up their minds to side-step rather than to await the results of their petition or to attack Edinburgh. Once they had started to move, the side-step became a retreat, and the little army poured back along the road to Linton and Biggar. At Rullion Green they paused to allow stragglers to catch up.

Meantime, Thomas Dalziel's forces had reached Currie on the other (northern) side of the Pentland Hills, and, hearing where the rebels were, Dalziel realized that he could catch them by striking south through the pass between Bell's Hill and Harbour Hill and down along the Glencorse Burn. The rebels took up a strong position on the flanks of the spectacular Turnhouse Hill, and Dalziel's forces did not have the battle all their own way, but in the end numbers told, and the rebels were defeated as the early winter night fell.

Many were taken prisoner, and about 50 rebels were killed. Dalziel had offered quarter as an inducement for them to lay down their arms, but the Covenanting prisoners were treated by the Privy Council as traitors and tried for their lives. About thirty were hanged at Edinburgh Cross and at various centres in the West Country, where several were sent to be hanged as a warning to their fellow citizens. (See *Glasgow, Ayr, Irvine, Dumfries, Hamilton, Newmilns* and *Fenwick,* as well as *Black Law, Kirk o'Shotts* and *Kells*. For fuller treatment of the whole subject readers are still recommended to C S Terry's *The Pentland Rising* 1666 [Glasgow 1905].)

The monument at Rullion Green is on the edge of a patch of woodland some distance across an open field from Rullion Green Farm, which lies north of Penicuik on the A702. There is a splendid view of Edinburgh and the Castle from the battle site.

Inscription

Here
And near to
this place lyes the
Reverend Mr John crookshank
and m^r Andrew m^ccormick
ministers of the Gospel and
About fifty other true covenanted Presbyterians who were
killed in this place in their own
Inocent self defence and defence of the covenanted
work of Reformation By
Thomas Dalzeel of Bins
upon The 28 of november
1666. Rev. 12-11. Erected
Sept. 28 1738.

(reverse)

A Cloud of Witnesses lyes here
Who for Christ's Interest did appear
For to Restore true Liberty
Overturned then by tyrrany.
And by proud Prelats who did Rage
Against the Lord's own heritage.
They sacrificed were for the laws
Of Christ their king, his noble cause.
These heroes fought with great renown
By falling got the martyrs crown.

Saint Andrews (NO 515 168)

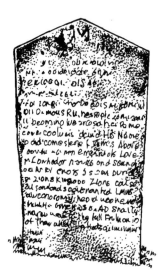

The tomb of Archbishop James Sharp, murdered on 3rd May, 1679, dominates one of the transepts in the Church of the Holy Trinity in South Street. It is unexpectedly beautiful, with rich and elaborate ornamentation, and a life-size carving of the Archbishop kneeling to receive the crown of martyrdom. Below the inscription is a powerfully-modelled bas-relief of the assassination on Magus Muir. The tomb itself is empty. In 1725 "certain ryotous and disorderlie persons" broke into the vault and made away with the body of the Archbishop, which has never been recovered.[1]

Rutherford's tomb

In the Cathedral churchyard stands the gravestone of Samuel Rutherford, at one time minister of Anwoth, who was appointed Professor of Divinity at St Andrews in 1639.

Inscriptions
(1) *Sharp (Church of Holy Trinity)*

DOM
SACRATISSIMI ANTISTITIS PRUDENTISSIMI SENATORIS
[SANCTISSIMI MARTYRIS CINERES PRECOSISSIMOS
SUBLIME HOC TEGIT MAUSOLEUM
HIC NAMQ JACET
QUOD SUB SOLE RELIQUUM EST REVERENDISSIMI IN X^TO
[PATRIS
D D Jacobi Sharp S^Ti ANDREAE ARCHIEPISCOPI TOTIUS SCOTIAE
[PRIMATIS &c
QUEM

PHILOSOPHIAE ET THEOLOGIAE PROFESSOREM ACADEMIA
[PRESBYTERUM DOCTOREM PRAESULEM ECCLESIA
TUM ECCLESIASTICI TUM CIVILIS STATUS MINISTRUM
[PRIMARIUM SCOTIA
SERENISSIMI CAROLI SECUNDI MONARCHICIQ IMPERII
[RESTITUTIONIS SUASOREM BRITANNIA
EPISCOPALIS ORDINIS IN SCOTIA INSTAURATOREM
[CHRISTIANUS ORBIS
PIETATIS EXEMPLUM PACIS ANGELUM SAPIENTIAE
[ORACULUM GRAVITATIS IMAGINEM BONI ET
[FIDELES SUBDITI

IMPIETATIS PERDUELLIONIS ET SCHISMATIS HOSTEM
[ACERRIMUM
DEI REGIS ET GREGIS INIMICI VIDERUNT AGNOVERUNT
[ADMIRABANTUR
QUEMQ

TALIS ET TANTUS CUM ESSET NOVEM CONJURATI PARICIDAE
[FANATICO FURORE PERCITI
IN METROPOLITICAE SUAE CIVITATIS VICINIO LUCENTE
[MERIDIANO SOLE CHARISSIMA FILIA
PRIMOGENITA ET DOMESTICIS FAMULIS VULNERATIS
[LACHRIMANTIBUS RECLAMANTIBUS
IN GENUA UT PROIPSIS ETIAM ORARET PROLAPSUM QUAM
[PLURIMIS VULNERIBUS
CONFOSSUM SCLOPETIS GLADIIS PUGIONIBUS HORRENDUM
IN MODUM TRUCIDARUNT
3^0 DIE MAIJ 1679 AETATIS SUAE 61

Translation

[DOM - Deo Optimo Maximo, to God, the best and the greatest]

THIS LOFTY MAUSOLEUM PROTECTS
THE MOST PRECIOUS ASHES OF A MOST HOLY PRELATE, A
[MOST SAGACIOUS SENATOR, A MOST SACRED MARTYR;
FOR HERE LIES
ALL THAT REMAINS UNDER THE SUN OF *JAMES SHARP*,
[DOCTOR OF DIVINITY, MOST REVEREND FATHER IN CHRIST,
ARCHBISHOP OF ST ANDREWS, PRIMATE OF ALL SCOTLAND
[ETC.,
WHO

WAS SEEN, RECOGNIZED AND ADMIRED
AS A PROFESSOR OF PHILOSOPHY AND THEOLOGY BY THE
[UNIVERSITY,
AS A PRIEST, A DOCTOR AND A CHIEF PRIEST BY THE CHURCH,
AS A PRIME MINISTER IN ECCLESIASTICAL AS IN CIVIL
AFFAIRS BY SCOTLAND,
AS AN ADVOCATE OF THE RESTORATION OF THE MONAR -
[CHICAL RULE OF THE MOST SERENE CHARLES THE
[SECOND BY BRITAIN,
AS A RENEWER OF THE ORDER OF BISHOPS IN SCOTLAND BY
[THE CHRISTIAN WORLD,
AS AN EXAMPLE OF PIETY, AN ANGEL OF PEACE, AN ORACLE
[OF WISDOM, AND AN IMAGE OF GRAVITY BY GOOD
AND FAITHFUL SUBJECTS AND AS A MOST KEEN ENEMY OF

IMPIETY, OF TREACHERY AND SCHISM BY THE
[ENEMIES OF GOD, THE KING AND THE FLOCK;

AND YET WHO,

FOR ALL THAT HE WAS OF SUCH A KIND AND SO GREAT,
                  [WAS SLAUGHTERED IN A HORRID MANNER,
HAVING FALLEN ON HIS KNEES THAT HE MIGHT YET PRAY
                            [FOR HIS OWN PEOPLE;
HE WAS PIERCED THROUGH BY VERY MANY WOUNDS OF
                  [PISTOLS, SWORDS AND DAGGERS,
BY NINE FORSWORN PARRICIDES EXCITED BY FANATICAL
RAGE IN THE FULL SUNLIGHT OF MIDDAY IN THE VICINITY
                  [OF HIS OWN METROPOLITAN CITY
IN SPITE OF THE TEARS AND PROTESTS OF HIS MOST DEAR
                            [FIRST-BORN DAUGHTER,
AND OF HIS DOMESTIC SERVANTS, WHO HAD BEEN
WOUNDED; ON THE THIRD DAY OF MAY, 1679, 61 YEARS OF
                                      [AGE.

(This monument, erected by his son, Sir William Sharp, was made in the
Netherlands from Greek and Italian marble, and placed in the church in
December of the same year, 1679).

On a May morning in 1679 Archbishop James Sharp was riding in his
carriage accompanied by his daughter when the party of eight or nine
murderers came upon him on a remote part of the road. These murderers
included James Russell, William Dingwall, John Balfour of Kinloch,
David Hackston of Rathillet and Andrew Guilline. They had started the
day by looking for an oppressive agent of the Archbishop, one William
Carmichael, but decided to go after the Archbishop himself when they
heard that his coach was in the neighbourhood.

They pursued the coach, fired shots after it, and succeeded in bringing it
to a standstill. Shots were fired into the coach but did not take effect, and
one of the assassins forced the Archbishop out with his sword. From the
start it seems to have been clear that they intended to kill Sharp, and once
he was out on the road he spent a great deal of time on his knees begging
for his life. Perhaps, also, the murderers needed some time to nerve
themselves for the deed, and they scolded their victim, casting up his past
misdeeds to him before firing a volley at him as he knelt on the road. This
did not kill him and Russell, the leader of the party, seems to have decided
that he must be finished off with swords, in case he was bullet-proof by
reason of his compact with the Devil. David Hackston of Rathillet was not
enthusiastic about completing the murder, and he united his pleas with

those of Sharp himself and his daughter, but to no avail.

The whole gruesome episode took three-quarters of an hour in the middle of a busy countryside, and yet the murderers got clean away. The only two who were ever caught and punished, ironically, were David Hackston and Andrew Guilline, both of whom had begged Russell to have mercy.[2] (See *Airdsmoss and Claremont* for their respective fates, as well as *Cupar* and *Magus Muir*. See also map II on p.74.)

This murder ushered in the last phase of the Covenanting episode of the 17th century, the Battles of Drumclog and Bothwell Brig following directly from it, and from them the three stages of the Cameronian phenomenon — Cameron's death at Airdsmoss in 1680, the Cargill excommunications at Torwood and the career of James Renwick from 1683 to 1688 including the Killing Time.

(2) *Rutherford (Cathedral churchyard)*

M

S   .   R

Here lyes the Reverend M[r] Samuell
Rutherfoord Professor of Divinity in
the University of S[t] Andreus who Died
March the 29 1661.

What tongu what Pen or Skill of Men
Can Famous Rutherfoord Commend
His Learning justly rasid his Fame
True GODliness Adornd HIS Name
He did converse with things Above
Acquainted with Emmanuels Love
Most orthodox He Was And Sound
And Many Errors Did Confound
For Zions King and Zions Cause
And Scotlands Covenanted LAWS
Mostly constantly he Did Contend
Until His Time Was At An End
Than He Wan TO the Full Fruition
OF That which He Had Seen in Vision.

For details of Samuel Rutherfo(o)rd's career, see *Anwoth*.

[1] Thomson p197
[2] For fuller treatments of the episode, see Wodrow iii   pp40-52,
  Kirkton pp403-482 &c.

Sanquhar (NS 796 096)

The village of Sanquhar was the scene of two dramatic episodes in Covenanting times: the declaration of war by Richard Cameron in 1680, the prelude to the Battle of Airdsmoss; and James Renwick's 1685 declaration against the new King James VII and II. (These are the two best known of a whole series of Sanquhar Declarations that continued until well into the eighteenth century.) Both are commemorated in the modern obelisk in the High Street. At the south of the village, on a high mound, stand the grim ruins of Crichton Peel, sometime stronghold of the Duke of Queensberry, Lord High Treasurer of Scotland and patron of John Graham of Claverhouse. (At the same point the A76 intersects with the Southern Upland Way, by which the energetic pedestrian may reach Allan's Cairn, the Enterkin Pass and other points of Covenanting interest.)

To the east of Sanquhar, in the high hills overlooking the Nithsdale Kirkconnel, an unlisted and partially unmetalled road will lead the visitor to Blackgannoch. See *Friarminnan* for details of Blackgannoch, Friarminnan and Auchtitench; see also *Airdsmoss* and Introduction pp16-21 for further details of the Sanquhar Declarations etc.

Inscription (Sanquhar obelisk)

IN COMMEMORATION OF
THE TWO FAMOUS
SANQUHAR DECLARATIONS
which were published
on this spot where stood
the ancient cross of the Burgh;
the one by
the Rev. Richard Cameron,
on the 22nd of June, 1680;
the other by
the Rev. James Renwick
on the 25th of May 1685;
"the Killing Time"

If you would know the nature of their crime
Then read the story of that killing time.

Sorn (NS 554 266)

HERE ... LYES ... CORC
WOOD WHO WAS SHOT
AT TINKHORN HILL BY BL
OODY JOHN REID TRUPER
FOR HIS ADHERANCE TO
THE WORD OF COD AND
THE COVENANTED VORK
OF REFORMOTION 1688

Sorn Parish Church stands at the west end of the charming village of Sorn, just over the hill from Mauchline (on the B743). Set into the church wall are two stones, an original and a replacement, commemorating George Wood, shot at Tincorn Hill outside Sorn in 1688 during a dragnet operation following the Houston rescue. (See *Stonepark*.) George Wood, who at 16 was perhaps the youngest Covenanting martyr, is also said to have been the last (following Renwick, who was hanged in February 1688). The style of the first stone in particular is primitive both in lettering and in spelling.

Sorn Parish was the birthplace of the great field-preacher Alexander Peden, who had the uncanny gift of prophecy. He also died within the boundaries of the parish in 1686 after a life of wandering, persecution and imprisonment. (For Peden see also *Cumnock*, *Kilmarnock*, *Tarbolton*, *Bass Rock*, *Ayr* and *Priesthill*.)

Inscriptions

(1)

HERE LIES GORG
WOOD WHO WAS SHOT
AT TINKHORN HILL BY BL
OODY JOHN ReID TRVPeR
FOR HIS ADHeRANCE TO
THe WORD OF GOD AND
THE cOVeNaNTeD VORK
OF ReFORMaTION 1688

(2)

TO
PRESERVE FROM OBLIVION
THE FATE OF
GEORGE WOOD
WHO WAS SHOT AT TINKHORNHILL
MDCLXXXIII
FOR HIS ADHERENCE TO THE WORD OF
GOD
AND THE COVENTED WORK OF
REFORMATION
AND TO MANIFEST GRATITUDE
FOR THE INVALUABLE
RELIGIOUS PRIVILEGES
NOW ENJOYED

(Note that the date on the second inscription is wrong.)

Stonehouse (NS 748 470)

Old St Ninian's graveyard contains one of the few Covenanters who fell at Drumclog, the sole battle won by the Covenanters over Government forces, on 1st June, 1679. Ironically, the commander on that occasion was John Graham of Claverhouse. For the other Drumclog victims, see *Loudoun, Newmilns, Strathaven* and *Lesmahagow.*

Inscription (older stone)

VIVE MEMOR LETHI FUGIT HORA

Here lays or near This Ia[s] Thomas
Who uas shot In . a : Rancounter . At .
Drumclog on June j[st] 1679 ~
By Bloody Graham of Clavers
House for his adherance to the
Word of God and Scotland[s]
Covenanted Work of Reform
ation. - Rev. j2 ii

(Illegible)

(reverse)

Memento Mori
This Hero brave Who doth Ly
here
In truth[s] defence he did Appear,
And to Crist[s] Cause He firmly Stood
Wntill He seal[d] it uith his blood.
With Swor[d] in han[d] upon the field
He lost his Life, yet did not Yeild.
His daYs did End in great Renown,
And he obtaine[d] the Martyr[s] ~
croun.

Stonehouse is a small village on the A71 between Strathaven and the M74.

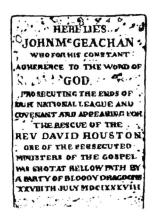

Stonepark (NS 593 195)

On 20th June,1688, an associate of the recently-executed James Renwick named David Houston, who had been arrested in Ireland, was being taken to Edinburgh under military escort to stand trial. After spending the night at Cumnock, the party had to make for Muirkirk along the line of the present A70, which runs beside the Bello Water. About 3 miles out of Cumnock, near the present village of Logan, a large party of armed Covenanters attacked the escort on the Bello Path. The Rev. Houston was rescued, but he had been bound to his horse and during the rescue he fell under the animal and was dragged upside down for some distance; he sustained brain injury and never recovered his faculties, although he lived for many years after.[1]

Several soldiers were killed or severely wounded during the action, and one rescuer, John MacGeachan, was mortally wounded: he made for his home at Auchengibbert but died before he could get there. The Stonepark monument marks the spot where he died.

Inscription (original)

> HeRe LYes JOHN MAC
> GeAGHAN WHO FOR HIS
> CONSTANT ADHeRANCe
> TO THe WORD OF GOD
> PROSeCUTING THe eNDS
> OF OUR NATIONAL AND
> SOLEMN LeAGUe AND COUe
> NANTS AND APPeARING
> FOR THe ReSCUe OF Mr
> DAVID HOUSTON ONe OF
> THe PeRSeCUTeD MINIS
> TeRS OF THe GOSPeL
>   SHOT AT BELLO
> PATH BY A PARTY OF THe
> BLOODY DRAGOONS
> JULY 28 1688
> eReCTeD ANNO 1728

[The original gravestone, inscribed as above, is half-buried and probably broken, alongside the commemorative stone of 1836 mentioned by Thomson. The date given on both monuments is probably wrong, the historian Wodrow supporting the date 20th June, 1688.]

The Stonepark site is south-east of Cumnock, to the east of the road connecting the village of Logan with the A76 that runs alonside the railway for part of its length; it is now enclosed in a quadrangle of trees reached by a rough track along one end of a field. Intending visitors are advised to consult A & I Patrick & Sons of Wee Auchengibbert (tel. Cumnock 20569) on whose ground the monument stands.

[1] Wodrow iv p442, Hewison ii p511, Thomson p341.

Straiton (NS 381 049)

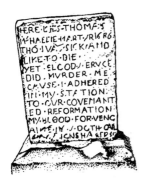

The original tombstone of Thomas McHaffie, together with a nineteenth-century replacement, stands at the west front of Straiton Parish Church. McHaffie, who was in flight (appearing in the List of Fugitives, 5th May, 1684), had been hiding out in a cave on Linfern Farm, but had become so ill that he had had to take refuge in a house; there, in 1686, he was discovered by a party of dragoons, taken out and, after refusing the Abjuration Oath, shot. According to local informants the cave, which was on the banks of the Palmullan Burn, is no longer traceable because of landslides. Thomson says that the stone marking the place where McHaffie was shot used to be visible on Linfern Farm, but I have been unable to trace it.[1]

Inscription

HERE . LIES . THOMAS
McHAFFIE . MARTYR . 1686
THO . I . WAS . SICK . AND .
LIKE . TO . DIE
YET . BLOODY . BRUCE
DID . MURDER . ME
CAUSE . I . ADHERED
IN . MY . STATION
TO . OUR . COVENANT
ED . REFORMATION .
MY . BLOOD . FOR . VENG
ANCE . NOU . DOTH . CALL
VPON . ZIONS . HATERS . (ALL)*

* Apparently missing from original inscription

Straiton is south-east of Maybole at the junction between the B7045 and the B741.

[1] Simpson *Traditions* p411, Thomson p316

Strathaven (NS 742 447)

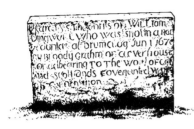

Strathaven is a point on the circle of Covenanting sites that has the remote Logan House as its hub. Other points on the circumference include Blackwood, Lesmahagow, Skellyhill, Priesthill, Muirkirk and Auchingilloch. The town of Strathaven is also on the direct route between Kilmarnock and Edinburgh, and it lay on Claverhouse's retreat from Drumclog in 1679. The townspeople tried to interdict his passage, and, according to Aiton, attacked him in a narrow road called the "Hole-closs".[1] Before they got away, Claverhouse wrote, the Government forces left "a dousain on the place" i.e. 12 dragoons were killed.[2] A location near Strathaven is called "The Trumpeter's Well"; at least one of the dragoons, a bugler of no more than 14 years, was trapped and ended his life at the bottom of a deep well.

One of the Covenanters who fell in the Drumclog action is buried in Strathaven churchyard: William Dingwall, who was also one of the assassins of Archbishop Sharp on 3rd May, 1679, less than a month before Drumclog. (See *Magus Muir* and *St Andrews*). For the other Whig victims of Drumclog, see *Loudoun, Newmilns, Stonehouse* and *Lesmahagow*.

The graveyard, which is high on a hill overlooking the town, also contains two martyrs, William Paterson and John Barrie, about whom little is known except that the date of their execution, April 1685, brings it within the most intense period of the "Killing Time". (See Introduction p21.)

Inscription
(1) Dingwall

(Erected in the year 1732, and renewed 1833)

>Heare Lys The Corps OF WILLIam
>DingWaLL Who Was Shot in a Ran
>counter at DrumCLog Jun 1 1679
>By BLOOdy GRahm OF Claverhouse.
>FOr adhearing TO The Word OF God,
>And Scotlands COVenanted WorK
>OF ReForrmations.

(reverse)

>This Hero Brave Who Here doth ly
>Was Persecute By Tyrrany -
>Yet To The Truth He Firmly StooD
>Gainst Foes Resisting To The BLOOD
>HimSeLF & Th' goSPeL did deFenD

TiLL For Christs Cause His Life
DiD enD -

(2) *Paterson/Barrie (flat table stone)*
Outer edge

> HERE LYES THE CORPSES
> OF WILLIAM PATERSON AND JOHN
> BARRIE VHO VAS
> SHOT TO DEATH FOR THER ADHERING TO THE

centre

> WORD OF GOD AND
> OUR COUENANTS
> —ANNO 1685.
> HERE LYS TUO MAR
> TYRS SEUERALLY
>   WHO FELL
> BY CAPTAIN
> INGLES AND BY
> BLOODY BELL
> POSTERITY SHALL
> KNOU THEYRE SHOT
> TO DEATH
> AS SACRIFICES
>   —TO POPISH
>   WRATH.

Strathaven lies at a crossroads between the A71, the A723 and the A726, on a direct route between Kilmarnock and Edinburgh. (See map on p.51.)

[1] Aiton p59
[2] Claverhouse p30

Tarbolton (NS 430 272)

The outlawed preacher Alexander Peden started his career as a schoolmaster in the village of Tarbolton. Later, in July 1685 (or 1684, according to Wodrow), William Shillilaw was buried here after having been shot at the Woodhead. According to local tradition, Shillilaw was arrested after Lieutenant Lauder "saw him cross the road". This might be another case of a completely arbitrary killing (cf. *Colmonell*), but Thomson says that the shooting took place "after a few of the usual questions". It is difficult to be sure in the absence of more positive evidence, but it is not unlikely that this was a case of refusal of the Abjuration Oath.

This Covenanter was only 18 years old at the time of his death. Wodrow says that after having shot Shillilaw, Lauder was going to execute his employer and two other people, but the soldiers restrained their lieutenant, on the grounds that "one in a day was sufficient."[1] The tombstone will be found against the wall of the Parish Church.

Inscription

HERE LYES
William Shillilau who
was shot at Woodhead
by lieut. Lauder for his
adherence to the word of
GOD and Scotlands cove
nanted work of *REFORMATION*
1685 Erected in 1727.
Renewed 1819 by Wm Drinnan.

Tarbolton is just off the A758 between Ayr and Mauchline.

[1] Wodrow iv p172

Tweedsmuir (NT 101 246)

Tweedsmuir graveyard contains one martyr stone, that of John Hunter. *A Cloud of Witnesses* says, "The said Col. James Douglas and his party shot to death John Hunter for no alleged cause but running out from the house of Corehead, in the parish of Moffat, the same year, 1685."[1] A whim of such brutality is unlikely, however, if only because the tombstone tells a different story. Sources say that Hunter was with a companion, Welsh, the farmer of Tweedhopefoot; when the soldiers approached, both ran from Corehead, a lonely place near the Devil's Beeftub. Hunter was caught and shot, but Welsh got away: he reached the farmhouse of Carterhope, and fell asleep from pure exhaustion in front on the fire. The dragoons reached the house too, not realizing that their quarry was already there, and the farmer's wife, to divert suspicion, hit Welsh between the shoulder-blades, and ordered him not to be so lazy but to go out and go about his work. The soldiers let him go without realizing who he was.[2]

Inscription

Here lyes
The body of John Hunter
Martyr who was cruely
Murdered at Corehead
By Col James Douglas and
His party for his adherance
To the Word of God and
Scotlands covenanted
Work of Reformation
1685.
Erected in the year 1726.

(reverse)

When Zions King was Robbed
of his Right
His witnesses in Scotland
put to flight
When popish prelats &
Indulgancie
Combin'd 'gainst Christ to
Ruine presbytrie
All who would not unto
their idols bow
They socht them out &
whom they found they slew
For owning of Christ's cause
I then did die
My blood for vengeance on
His en'mies did cry.

A nineteenth-century obelisk also stands in the churchyard,
inscribed

IN MEMORY OF / JOHN HUNTER / MARTYR /
WHOSE / GRAVESTONE / IS IN / THE LOWER PART /
OF THIS / CHURCHYARD / 1837.

JOHN HUNTER
a Tweedsmuir lad
was accidentally visiting a
sick friend at Corehead when
timely in the morning he was
surprised with Douglas and
his dragoons. He fled to the
hill a great way, but one

named Scott, being well horsed
compassed him and came
before him. He was most
barbarouslie shot through
the body, felled on the
head with the neck of a
gun, and casted headlong
over a high steep craig.
- *CONTEMPORARY RECORD*

J. H.
1660-1685

A monument stands at the side of the A701 overlooking the Devil's
Beeftub and Corehead. The Devil's Beeftub, a colossal hole in the hills
north of Moffat, is probably the place where John Hunter was shot, trying
to run up the steep slope which within the Beeftub is more than 150 metres
high, and another stone on the slope marks the spot.

Tweedsmuir lies about 12 kilometres north of the Devil's Beeftub on the
A701.

[1] *Cloud* Appendix p383
[2] Simpson p114; Thomson pp447-449

Twynholm (NX 664 543)

Twynholm Parish Churchyard is the rest-
ing-place of one of the party of five men
surprised and summarily executed on
Kirkconnel Moor just north of here by Sir
Robert Grierson of Lagg in 1685. (For
further details, see *Anwoth, Balmaghie* and
Kirkconnel Moor.)

Inscription

MEMEN (Skull & Crossbones)
TO MORI
HERE
LYES ANDREU
MCROBERT WHO WAS
SURPRJSED AND
SHOT TO DEATH
IN THE PAROCH OF

(reverse)   (skull)
                         TONGLAND BY
                         GRIER OF LAGG
                         FOR HIS ADHERE
                         ENCE TO SCOT
                         LANDS REFORMATION
                         COVENANTS NATION
                         AL AND SOLEMN
                         LEAGUE   1685.

Twynholm is a small village on the A75 north-west of Kirkcudbright.

Tynron (NX 808 931)

This small parish churchyard near Moniaive (A702) is the resting place of a boy of 19, William Smith, who was shot by order of Sir Robert Laurie of Maxwelton after Smith had been arrested while working in the fields belonging to his father, the tenant farmer of Hill. Smith had refused to answer under interrogation; he may have been a Renwickite, and he may therefore have refused the Abjuration Oath. The historian Wodrow gives 3rd March, 1685, as the date of execution, but the tombstone gives 29th March.[1]

The story goes that when Smith was arrested and questioned, his father waited upon his laird, Sir Robert Laurie: Sir Robert had had a daughter married that day, and old Smith thought that this might soften his mood. Unfortunately, Sir Robert not only threatened the arresting officer, Cornet Bailie, with being reported to the Council for delaying the execution, but ordered the body to be buried at the threshold of Hill farmhouse, so that everybody entering or leaving had to step over the body of the executed son of the household. The body, according to the sources, was not reburied in Tynron Churchyard until after the 1688 Revolution.[2]

Inscription

                         HERE LYETH WILLIAM
                         SMITH SON TO WILLIAM
                         SMITH IN HILL WHO FOR
                         HIS ADHERING TO THE COVE
                         NANTED WORK OF REFOR
                         MATION WAS SHOT AT
                         MINNYHIVE MOSS THE 29
                         DAY OF MARCH 1685 HIS AGE

19 YEARS, THIS DEED WAS
NOT DONE BY A COUNCIL
OF WAR BUT BY COUNTRYMEN
WITHOUT SYSE

(at foot of and at right angles to main inscription)
I WILLIAM SMITH NOW HERE DO LY
ONCE MARTYR'D FOR CHRIST'S VERITY
DOUGLAS OF STENHOUSE LAWRIE OF MAXWELTOU
N
CAUSED CORONET BAILIE GIVE ME MARTRDOM
WHAT CRUELTY THEY TO ME CORPSE THEN US'D
LIVING MAY JUDGE: ME BURIAL THEY REFUSED.

The last line of the verse transcribed above may hint at some confusion of evidence with regard to Smith's burial allegedly in his father's house; the practice of refusing normal Christian burial to executed Covenanters was widespread. See e.g. *Kilmarnock, Ayr* and *Auchencloy*. It may account for the fact that many recorded victims of the persecution do not have identifiable graves.

[1] Wodrow iv p202   [2] Shields p37; Hewison ii p468

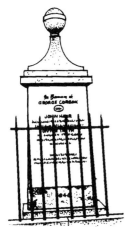

Waistland (NS 664 127)

This monument is situated two miles east of Afton Bridgend (New Cumnock) on rising farm-land bordering the A76. It is quite prominent on the skyline on the west side of the road. See *Corsgellioch* for a conjectural and partial reconstruction of what may have happened when George Corson and John Hair were shot here in 1685.

Inscription

In Memory of
GEORGE CORSON
and
JOHN HAIR
who were shot near this place
in 1685 for their adharance to
DIVINE TRUTH
and attachment to the

Covenanted Reformation
of 1638-50
"They lived unknown
"Till persecution dragged them into fame
"And chased them up to Heaven."
1845

I do not know if there was an earlier stone at Waistland.

The owner of the property at Waistland is Mr Alan Young of Barshare Farm, Cumnock (tel Cumnock [01290] 420731).

Wellwood (NS 674 256)

The farm on which this monument is situated is Upper Wellwood, which is reached along a farm road running south and west from the A70 just beyond the western boundary of Muirkirk. The stone commemorating William Adam is on the banks of the Proscribe Burn, which has to be reached through the complex of venerable farm buildings (the principal one dated 1605). The owner of Upper Wellwood, who should be contacted by intending visitors, is Mr Anderson (tel Muirkirk [01290] 661206).

Traditional sources state that William Adam was waiting at a rendezvous beside the Proscribe Burn for the arrival of his fiancée, who was a pious young woman. To pass the time he took out his Bible and started to read it. Becoming engrossed, he failed to notice the approach of the dragoons, who rode up to him and shot him on the spot. His fiancée approached, passing the dragoons as they rode away across a wooden bridge over the River Ayr. One of the soldiers tried to push her off the bridge with the flat of his sword, whereupon the spirited girl seized the sword, snapped it in two and threw the bits in the river. She then ran forward and found William lying dead on the ground, as she had feared hearing the sound of gunfire a few minutes earlier.[1]

This account has echoes of the case at Cambusnethan (q.v.) where dragoons were rendered suspicious by the sight of Arthur Hislop reading a Bible: anybody doing that would be sure to be a rebel or a conventicler —so they shot at him, startled him so much that he threw the Bible in the air, and rode up to him and killed him with a sword. Also, at Barrhill, Murchie and Meiklewrick were supposed to have been shot merely because they were carrying Bibles. In that case the fiancée of one of the victims comes into the story too; she and another girl are said to have buried the bodies at night.

John Cochrane of Waterside (son of the rebel Sir John Cochrane of Ochiltree) has a different version: he says that Dalzeal and Strachan, finding William Adam "hiding himself in a bush, did stick him dead without ever speaking a word unto him."[2] Wodrow says Adam was not being sought for any specific offence—merely that he was caught, perhaps acting suspiciously, and shot out of hand.[3] The epitaph, however, does not imply random, arbitrary or careless killing.

Inscription

Here lies WILLIAM ADAM
who was
shot in
this place
by CAP[T] DALZEAL
and his party for his
adherance to the
word of GOD
and Scotlands
covenanted work
of reformation
March 1685

[1] Simpson p9; Thomson p150
[2] Quoted Hewison ii p460.
[3] Wodrow iv p241

Wigtown NX 437 556)

This one-time county town on the shores of the Solway was the scene of one of the most celebrated executions of the Covenanting period, the drowning of Margaret Wilson and Margaret Maclauchlan. The justiciary commission which ordered the drowning included Sir Robert Grierson of Lagg.

Margaret and Agnes Wilson, both radical Conventiclers and probably Renwickites, appear to have ventured back into their home town where they were arrested and brought to trial on charges of conventicling, together with an older woman, Margaret Mclauchlan, and one other, Margaret Maxwell. The last-named took the Abjuration Oath, and it seems the other three did not. The three were all condemned to death by drowning, the preferred method of execution for women, and one endorsed in a Privy Council instruction (13th January, 1685).

Agnes Wilson, a child of thirteen, was released after her father had paid a bond of £100, but her sister Margaret and Margaret Maclauchlan were tied to stakes below high water mark at the Bladnoch outside Wigtown on 11th May, 1685. Both were drowned by the incoming tide although, after Margaret Maclauchlan had been drowned, Margaret Wilson, a girl of only eighteen, was half released and asked again whether she would take the Abjuration Oath. She refused and was thrust back under the water where she drowned. This was done apparently in spite of a stay of execution ordered by the Privy Council on 30th April, 1685.[1]

Some of the above detail may be apocryphal — the first account of the executions was given only in 1711 — but there is nothing inherently improbable in any of it; some historians and commentators have tried to suggest that the drownings may not have taken place at all. It may be worth noting that to go by the inscription at Allan's Cairn (q.v.), Lagg's soldiers were involved in the killing of another woman, Margaret Gracie, and such killings were very rare indeed in the Covenanting period. (See *Corsgellioch*, and Introduction p21 , for discussions of this issue, and of the timing of the Wigtown and other executions in "The Killing Time".)

Three other martyrs —Johnston, Milroy and Walker—who were hanged for refusing the Abjuration Oath— are also buried at Wigtown.

Inscriptions
(1) *Wilson*
(i) *At right angles to main inscription, at side of stone*

> HERE LIES MARGRAT
> WILLSON DOUGHTER
> TO GILBERT WILLSON
> IN GLENVERNOCH
> WHO WAS DROUNED
> ANNO 1685 AGED 18 C

(ii) *Main inscription*

> LET EARTH AND STONE STILL WITNES BEAR
> HEIR LYES A VIRGINE MARTYRE HERE
> MURTHER'D FOR OUNING CHRIST SUPREAME
> HEAD OF HIS CHURCH AND NO MORE CRIME
> BUT NOT ABJURING PRESBYTRY
> AND HER NOT OUNING PRELACY

THEY HER CONDEM'D, BUT UNJUST LAW,
OF HEAVEN NOR HELL THEY STOOD NO AW
WITHIN THE SEA TYD TO A STAKE
SHE SUFFERED FOR CHRIST JESUS SAKE
THE ACTORS OF THIS CRUEL CRIME
WAS LAGG . STRACHAN . WINRAM . AND GRHAME
NEITHER YOUNG YEARES NOR YET OLD AGE
COULD STOP THE FURY OF THERE RAGE

(2) *Maclauchlan*

MEMENTO MORI
HERE LYES
MARGRET LACHLANE
WHO WAS BY UN
JUST LAW SENTENC
ED TO DIE BY LAGG[*]
STRACHANE WIN
RAME AND GRHAME
AND TYED TO A
STAKE WITHIN THE
FLOOD FOR HER

(reverse)

(skull and crossbones)

ADHERENCE
TO SCOTLANDS RE
FORMATION COVE
NANTS NATIONAL
AND SOLEMN LEAGUE
AGED 63   1685

[* *Vertically, at right angles to the ends of the lines, the words*
SURNAMED GRIER]

(3) Johnston / Milroy / Walker
(i) *Upper edge*

MEMENTO MORI

(ii) *Main inscription*

N
HERE LYES WILLIAM JOHNSTO
JOHN MILROY GEORGE WALKER
WHO WAS WITHOUT SENTE
NCE OF LAW HANGED BY MA
JOR WINRAM FOR THEIR ADHER

ANCE TO SCOTLAND'S REFOR
MATION COVENANTS NATIO
NAL AND SOLAM LEAGWE.
1685

The three commemorative stones mentioned above have been gathered together into one railed enclosure in the Old Churchyard in Wigtown.

Also at Wigtown are a tall obelisk (just outside the town), and at the reputed site of the drowning— now dry land— the free-standing stone representation of a stake.

[1] Walker i p329; Defoe p266; Hewison ii pp474-477; Thomson pp420-429; Cowan pp126-128

Appendix 1

Covenanters and associates executed or otherwise killed through government action during the period 1660-1688 (A) In Edinburgh, (B) In the
rest of the country excluding Orkney and (C) In Orkney

A   In Edinburgh

"From may 27th 1661 that the noble Marquess of Argyle suffered to the
17th of feb 1688 that Mr James Renwick suffered were execut at Edinburg
about an hundered of Noblemen Gentlmen Ministers & others noble
martyres for JESUS CHRIST — the most part of them lys here."
*(Original Martyrs' Monument at Greyfriars Churchyard, Edinburgh —now at
Huntly House Museum)*

No.	Name of martyr, place of origin where known, brief details and/or references	Execution
1660-1665		
1	Archibald Campbell, Marquis of Argyll	27/5/1661
2	James Guthrie, Minister of Stirling	1/6/1661
3	Lieutenant William Govan	1/6/1661
4	Archibald Johnston, Lord Wariston	22/7/1663
1666: the aftermath of the Pentland Rising		
5	Captain Andrew Arnot	7/12/1666
6	Major John McCulloch	7/12/1666
7	Gavin Hamilton in Maudslie in Carluke	7/12/1666
8	John Gordon of Knockbreck	7/12/1666
9	Robert Gordon	7/12/1666
10	Cristall Strang, Kilbride	7/12/1666
11	John Parker, waulker in Kirkbride Parishin	7/12/1666
12	John Ross in Mauchline	7/12/1666
13	James Hamilton, tenant in Kithemoor	7/12/1666
14	John Shiells in Titwood	7/12/1666

*According to Defoe (p163) Thomas Paterson died of his wounds before execution. The right hands
of the foregoing ten were sent to Lanark; the heads of the Hamiltons, Parker and Strang were sent to
Hamilton (see entry), of Ross and Shiells (Shields) to Kilmarnock (see entry), of the Gordons and of
McCulloch to Kirkcudbright and of Arnot to the Watergate.*

No.	Name of martyr, place of origin where known, brief details and/or references		Execution
15	John Neilson of Corsock		14/12/1666
16	Alexander Robertson		14/12/1666
17	George Crauford in Cumnock		14/12/1666
18	John Gordon in Irongray		14/12/1666
19	Hugh McKail		22/12/1666
20	Humphrey Colquhoun		22/12/1666
21	Mungo Kaip in Evandale		22/12/1666
22	Ralph Shiells collier in Ayr		22/12/1666
23	John Wodrow merchant in Glasgow		22/12/1666
24	John Wilson in Kilmaurs		22/12/1666

A fifth man may have died on 14th December; his name may have been John Lindsay.

1667-1677

No executions of Covenanters are recorded in Edinburgh during these years.

1678-1688

No.	Name		Execution
25	James Mitchell		18/1/1678
26	James Learmont		27/9/1678
27	John Kid		14/8/1679
28	John King		14/8/1679
29	David Hackston of Rathillet		30/9/1680
30	Archibald Alison (Evandale)		13/8/1680
31	John Malcolm of St John's Clachan of Dalry		13/8/1680

Mitchell was the perpetrator of a bungled attempt on the life of Archbishop Sharp 10 years earlier on 11/7/1668. Learmont was concerned in the killing of John Hogg, a soldier, at the Whitekirk conventicle on 5th May 1678. Kid and King were conventicling preachers captured at the Battle of Bothwell Brig after having been present at Drumclog. Hackston was one of the assassins of Archbishop Sharp and was captured at Airdsmoss as were Alison and Malcolm.

No.	Name		Execution
32	James Skene	Cargillite	1/12/1680
33	Archibald Stewart (Bo'ness)	Cargillite	1/12/1680
34	John Potter (Uphall)	Cargillite	1/12/1680
35	Isobel Alison (Perth)	Cargillite	26/1/1681
36	Marion Harvey (Bo'ness)	Cargillite	26/1/1681
37	William Gougar (Bo'ness)	Cargillite	11/3/1681
38	Robert Sangster (Stirlingshire)	Cargillite	11/3/1681
39	Christopher Miller (Stirlingshire)	Cargillite	11/3/1681
40	Adam Philip (Fife)	Cargillite	13/7/1681
41	Laurence Hay (Fife)	Cargillite; *see entry for Cupar.*	13/7/1681
42	Andrew Pitulloch (Largo)	Cargillite; *see entry for Cupar.*	13/7/1681

No.	Name of martyr, place of origin where known, brief details and/or references		Execution
43	Rev. Donald Cargill		27/7/1681
44	Walter Smith		27/7/1681
45	James Boig (student)		27/7/1681

The Rev Donald Cargill, the successor to Richard Cameron, was a radical field-preacher and co-author of the"Queensferry Paper" and excommunicated King Charles II and his advisers at Torwood, Stirlingshire, in September 1680. Smith and Boig were arrested with Cargill at Covington Mill on 12th July, 1681.

46	William Thomson (Fife)	Cargillite	27/7/1681
47	William Cuthill (Bo'ness)	Cargillite	27/7/1681
48	Robert Garnock (Stirling)		10/10/1681

Garnock, a Stirling hammerman or blacksmith, was the leader of the irreconcilable prisoners in Greyfriars Churchyard (see entry for Edinburgh) after the Battle of Bothwell Brig.

49	Patrick Forman (Alloa)	Cargillite	10/10/1681
50	David Farrie	Cargillite	10/10/1681
51	James Stewart	Cargillite	10/10/1681
52	Alexander Russell	Cargillite	10/10/1681
53	Robert Gray (Northumberland)		19/5/1682
	(Refused Test; repudiated King's authority).		
54	Thomas Lauchlan *(participant in Battle of Bothwell Brig)*		16/8/1682
55	James Robertson (Stonehouse)	Cargillite	15/12/1682
56	William Cochran (Carnduff)	Cargillite	15/12/1682
57	John Finlay (Kilmarnock)	Cargillite	15/12/1682
	(See entry for Kilmarnock)		
58	Alexander Home (Humetoun) conventicler; "armed rebellion".		21(?) or 29/12/1682
59	John Wilson (Lanark) *(participant in the Battle of Bothwell Brig)*		16/5/1683
60	David MacMillan *(participant in Battle of Bothwell Brig)*		16/5/1683
61	Andrew Guilline *(assassin of Archbishop Sharp; see entry for Claremont).*		13/7/1683
62	John Whitelaw (New Monkland)		30/11/1683
	(participant in Drumclog, Bothwell Brig etc.)		
63	Arthur Bruce (Dalserf)		30/11/1683
	(as Whitelaw; refused to call Archbishop's death "murder").		
64	John Cochran (Lesmahagow) (as Whitelaw and Bruce)		30/11/1683
65	George Martin (Old Dailly)		22/2/1684
	(denial of King's authority; see entry for Old Dailly.)		
66	John Kerr or Gilry (Hounam), *as Martin,*		22/2/1684
67	James Muir (Cessford-Boat), *as Martin and Kerr,*		22/2/1684
68	James Dick (Edinburgh)		5/3/1684

Dick was a participant in the Battle of Bothwell Brig and a follower of John Welch. (See entry for Irongray). He escaped while under sentence to death in a mass breakout from Edinburgh Tolbooth on 16th September, 1683, but was recaptured in March 1684.

| 69 | Captain John Paton of Meadowhead | 9 / 5 / 1684 |
| | *See Intorduction p.17 and entry for Fenwick* | |

No.	Name of martyr, place of origin where known, brief details and/or references	Execution
70	Arthur Taiket (Hamilton) *(Blackloch conventicler; Bothwell participant)*	30/7/1684
71	Thomas Harkness (Locherben)	15/8/1684
72	Andrew Clark (Leadhills)	15/8/1684
73	Samuel McEwen (Glencairn)	15/8/1684
74	Thomas Wood (Kirkmichael)	15/8/1684
75	James Nicol (Peebles)	27/8/1684

Harkness, Clark, McEwen and Wood were all participants in the Enterkin Pass rescue. (For details, see Introduction, p18 and entries for Enterkin, Dalgarnock and Auchencloy.) According to Hewison a fifth man, unnamed, was also executed on 15/8/1684. James Harkness, the leader of the rescuers and brother of Thomas, had earlier escaped from Dumfries Jail, after being arrested with his five companions in Closeburn, Dumfriesshire, by Claverhouse himself. James Nicol, a participant in the Battle of Bothwell Brig and a "recusant", was arrested at the execution of these Enterkin rescuers for "muttering too loudly" against the hangings.

76	William Young (Evandale) *(escapee from the Canongate Tolbooth on 21/8/1684)*	27/8/1684
77	John Semple (Glassford) *(refused Abjuration Oath).*	24/11/1684
78	John Watt (Kilbride) *(as above)*	24/11/1684
79	Gabriel Thomson *(as above) (Compare entry for Eaglesham.)*	24/11/1684
80	Thomas Wood *(as Semple, but compare 74 above; some confusion may exist.)*	9/12/1684
81	George Jackson (Nether Pollock) *(as above)*	9/12/1684
82	Thomas Robertson *(as above)*	9/12/1684
83	James Graham *(as above; see entry for Crossmichael.)*	9/12/1684
84	Robert Baillie of Jerviswood *(See Introduction p20.)*	23/12/1684

Accused of complicity in treason, Baillie, a scholarly anti-Prelatist, was hanged when dying, possibly to satisfy the spite of the Duke of York, later James VII and II.

85	Robert Pollock (East Kilbride) *(Refused Abjuration Oath)*	23/1/1685
86	Robert Miller (Rutherglen) *(as above)*	23/1/1685
87	Colonel Richard Rumbold *(associate of Argyll: see 88.)*	?26/6/1685
88	Archibald Campbell, 9th Earl of Argyll: *cf.1 above and see Introduction p23*	30/6/1685
89	Thomas Stodhart *(hanged for treason and rebellion)*	12/8/1685
90	Gavin Russell *(as above)*	12/8/1685
91	James Wilkinson *(as above)*	12/8/1685
92	Thomas Archer *(associate of Argyll; see 88)*	21/8/1685
93	Captain John Nisbet of Hardhill *(see Introduction p23 , Fenwick, Newmilns)*	4/12/1685
94	Edward Marshall of Muiravonside *(Cameronian/Renwickite)*	4/12/1685
95	James Renwick: *the last major Covenanting martyr; see Introduction p24 and* Moniaive.	17/2/1688

Appendix IB

Covenanters killed in the rest of the country (excluding Orkney) 1666-1688

This list includes isolated shootings and some but not all deaths in battles and skirmishes. For details of individual cases and variations in spelling etc. see the appropriate Gazetteer entry. I have not attempted to make a distinction between those cases in which the victim is alleged to have been "murdered" and those in which the killing was apparently legal.

No.	Date	Name	Site	Note
1666-1667: Rullion Green (Pentland Rising) and aftermath				
1	28th Nov 1666	Rev. John Crookshank	Rullion Green	Tombstone: "and About fifty other[s]"
2	28th Nov 1666	Rev. Andrew McCormick	Rullion Green	Same tombstone as 1
3	19th Dec 1666	Robert Buntine (Fenwick)	Glasgow	See entry for Fenwick.
4	19th Dec 1666	John Hart (Glassford)	Glasgow	
5	19th Dec 1666	Robert Scott (Shavock, Dalserf)	Glasgow	
6	19th Dec 1666	Matthew Paton (Newmilns)	Glasgow	See entry for Newmilns.
7	27th Dec 1666	John Graham of Midtoun	Ayr	
8	27th Dec 1666	James Smith in Old Crachan	Ayr	
9	27th Dec 1666	Alexander MacCulloch in Carsphairn	Ayr	
10	27th Dec 1666	James MacMillan in Marduchat	Ayr	
11	27th Dec 1666	George MacCartney in Blairkennie	Ayr	
12	27th Dec 1666	John Short (Dalry)	Ayr	
13	27th Dec 1666	James Muirhead (Irongray)	Ayr	
14	31st Dec 1666	James Blackwood (Fenwick)	Irvine	
15	31st Dec 1666	John McCoull (Carsphairn)	Irvine	
16	2nd Jan 1667	John Grier (Fourmerkland)	Dumfries	
17	2nd Jan 1667	William Welsh (Kirkpatrick)	Dumfries	

The four men executed in Irvine and Dumfries were sentenced in Ayr at the same time as the others. Another man, Cornelius Anderson, was condemned then but was reprieved on condition that he hanged his friends at Ayr and Irvine. See site entry. Four further deaths are associated with the aftermath of the Battle of Rullion Green.

18	1666	Unknown	Black Law	
19	1666	David Findlay	Newmilns	
20	1666	William Smith of Moremell	Kirk o'Shotts	
21	6th Jan 1667	John Gordon of Largmore	Kells	

No.	Date	Name	Site	Note

1667-1678

Apart from the Rullion Green casualty listed above, only two Covenanters are reported to have lost their lives as a result of Government action outside Edinburgh during this period of eleven years:

No.	Date	Name	Site	Note
22	Apr 1673	James Davie of Blackdub	Bathgate	
23	Oct 1678	Andrew Brodie	Forgandenny	

1679

Dragnet after the assassination of Archbishop James Sharp:

No.	Date	Name	Site	Note
24	3rd May 1679	Andrew Aytoun	Cupar	No gravestone

The Battle of Drumclog:

No.	Date	Name	Site	Note
25	1st June 1679	Thomas Flem(m)ing	Loudoun	
26	1st June 1679	John Gebbie in Feoch	Newmilns	
27	1st June 1679	John Morton in Broomhill	Newmilns	
28	1st June 1679	William Dingwall	Strathaven	
29	1st June 1679	James Thomson	Stonehouse	
30	1st June 1679	Thomas Weir	Lesmahagow	

The Battle of Bothwell Brig (associated circumstances):

No.	Date	Name	Site	Note
31	22nd June 1679	William Gordon of Earlston	Glassford	
32	June 1679	Andrew Richmond	Galston	
33	July 1679	Arthur Inglis in Netherton	Cambusnethan	

Revenge for the assassination of Archbishop Sharp (The five men listed below were not connected with Sharp's murder.)

No.	Date	Name	Site	Note
34	18th Nov 1679	Thomas Brown (Edinburgh)	Magus Muir	
35	18th Nov 1679	Andrew Sword (Borgue)	Magus Muir	
36	18th Nov1679	John Waddell (New Monklands)	Magus Muir	
37	18th Nov 1679	John Clide	Magus Muir	
38	18th Nov 1679	James Wood Newmilns	Magus Muir	

SEE ALSO APPENDIX IC FOR DROWNED AND SURVIVING DEPORTEES IN THE SHIPWRECK IN ORKNEY.

The Queensferry incident 1680

No.	Date	Name	Site	Note
39	3rd June 1680	Henry Hall of Haughhead	Queensferry	(no tombstone)

The Battle of Airdsmoss:

No.	Date	Name	Site	Note
40	22nd Jul 1680	Richard Cameron	Airdsmoss	
41	22nd Jul 1680	Michael Cameron	Airdsmoss	
42	22nd Jul 1680	John Hamilton	Airdsmoss	
43	22nd Jul 1680	John Gemmel	Airdsmoss	
44	22nd Jul 1680	James Gray	Airdsmoss	
45	22nd Jul 1680	Robert Dick	Airdsmoss	
46	22nd Jul 1680	Captain John Fuller (Fowler)	Airdsmoss	
47	22nd Jul 1680	Robert Paterson	Airdsmoss	
48	22nd Jul 1680	Thomas Watson	Airdsmoss	

1681

In 1681 no deaths of Covenanters were caused by
Government action outside the Edinburgh area.

No	Date	Name	Site	Note
		1682		
49	2nd Mar 1682	William Harvey	Lanark	
50	15th Mar 1682	William Graham	Crossmichael	
		1683		
51	14th Apr 1683	John Nisbet of Glen or Know(e)	Kilmarnock	
52	14th Jun 1683	William Boick of Auchinreoch	Campsie	Executed in Glasgow
53	14th Jun 1683	John Wharrie (Lesmahagow)	Inchbelly	Executed in Glasgow
54	14th Jun 1683	James Smith (Lesmahagow)	Inchbelly	Executed in Glasgow
		1684		
55	19th Mar 1684	John Richmond, younger, of Know(e)	Glasgow	See entry for Galston
56	19th Mar 1684	James Winning	Glasgow	
57	19th Mar 1684	Archibald Stewart (Lesmahagow)	Glasgow	See entry for Lesmahagow.
58	19th Mar 1684	James Johnston (Cadder)	Glasgow	
59	19th Mar 1684	John Main (Old Monklands)	Glasgow	
60	5th Jun 1684	James Nisbet of Highside	Glasgow	
61	24th Oct 1684	James Lawson	Glasgow	
62	24th Oct 1684	Alexander Wood	Glasgow	
63	Nov 1684	Andrew McGill (Ballantrae)	Ayr	(No gravestone)
The Killing Time (1)		*The Auchencloy Incident:*		
64	18th Dec 1684	James McMichael	Auchencloy	No gravestone
65	18th Dec 1684	Robert Ferguis or Ferguson	Auchencloy	
66	18th Dec 1684	Robert Stewart	Dalry	See also entry for Auchencloy.
67	18th Dec 1684	John Grierson	Dalry	See also entry for Auchencloy.
68	18th Dec 1684	Archibald Stewart	Auchencloy	No tombstone; burial unknown.
69	Dec 1684	William Hunter	Kirkcudbright	See entry for Auchencloy.
70	Dec 1684	Robert Smith	Kirkcudbright	See entry for Auchencloy.
		1685		

The Killing Time (2) — Events surrounding Charles II's death and the Argyll revolt:

(i) Executions &c datable by month January - May 1685

71	23rd Jan 1685	James Dun	Caldons Wood	
72	23rd Jan 1685	Robert Dun (Benwhat)	Caldons Wood	
73	23rd Jan 1685	Robert Stevenson (Barbeath Straiton)	Caldons Wood	

No	Date	Name	Site	Note
74	23rd Jan 1685	John Stevenson (Star, Straiton)	Caldons Wood	
75	23rd Jan 1685	Andrew McCall (or Alexander McAuley)	Caldons Wood	
76	23rd Jan 1685	James McClive (or John McClure)	Caldons Wood	
77	31st Jan 1685	Daniel McMichael	Durisdeer	See also entry for Dalveen.
78	3rd Feb 1685	John Park	Paisley	
79	3rd Feb 1685	James Algie	Paisley	
80	21st Feb 1685	James Clement	Kirkconnel Moor	
81	21st Feb 1685	John Bell of Whiteside	Anwoth	See also entry for Kirkconnel Moor.
82	21st Feb 1685	Andrew McRobert	Twynholm	See also entry for Kirkconnel Moor.
83	21st Feb 1685	Robert Lennox of Irelandtoun	Girthon	See also entry for Kirkconnel Moor.
84	21st Feb 1685	David Halliday of Mayfield	Balmaghie	See also entry for Kirkconnell Moor.
85	28th Feb 1685	Edward M'Keen	Barr	
86	Feb 1685	John Smith	Muirkirk	
87	2nd Mar 1685	William Herron (Glencairn)	Lochenkit	
88	2nd Mar 1685	John Gordon (Garryhorn)	Lochenkit	
89	2nd Mar 1685	William Stewart (Crofts)	Lochenkit	
90	2nd Mar 1685	John Wallace (Rosehill)	Lochenkit	
91	3rd Mar 1685	Alexander McCubine (Glencairn)	Irongray (Hallhill)	See also entry for Lochenkit.
92	3rd Mar 1685	Edward Gordon (Blacke)	Irongray (Hallhill)	See also entry for Lochenkit.
93	29th Mar 1685	William Smith	Tynron	
94	Mar 1685	John Brown	Blackwood	
95	Mar 1685	William Adam	Wellwood	
96	4th Apr 1685	Thomas Richard	Cumnock	
97	28th Apr 1685	John Gibson (Ingliston)	Glencairn	See also entry for Ingliston.
98	28th Apr 1685	James Bennoch (Glencairn)	Glencairn	See also entry for Ingliston.
99	28th Apr 1685	Robert Edgar	Glencairn	See also entry for Ingliston.

No	Date	Name	Site	Note
100	28th Apr 1685	Robert Mitchell (Cumnock)	Glencairn	See also entry for Ingliston.
101	28th Apr 1685	Robert Grierson (Galloway)	Balmaclellan	See also entry for Ingliston.
102	Apr 1685	James White	Fenwick	See also entry for Ingliston.
103	Apr 1685	David Findlay	Fenwick (no gravestone)	See also entry for Newmilns.
104	Apr 1685	John Law	Newmilns	
105	Apr 1685	James Smith	Mauchline	See entries for Newmilns & Galston
106	Apr 1685	William Paterson	Strathaven	
107	Apr 1685	John Barrie	Strathaven	
108	1st May 1685	John Brown	Priesthill	See also entry for Newmilns.
109	1st May 1685	Gabriel Thomson	Eaglesham	
110	1st May 1685	Robert Lockhart	Eaglesham	
111	6th May 1685	John Browning	Mauchline	See entries for Newmilns & Priesthill
112	6th May 1685	Peter Gillies	Mauchline	
113	6th May 1685	John Brice	Mauchline	
114	6th May 1685	Thomas Young	Mauchline	
115	6th May 1685	William Fiddison	Mauchline	
116	10th May 1685	Adam MacQuhan	Kells	
117	11th May 1685	Margaret Wilson	Wigtown	
118	11th May 1685	Margaret MacLauchlan	Wigtown	
119	11th May 1685	Andrew Hislop	Craighaugh	
120	11th May 1685	Thomas Cook	Cathcart (Polmadie)	
121	11th May 1685	John Urie	Cathcart (Polmadie)	
122	11th May 1685	Robert Thom	Cathcart (Polmadie)	
123	13th May 1685	James Kirko (or Kirk, or Kirka)	Dumfries	

(ii) Executions &c datable by month for the rest of 1685:

No	Date	Name	Site	Note
124	11th July 1685	David Halliday	Balmaghie	
125	July 1685	William Shillilaw	Tarbolton	
126	November 1685	Peter Gemmel	Fenwick	
127	November 1685	George Woodburn	Fenwick	
128	November 1685	John Fergushill	Fenwick	

(iii) Executions &c not securely datable by month in 1685:

No	Date	Name	Site	Note
129	1685 (?April)	David Dun (Closs or Glass)	Cumnock	
130	1685 (?April)	Simon Paterson	Cumnock	

No	Date	Name	Site	Note
131	1685 (?April)	Joseph Wilson	Corsgellioch	
132	1685 (?Apr)	John Jamieson	Corsgellioch	
133	1685 (?Apr)	John Humphrey	Corsgellioch	
134	1685 (?Apr)	George Corson	Waistland	
135	1685 (?Aprl)	John Hair	Waistland	
136	1685 (?Apr)	Margaret Dun	Dalgig	No tombstone at Dalgig
137	May-Aug 1685	John Stot	Dunnottar Churchyard	See also entry forDunnottar Castle.
138	May-Aug 1685	James Atchison	Dunnottar Churchyard	See also entry for Dunnottar Castle.
139	May-Aug 1685	James Russell	Dunnottar Churchyard	See also entry for Dunnottar Castle.
140	May-Aug 1685	William Broun	Dunnottar Churchyard	See also entry for Dunnottar Castle.
141	May-Aug 1685	? John White	Dunnottar Churchyard	See also entry for Dunnottar Castle.
142	May-Aug 1685	? William Breadie	Dunnottar Churchyard	See also entry for Dunnottar Castle.
143	May-Aug 1685	? Mary Gibson	Dunnottar Churchyard	See also entry for Dunnottar Castle.
144	May-Aug 1685	? Jean Muffet	Dunnottar Churchyard	See also entry for Dunnottar Castle.
145	May-Aug 1685	James Watson	Dunnottar Churchyard	See also entry for Dunnottar Castle.
146	1685	George Short	Balmaghie	
147	1685	Matthew McIlwraith	Colmonell	
148	1685	John Murchie	Barrhill	
149	1685	Daniel McIlwrick	Barrhill	
150	1685	Alexander Lin(n)	Craigmoddie	
151	1685	Gilbert McAdam	Kirkmichael	
152	1685	John Semple	Old Dailly	
153	1685	Thomas McClorgan	Old Dailly	
154	1685	Unknown (Black Clauchrie)	Old Dailly	
155	1685	Unknown (Killoup)	Old Dailly	

No	Date	Name	Site	Note
156	1685	Robert M'Whae	Kirkandrews	
157	1685	John Hallam (Hallume)	Kirkcudbright	
158	1685	William Johnston	Wigtown	
159	1685	John Milroy	Wigtown	
160	1685	George Walker	Wigtown	
161	1685	John Hunter	Tweedsmuir (Corehead)	
162	1685	Robert (or William) Auchenleck	Carlinwark	Not in Gazetteer
163	1685	William McKergue	Blairquhan	No gravestone
164	1685	John Blackadder	North Berwick (Bass Rock)	See entry for Dumfries (Troqueer)
165	1685(?)	Mowat	Fleet-Dee	Not in Gazetteer.
166	1685(?)	George Allan	Allan's Cairn	
167	1685(?)	Margaret Gracie	Allan's Cairn	
168	1685(?)	Unknown	Windshields	(See entry for Craighaugh p206.)
169	1686	Thomas McHaffie (or McHassie)	Straiton	"Cloud" states January 1685.
170	20th Dec 1686	David Steel	Lesmahagow (Skellyhill)	
171	20th June 1688	John MacGeachan	Stonepark	
172	June 1688	George Wood	Sorn	

Appendix IC

Prisoners deported after the battle of Bothwell Brig and shipwrecked when the vessel Crown of London *foundered off Muil Head of Deerness, Orkney, on 10th December 1679.*

Gazetteer entries for Edinburgh Greyfriars, Orkney and Bothwell Brig.

The following is extracted from pp 333-337 of the Appendix to *A Cloud of Witnesses* (1796 edition):

> "... *item, anno 1679, of the prisoners taken at Bothwel, were banished to America 250; who were taken away by — — Paterson merchant at Leith, who transacted for them with Provost Milns, laird of Barnton, the man that first burnt the covenant; whereof 200 were drowned by shipwreck at a place called the Mule-head of Darness near Orkney, being shut up by the said Paterson's order beneath the hatches; 50 escaped, whereof the names, so many of them as could be had, follow; these who escaped are printed in Italic characters, for distinction's sake.*" [Numbers, letters and side-headings added]

(A) CLYDESDALE

(a) Out of the shire of Clydesdale and city of Glasgow,
(1) Francis Wodrow, (2) Walter M'Kechnie, (3) Alexander Pirie, (4) William Miller.

(b) Out of the parish of Govan, (5) Andrew Snodgrass.

(c) Out of the parish of Kilbride, (6) Robert Auld, (7) John Struthers, (8) James Clark, (9) John Clark, (10) William Rodger.

(d) Out of the parish of Shotts, (11) Peter Lermont, (12) John Aitken, (13) Robert Chalmers, (S1) *John Thomson*, (14) John Killen, (15) Alexander Walker.

(e) Out of the parish of Cambusnethan, (S2) *William Scular.*

(f) Out of the Monklands, (S3) *William Waddel*, (16) William Grinlaw, (17) Thomas Mathie, (18) William Miller, (19) John Wynet, (20) James Waddel, (S4) *John Gardner*, (21) Thomas Barton.

(g) Out of the parish of Bothwel, (S5) —— *More,* (22) William Breakenrig.

(h) Out of the parish of Evandale, (23) John Cairnduff, (24) John Cochran, (25) Robert Alison, (26) Andrew Torrence, (27) Thomas Brownlee, (28) John Watson, (29) William Alison, (30) Andrew Aiton.

(i)   Out of the parish of Calder, (S6) *William Fram.*

(j)   Out of the parish of Glassford, (31) John Miller, (32) John Craig.

(k)   Out of the parish of Carnwath, (33) Thomas Crichton, (34) James Couper.

(l)   Out of the parish of Quathquhan, (S7) *James Penman,* (35) James Thomson, (36) Thomas Wilson.

(m)   Out of the parish of Carstairs, (S8) *Thomas Swan.*

(n)   Out of the parish of Biggar, (37) John Rankin.

(o)   Out of the parish of Lesmahego, (38) George Wier, (39) Robert Wier, (S9) *George Drafin.*

(B) AYRSHIRE

(a)   Out of the shire of Air and parish of Finnick, (40) James Gray, (41) Andrew Buckle, (42) David Currie, (43) David Bitchet, (44) Robert Tod, (45) John White, (S10) *Robert Wallace,* (46) John Wylie, (47) William Bitchet.

(b)   Out of the parish of Loudon, (48) Thomas Wylie.

(c)   Out of the parish of Dalmellington, (50) Hugh Simpson, (51) Walter Humper (S11) *Walter Humper,* younger, (S12) *Hugh Cameron,* (S13) *Quintin M'Adam.*

(d)   Out of the parish of Cumnock, (52) John Gemil, (53) James Mirrie.

(e)   Out of the parish of Ochiltree, (54) Andrew Welch.

(f)   Out of the parish of Auchinleck, (55) Andrew Richmond.

(g)   Out of Dundonald, (S14) *Andrew Thomson.*

(h)   Out of Mauchlin, (56) William Reid, (57) William Drips.

(i)   Out of the parish of Muirkirk, (58) John Campbell, (59) Alexander Paterson.

(j)   Out of the parish of Digen [Dreghorn], (60) James Bouston.

(k)   Out of the parish of Galston, (61) James Young, (62) George Campbell.

(l)   Out of the parish of Kilmarnock, (63) Thomas Finlay, (64) John Cuthbertson, (65) William Brown, (S15) *Patrick Watt,* (66) Robert Anderson, (67) James Anderson.

(m)   Out of the parish of Stewarton, (68) Thomas Wylie, (69) Andrew Wylie, (70) Robert Wylie.

(n)   Out of the parish of Bar, (71) Alexander Burden.

(o)   Out of the parish of Colmonel, (72) Thomas M'Clurg, (73) John M'Cornock, (74) John M'Clellen.

(p)   Out of the parish of Girvan, (75) William Caldwel.

(q)   Out of the parish of Dalry, (76) David M'Cubin, (77) William M'Culloch.

(r)   Out of the parish of Maybole, (78) William Rodger, (79) Mungo Eccles, (80) John M'Whirter, (81) Thomas Horn, (82) Robert M'Garron, (83) John M'Harie.

(s)   Out of the parish of Craigie, (S16) *George Dunbar.*

(t)   Out of the parish of Straiton, (84) James M'Murrie, (85) Alexander Lamb, (86) George Hutcheson.

(u)   Out of the parish of Kirkmichael, (87) John Brice, (88) Robert Ramsay, (89) John Douglas, (90) John M'Tire, (91) James M'Connell.

(v)   Out of the parish of Kirkoswald, (92) John White, (93) Thomas Germont.

(C) FIFE

(a)   Out of the shire of Fife and parish of Newburn, (94) James Beal.

(b)   Out of the parish of Largo and Kilconquhar, (95) Andrew P [?i] rie, (96) James Kirk.

(c)   Out of the parish of Ceres, (97) John Kirk, (S17) *Thomas Miller.*

(d)   Out of the parish of Strathmiglo, (98) Robert Bog.

(e)   Out of the town of Kinross, (99) James Lilburn.

(f)   Out of the parish of Orwel, (S18) *Robert Kirk*, (S19) *Robert Sands.*

(D) PERTHSHIRE

(a)   Out of the shire of Perth and parish of Kilmadock, (100) John Christison.

(b)   Out of the parish of Kincardine, (101) Patrick Keir, (102) John Donaldson.

(c) Out of the parish of Glendovan, (103) John Muire, (104) Andrew Muire.

(E) RENFREWSHIRE

(a)   Out of the shire of Renfrew and parish of Eastwood, (105) James Cunningham.

(b) Out of the parish of Neilston, (106) John Govan.

(c) Out of Paisley, (107) William Buchan, (108) William Auchinclose.

(F) LENNOX

(a) Out of the shire of Lennox and parish of New Kilpatrick, (109) James Finlayson.

(G) STIRLINGSHIRE

(a) Out of the shire of Stirling and parish of Drummond, (110) Daniel Cunningham.

(b) Out of the parish of Kippen, (111) James Galbraith.

(c) Out of Gargunnock, (112) Thomas Miller, (113) Patrick Gilchrist, (S20) *James Sands,*
     (114) Thomas Brown, (115) James Buchannan.

(d) Out of the parish of St. Ninians, (S21) *Thomas Thomson,* (S22) *Andrew Thomson,*
     (116) John Neilson, (117) John M'Nure.

(e) Out of the parish of Denny, (118) James M'Kie.

(f) Out of the parish of Airth, (119) Andrew Young, (120) John Morison,
     (121) Robert Hendrie.

(g) Out of the parish of Falkirk, (S23) *Hugh Montgomerie.*

(h) Out of Morrenside, (122) Thomas Phalp.

(H) WEST LOTHIAN

(a) Out of the shire of West Lothian, in the parish of Torphichen, (123) John Allan,
     (124) John Thomson, (S24) *John Pender,* (125) James Easton, (S25) *John Easton,*
     (126) Andrew Easton, (127) John Addie, (128) Alexander Bishop.

(b) Out of Dalmannie, (129) John Thomson.

(c) Out of Livingstoun, (130) Thomas Ingles, (131) Patrick Hamilton, (132) John Bell,
     (133) Patrick Wilson, (134) William Younger, (135) William Henderson,
     (136) John Steven.

(d) Out of the parish of Kirklistoun, (137) John Govan.

(e) Out of Bathgate, (138) David Ralston.

(f) Out of the parish of Abercorn, (139) John Gib, (140) James Gib.

(g) Out of the parish of Linlithgow, (141) Thomas Borthwick.

(h) Out of the parish of Kinneil, (142) Andrew Murdoch.

(I) MIDLOTHIAN

(a) Out of the shire of Mid-Lothian and parish of Calder, (143) James Steel,
(144) Thomas Gilchrist, (145) James Graze, (146) Alexander Russel.

(b) Out of Mid-Calder, (147) John Brown, (148) Alexander Mutray [?Murray].

(c) East-Calder, (S26) *David Samuel*, (149) Alexander Bisset.

(d) Out of the parish of Stow, (150) Thomas Pringle.

(e) Out of the parish of Temple, (151) James Tinto.

(f) Out of the parish of Liberton, (S27) *Thomas M'Kenzie.*

(g) Out of the parish of Crichtoun, (152) James Fork.

(h) Out of the parish of Cranstoun, (153) Thomas Williamson, [sic]

(i) Out of the town of Musselburgh, (154) William Reid.

(J) EAST LOTHIAN

(a) Out of the shire of East-Lothian, and parish of Dunbar, (155) James Tod.

(K) NITHSDALE

(a) Out of the shire of Nithsdale, and parish of Glencairn, (156) David Mackervail,
(157) John Ferguson, (158) Robert Milligan, (S28) *John Milligan,* (S29) *John Murdoch,*
(S30) *John Smith,* (S31) *William Ferguson,* (159) James Colvil, (160) Thomas Rosper.

(b) Out of the parish of Closeburn, (161) Thomas Milligan, (162) John Kennedy.

(L) GALLOWAY

(a) Out of the shire of Galloway, and parish of Kirkcudbright, (163) James Corsan,
(S32) *Andrew Macquhan,* (S33) *John Macartney,* (S34) *John Macgie.*

(b) Outof [sic] the parish of Balmaghie, (S35) *Robert Caldow,* (164) James Houston.

(c) Out of the parish of Kelton, (165) James Donaldson.

(d) Out of the parish of Kirkmabreck, (166) Robert Brown, (167) Samuel Beck, (168) Samuel
Hannay.

(e) Out of the parish of Penningham, (169) John Mactagart, (S36) *Alexander Murray.*

(f) Out of the parish of Borgue, (170) Andrew Sprot, (171) Robert Brice,
(S37) *John Richardson*, (S38) *John Martin*, (172) John Brice, (173) William Thomson.

(g) Out of the parish of Girthon, (174) Andrew Donaldson.

(h) Out of the parish of Dalry, (S39) *John Smith*, (S40) *John Malcolm*.

(i) Out of Irongray, (175) Andrew Wallet.

(j) Out of Balmaclellan, (S41) *John Edgar*.

(k) Out of Lochrutan, (S42) *Andrew Clark*.

(l) Out of Etrick [?] or Forrest, (176) John Scot.

(m) Out of the parish of Gallashields, (S43) *Robert Macgill*, (177) Robert Young.

(M) Merse and Teviotdale

(a) Out of the shires of Merse and Teviotdale, and parish of Nethen, (178) Samuel Nisbet,
(S44) *James Aitchison*.

(b) Out of the parish of Cavers, (S45) *James Leidon*, (S46) *James Glasgow*,
(S47) *William Glasgow*, (179) John Greenshields, (180) Richard Young,
(181) Samuel Douglas, (S48) *James Young*, (182) James Hobkirk.

(c) Out of the town of Kelso, (183) William Hardie.

(d) Out of the town of Jedburgh, (184) John Mather

(e) Out of the parish of Sprouston, (185) Walter Waddel, and (186) Thomas Cairns.

(f) Out of the parish of Melross, (187) John Young and (188) Andrew Cook.

(g) Out of the parish of Castletoun, (189) William Scot, (190) John Pringle,
(191) Alexander Waddel, and (192) John Unnes.

(h) Out of the parish of Ashkirk, (193) William Herd.

(i) Out of the parish of Bandon, (194) Andrew Newbigging.

(j) Out of the parish of Sudon, (195) James Custon, (S49) *William Swanston*,
(196) John Elliot.

(k) Out of the parish of Hobkirk, (197) John Oliver.

Appendix II

Covenanting sites and memorials (mainly of lesser importance) which have not been covered in the main survey.

AUCHINLECK (NS 552 215)
A modern (nineteenth century) memorial just inside the old parish graveyard commemorating the fallen at Airdsmoss and Alexander Peden, who was briefly buried in the graveyard.

BENHAR (NS 902 628)
A modern (nineteenth century) cast iron monument to conventicles held here by Alexander Peden and others.

BLACKNESS CASTLE (NT 056 802)
A state prison in Covenanting times; John Welch of Irongray was among Conventiclers confined here.

CARNWATH (NS 976 465)
Memorials to two local Covenanting worthies (Sir William Denham and Sir Thomas Steuart) and to two Carnwath victims (Crichton and Couper) of the 1679 Orkney shipwreck (see Appendix Ic) will be found in the graveyard behind St Mary's Aisle.

CARSPHAIRN (NX 567 932)
Scene of the murder of the Curate of Carsphairn, Peter Peirson, by Black James McMichael. (See *Auchencloy*).

CESSNOCK CASTLE (NS 512 355)
Associated from the earliest times with the reformed religion. A Campbell of Cessnock was one of the Lollards of Kyle and Sir Hew Campbell of Cessnock was imprisoned on the Bass Rock from 1684 to 1686. Now a private residence.

CLOSEBURN (NX 904 924)
Burial place of John Mathieson, returned Covenanting deportee. (d. 1709).

COVINGTON MILL (NS 975 398)
Spot where James Irvine of Bonshaw arrested the great Donald Cargill on 12th July, 1681; now marked by a modern memorial.

CRAIGDOW (NS 257 059)
A famous conventicle site south of Maybole, where Cameron, Cargill and others preached.

DALMELLINGTON (NS 481 061)
Scene of much Covenanting activity and persecution of Covenanters (e.g. by the "Highland Host" of 1678). Long the garrison headquarters of Colonel Thomas Buchan after the Restoration. A modern cross has been erected in the old graveyard.

DARMEID (NS 902 554)
Famous conventicle site known to Cameron, Cargill, Renwick *et al.*

DISTINKHORN HILL (NS 586 332)
This, the highest hill in Galston Parish, was another famous conventicle site where, in April 1688, Alexander Shields bitterly denounced the execution two months previously of James Renwick. The eccentric-seeming name means "the house (*horn*) of the Dish-thegn (= *dapifer*, Steward)". Distinkhorn Hill is in Kyle Stewart.

DOUGLAS (NS 835 306)
In the main street is a memorial to James Gavin, a Cameronian tailor who was banished to the Barbados after having his left ear cut off with his own shears on 4th August, 1685.

EASTWOOD (NS 552 600)
Cemetery (adjacent to Thornliebank Station) containing the tomb of Robert Wodrow, famous historian of the Covenanting times; visible from the main road.

GIB'S CORSE (AE FOREST)
On some Ordnance Survey maps this is marked as a "Covenanters' Stone' but the attribution is dubious and the actual stone (an unmarked boulder) cannot now be traced.

GLENBUCK (NS 749 296)
A plaque commemorating local Covenanters was affixed to the now disused church at Glenbuck by a laird of Glenbuck when it was opened for worship in 1882. This tiny settlement is only a mile or so from Priesthill (*q.v.*).

KIRKPATRICK DURHAM (NX 786 703)
In the churchyard will be found a flat tombstone commemorating John Neilson of Corsock, a Pentland Martyr executed in Edinburgh on 14th December 1666.

MAYBOLE (NS 295 110)
At the side of the Cross Road just above Maybole to the north stands the modern Cargill Monument bearing the name of the famous martyr (executed 1681) and

the names of six Carrick men who perished on 10th December 1679 when the vessel deporting them to the Americas after the Battle of Bothwell Brig foundered off Orkney. (See Appendix 1c.) Donald Cargill is said to have preached at this site two months before his arrest, and to have used a large rock as a pulpit; this rock, broken up, forms the basis of the monument, and another portion of it has been incorporated in the now disused Cargill Memorial Church in Maybole itself.

TYNWALD (NY 003 816)
Burial place (parish churchyard) of John Corbet (*d*. 17th March 1706), returned Covenanting deportee.

WINDSHIEL(D)S (NY 156 930)
Epitaph: 'Grave of a Covenanter for sheltering whom nearby Andreu Hislop was taken by Claverhouse and shot at Craighaugh 12 May 1685. Two fugitives to mid Windshields lie here.'
For further details see Craighaugh *passim* and n.1

Appendix III

(See *Newmilns, Priesthill, Mauchline,* and Introduction p22.)

Letter written by John Graham of Claverhouse to the Duke of Queensberry from Galston on 3rd May 1685, describing the arrest and execution of John Brown and attendant circumstances:

MAY IT PLEASE YOUR GRACE, —

On Frayday last, amongst the hilles betuixt Douglas and the Plellands, we perseued tuo fellous a great way throu the mosses, and in end seized them. They had no armes about them and denayed they had any, but being asked if they would take the abjuration, the eldest of tuo, called John Broun, refused it, nor would he swear not to ryse in armes against the King, but said he kneu no King; upon which, and there being found bullets and match in his house and treasonable peapers, I caused shoot him dead, which he suffered very inconcernedly. The other, a yong fellou, and his nepheu, called John Brounen, offered to take the oath; but would not swear that he had not been at Neumilles in armes at the rescuing the prisoners. So I did not knou what to doe with him. I was convinced that he was guilty, but saw not hou to proceed against him; wherfor after he had said his prayers and carabins presented to shoot him, I offered to him that if he would make ane ingeneous confession and make a discoverie that might be of any importance for the Kings service, I should delay puting him to death, and plead for him; upon which he confessed that he was at that attake of Neumilles, and that he had com straight to this house of his uncles on Sunday morning. In the mean time he was making the souldiers found out a house in the hille under ground, that could hold a dusen of men, and there were swords and pistolles in it; and this fellou declaired that they belonged to his uncle, and that he had lurked in that place ever since Bothwell, where he was in armes. He confessed that he had a halbart and told who gave him it about a month agoe, and we have the feleou prisoner. He gave account of the names of the most pairt of those that wer there. They were not above sixty, and they wer all Gaston and Neumilles men, saive a feu out of Streven parish. He gave also acount of a conventicle keeped by Renek [Renwick] at the bak of Carantable [Cairntable], where there wer threttin scor of men in armes mustered and exercised, of which number he was with his hallard. He tells of ane other conventicle about three moneths agoe keeped near Louden Hille, and gives acount of the persons wer at both, and what childring wer baptised, particularly that at Carntable, which was about the time that Liev: Muray and Crichton should have laiten them eskeap. He also gives acount of those who gave any assistance to his uncle, and we have seised there upon the good man of the upmost Plellands and ane other tenent about a myll belou, that is flaid upon it. I dout not but if we had time to stay, good use might be made of his confession. I have acquyted my self when I have told your Grace the caise. He has been but a moneth or tuo with his halbart; and if your Grace thinks he deserves no marcy, justice will pass on him, for I, having no comission of justiciary myself, have delyvered him up to the Lievetenent Generall to be disposed of as he pleases. - I am, my Lord, your Graces most humble servant,

J Grahame.

(Reports of the Royal Commission on Historical Manuscripts [London 1870 —], xv, part viii, p 292).

Appendix IV

Martyrs named on the Nithsdale Cross (Dalgarnock) (Some of the martyrs named in this appendix have not yet been traced)

No.	Name	Other references
1	George Allan	Allan's Cairn
2	James Bennoch	28/4/1685: shot Ingliston, buried Glencairn
3	William Brown	Shot at Craignorth, see Corsgellioch
4	James Carsan (?Corsan)	Orkney App1(c): Galloway - Kirkcudbright
5	James Colvin(?-il)	Orkney App 1(c): Nithsdale - Glencairn
6	George Corson	Shot Waistland 1685
7	Thomas Dinwiddle	Not traced
8	Robert Edgar	28/4/1685: shot Ingliston, buried Glencairn
9	Andrew Ferguson	Not traced
10	Elizabeth H Ferguson	(?) Died being deported 1685*
11	John Ferguson	Orkney App 1(c): Nithsdale - Glencairn
12	Robert Ferguson	Not traced: see, however, Auchencloy.
13	Robert Ferguson (2)	Not traced
14	M James Forsyth	Lochmaben: ? died in Dunnottar 1685
15	John Gibson	28/4/1685: shot Ingliston, buried Glencairn
16	James Glover	Tynwald: died in prison (Edinburgh) 1685*
17	Edward Gordon	3/3/1685: hanged Irongray (Hallhill)
18	Margaret Gracie	Allan's Cairn
19	Robert Grierson	28/4/1685: shot Ingliston, buried Balmaclellan
20	William Grierson	Dumfries (Pentland): hanged 2/1/1667
21	John Hair	Shot Waistland 1685
22	Thomas Harkness	15/8/1684: hanged Edinburgh
23	William Heron	2/3/1685: shot Lochenkit
24	Andrew Hunter	Dumfries: died in prison 1685*
25	Elizabeth G Hunter	Dumfries: died in Holland 1685*
26	William Hunter	1684: hanged Kirkcudbright
27	John Johnstone	Not traced
28	John Kennedy	Orkney - App 1(c): Nithsdale - Closeburn
29	James Nimmo	Not traced
30	James MacCall	Not traced
31	Alexander MacCubine	3/3/1685: hanged Irongray (Hallhill)

No.	Name	Other references
32	Samuel MacEwen	15/8/1684: hanged Edinburgh
33	Thomas MacGirr	Not traced
34	David MacKervall	Orkney - App.1(c): Nithsdale - Glencairn
35	John MacLamroes	Not traced
36	Andrew MacLellan	Dumfries: died being deported 1685
37	Daniel MacMichael	1685: shot Dalveen, buried Durisdeer
38	James MacMichael	Auchencloy: killed 18th December 1684
39	Robert Milligan	Orkney - App.1(c): Nithsdale - Glencairn
40	Thomas Milligan	Orkney - App. 1(c) Nithsdale - Closeburn
41	Robert Mitchell	28/4/1685: shot Ingliston, buried Glencairn
42	Robert Morris	Shot at Craignorth (see Corsgellioch)
43	James Muirhead	Irongray - Pentland: hanged Ayr 27/12/1666
44	James Muncie	Dumfries: died in prison (Edinburgh) 1685*
45	John Mundell	Nithsdale: died in prison (Edinburgh) 1685*
46	Rev James Renwick	born Moniaive: hanged 17/2/1688 Edinburgh
47	John Renwick	Dumfries: died being deported 1685*
48	James Robson	Not traced
49	Thomas Rosper	Orkney - App. 1(c): Nithsdale - Glencairn
50	Robert Sitlington	? Dunscore - died being deported 1685
51	Thomas Sitlington	Not traced
52	James Smith	Lesmahagow: hanged 14/6/1683 b Inchbelly
53	Rev Robert Smith	(?) 1684: hanged Kirkcudbright
54	William Smith	3/3/1685 or 29/3/1685: shot Tynron
55	John Stot	Dunnottar Churchyard: d Dunnottar 1685
56	William Welsh	Dumfries (Pentland): hanged 2/1/1667
57	Andrew Wallet	Orkney - App. 1(c): Galloway - Irongray

*Mentioned in Wodrow Book 4 Chapters IX and X and passim.
See also "The Tryst of Dalgarnoc" by James King Hewison DD
(reprinted from the Dumfries and Galloway Courier & Herald of dates 31st August and 3rd September 1927.)

Bibliography & Abbreviations

APS
Acts of the Parliaments of Scotland, eds. T Thomson and G Innes, 12 vols. Edinburgh 1814-1875

Aiton
Willliam Aiton, *A History of the Rencounter at Drumclog and Battle at Bothwell Bridge*, IN THE MONTH OF JUNE 1679. Hamilton 1821

Brown
Rev. Peter J Brown, *Historical Sketches of the Parish of Cambusnethan,* Wishaw 1859

Burnet *History*
Gilbert Burnet, *History of My Own Times, ed* O Airy. 2 vols., Oxford 1897-1900

Burnet *Memoires*
Gilbert Burnet, *The Memoires of the Lives and Actions of James and William Dukes of Hamilton.* Oxford 1852

Claverhouse
Letters of John Graham of Claverhouse, Viscount of Dundee, The Bannatyne Club, Edinburgh 1826

Cloud
A CLOUD of WITNESSES, FOR THE *Royal Prerogatives* of JESUS CHRIST: OR, THE LAST *Speeches and Testimonies* of those who have suffered for the TRUTH in SCOTLAND *Since* the *Year* 1680. Glasgow 1741

Cowan
Ian B Cowan, *The Scottish Covenanters 1660-1688,* London 1976

Creichton
Memoirs of Captain John Creichton from his own Materials ..... drawn up and digested by Dr J Swift. In Swift's *Works* xii, 2nd edition (*ed* Sir Walter Scott) Edinburgh 1824

Defoe
Daniel Defoe, *Memoirs of the Church of Scotland,* London 1717

Donaldson
Gordon Donaldson, *Scottish Historical Documents,* Edinburgh and London 1974

Dunlop
A Ian Dunlop, *William Carstares and The Kirk by Law Established,* Edinburgh 1967

Findlay
Thomas Findlay, *Garan 1631 to Muirkirk 1950,* unpublished, Kyle and Carrick District Council Libraries (Headquarters), Ayr: local collection

Fountainhall *Historical Notices*
Sir John Lauder of Fountainhall, *Historical Notices of Scotish Affairs 1661-1688* (in two parts), The Bannatyne Club, Edinburgh 1848

Fountainhall *Observes*
Sir John Lauder of Fountainhall, *Historical Observes of Memorable Occurrents in Church and State from October 1680 to April 1686*, The Bannatyne Club, Edinburgh 1840

Fountainhall *Decisions*
Sir John Lauder of Fountainhall, *The Decisions of the Lords of Council and Session from June 6th 1678 to July 30th 1702* (2 vols.), Edinburgh 1759-61

Gibson
James Gibson, *Inscriptions on the Tombstone and Monuments erected in memory of the Covenanters*, Glasgow ND

Hendrie
J Hendrie, *History of Galston Parish Church,* Paisley 1909

Hewison *History*
James King Hewison DD, *A History of the Church in Scotland from the Reformation to the Revolution*, 2 vols., Glasgow 1908

Hewison *Allan's Cairn*
James King Hewison DD, *A Covenanting Memorial: Allan's Cairn* Dumfries 1936

Hewison *Dalgarnoc*
James King Hewison DD *The Tryst of Dalgarnoc* (reprinted from the Dumfries and Galloway Courier & Herald 31st August & 3rd September 1927.

Howie of Lochgoin
John Howie of Lochgoin, *Biographia Scoticana, or, a Brief Historical Account of the most eminent SCOTS WORTHIES, Noblemen, Gentlemen, Ministers and others, who testified or suffered for the Cause of Reformation in Scotland from the beginning of the Sixteenth Century to the year 1688*, Edinburgh 1775 Shorter edition, ed Carslaw, Edinburgh 1870.

Kirkton
James Kirkton, *The Secret and True History of the Church of Scotland from the Restoration to the year 1688*, ed C K Sharpe, Edinburgh 1817

Knox
John Knox, *History of the Reformation*, 2 vols., *ed* William Croft Dickinson, London 1949

Lawson *Covenanters*
Rev. Roderick Lawson, *The Covenanters of Ayrshire: Historical and Biographical.* 2nd edition, enlarged. Paisley etc. ND

Lawson *Maybole*
Rev. Roderick Lawson, MAYBOLE *and its Historical Associations.* A Lecture delivered by the Rev. R Lawson, West Church, Maybole. 2nd edition, Stirling 1868

M'Kay
Archibald M'Kay, *The History of Kilmarnock*, 4th edition, Kilmarnock 1880

MacKenzie 1933
Rev. Archibald MacKenzie, *William Adair and his Kirk, The Auld Kirk of Ayr 1639-1684*, Ayr 1933

MacKenzie 1953 (*RBA*)

Rev. Archibald MacKenzie, "The Church from the Reformation till the end of the Eighteenth Century" in *The Royal Burgh of Ayr*, *ed* Annie I Dunlop. Edinburgh and London 1953

Macleod *NSA*

Rev. Norman Macleod, writer of article on Loudoun Parish in the *New Statistical Account of Scotland* (1845) vol v

Napier

Mark Napier, *Life and Times of John Graham of Claverhouse* (3 vols.) Edinburgh 1862

Paterson

James Paterson, *History of the County of Ayr*, 2 vols., Edinburgh and Ayr 1852

Peterkin

A Peterkin (*ed*), *Records of the Kirk of Scotland*, *Containing the Acts and Proceedings of the General Assemblies* Edinburgh 1838

Privy Council

The Register of the Privy Council of Scotland, Edinburgh 1908

Renwick

See Shields

Robertson

William Robertson, *Ayrshire, Its History and Historic Families*, 3 vols., Kilmarnock and Ayr 1908

Scott *OM*

Sir Walter Scott, *Old Mortality* Edinburgh 1823

Shields *Hind*

Rev. Alexander Shields or Shiells, *A Hind let loose: OR, AN Historical REPRESENTATION of the TESTIMONIES OF THE Church of Scotland &c*, Edinburgh 1744

Shields *Memorial*

Rev. Alexander Shields or Shiells, *A Short Memorial of the Sufferings and Grievances, past and present, of the Presbyterians in Scotland* (1690)

Shields *Vindication*

Rev. Alexander Shields or Shiells, with James Renwick: An Informatory Vindication of a Poor, wasted, misrepresented Remnant of the suffering, Antipopish, Anti-prelatick, Anti-Erastian true Presbyterian Church of CHRIST in *Scotland* &c. Written at the *Leadhills* in the Year 1687 conjunctly by MR. JAMES RENWICK and MR. ALEXANDER SHIELLS Author of the *Hind let loose*. Edinburgh 1744

Simpson

Rev. Robert Simpson, *Traditions of the Covenanters* or *Gleanings Among the Mountains*, 3rd Edition, Edinburgh 1850

Stevenson D 1972

David Stevenson, "Conventicles and the Kirk 1619-1637: The Emergence of a Radical Party", *Records of the Scottish Church History Society* xviii (1972-74) pp 99-114

Stevenson D 1973

David Stevenson, *The Scottish Revolution 1637-1644: The Triumph of the Covenanters*, Newton Abbot 1973

Stevenson D 1973 (MM)
David Stevenson, "The Battle of Mauchline Moor 1648", *Ayrshire Collections* XI i (1973) pp 3-24

Stevenson D 1975
David Stevenson, "The Massacre at Dunaverty, 1647" *Scottish Studies* 19 (1975) pp 27-37

Stevenson D 1977
David Stevenson, *Revolution and Counter-Revolution in Scotland 1644-1651*, London 1977

Stevenson D 1988
David Stevenson, *The Covenanters: the National Covenants and Scotland*, The Saltire Society 1988

Stevenson J
John Stevenson of Camregan, *A Soul Strengthening and Comforting Cordial for Old and Young Christians*, Glasgow 1729

Stevenson R L
Robert Louis Stevenson, "The Tale of Tod Lapraik" in *Catriona*, London 1893

Sutherland W
William Sutherland, *The Genuine Declaration of William Sutherland*, Hangman at Irvine, wherein his *Knowledge of the Scriptures, his Courage and Behaviour towards the Persecutors, and their Barbarous Treatment of him at Air are plainly set forth.* Edinburgh 1821 (first published in Wodrow's *History*).

Terry *Claverhouse*
C S Terry, *John Graham of Claverhouse Viscount of Dundee 1648-1689*, London 1905

Terry *Pentland*
C S Terry, *The Pentland Rising 1666*, Glasgow 1905

Thomson
J H Thomson, *The Martyr Graves of Scotland, Edinburgh and London* ND

Torfoot
Narratives of the **Battles of Drumclog** and *Bothwell Bridge*; the former fought on the 1st, and the latter on the 22d of June, 1679. *Between the King's Troops and the Covenanters.* BY THE LAIRD OF TORFOOT
KILMARNOCK: *Printed by* H. Crawford Bookseller 1825

Turner
Sir James Turner, *Memoirs of his Life and Times, ed.* T. Thomson, Bannatyne Club, Edinburgh 1829

Walker
Patrick Walker, *Six Saints of the Covenant, ed* Hay Fleming

Warrick
Rev. John Warrick, *The History of Old Cumnock*, London 1899

Wodrow History
Rev. Robert Wodrow, *The History of the Sufferings of the Church of Scotland from the Restoration to the Revolution, ed* Rev. Robert Burns, Glasgow 1828-36 (4 vols)

Wodrow MSS
Rev. Robert Wodrow, MSS (National Library of Scotland)

Index

Some Saltire Publications

J D McClure	*Why Scots Matters*	0 85411 039 9	£2.95
Geoffrey Barrow	*Robert the Bruce and the Scottish Identity*	0 85411 027 5	£1.00
I B Cowan	*Mary Queen of Scots*	0 85411 037 2	£2.50
David Stevenson	*The Covenanters*	0 85411 042 9	£2.95
Kenneth MacKinnon	*Gaelic: a Past and Future Prospect*	0 85411 047 X	£7.95
Meston, Sellars and Cooper	*The Scottish Legal Tradition (New Ed.)*	0 85411 045 3	£5.99
Rosalind Mitchison (ed.) (contribs from Geoffrey Barrow, A A M Duncan, Alexander Grant, Michael Lynch, David Stevenson, Bruce P Lenman, T M Devine, R H Campbell, Christopher Harvis)	*Why Scottish History Matters*	0 85411 048 8	£5.99
William Neill	*Tales frae the Odyssey o Homer owreset intil Scots*	0 85411 049 6	£7.95
William Ferguson	*Scotland's Relations with England: a Survey to 1707*	0 85411 058 5	£12.99
Paul Scott	*Andrew Fletcher and the Treaty of Union*	0 85411 057 7	£12.99
Paul Scott	*Walter Scott and Scotland*	0 85411 056 9	£7.99
David Stevenson	*Highland Warrior: Alasdair MacColla and the Civil Wars*	0 85411 059 3	£12.99
David Daiches	*Robert Burns, the Poet*	0 85411 060 7	£12.99

Saltire New Poetry

Raymond Vettese	*A Keen New Air*	0 85411 063 1	£12.99

Forthcoming Editions

Ed. David Daiches et al.	The Scottish Enlightenment 1730-1790: a Hotbed of Genius	0 85411 069 0	£12.99
John Sibbald Gibson	Edinburgh in the '45' Bonnie Prince Charlie at Holyroodhouse	0 85411 067 4	£7.99

Complete list (and details of Saltire Society membership etc.) available from the
Saltire Society,
9 Fountain Close, 22 High Street, Edinburgh EH1 1TF